Living with water

Manchester University Press

Living with water
Everyday encounters and liquid connections

Edited by Charlotte Bates and Kate Moles

Manchester University Press

Copyright © Manchester University Press 2023

While copyright in the volume as a whole is vested in Manchester University Press, copyright in individual chapters belongs to their respective authors, and no chapter may be reproduced wholly or in part without the express permission in writing of both author and publisher.

Published by Manchester University Press
Oxford Road, Manchester M13 9PL

www.manchesteruniversitypress.co.uk

British Library Cataloguing-in-Publication Data
A catalogue record for this book is available from the British Library

ISBN 978 1 5261 6172 7 hardback
ISBN 978 1 5261 9135 9 paperback

First published 2023
Paperback published 2025

The publisher has no responsibility for the persistence or accuracy of URLs for any external or third-party internet websites referred to in this book, and does not guarantee that any content on such websites is, or will remain, accurate or appropriate.

Typeset
by Cheshire Typesetting Ltd, Cuddington, Cheshire

Contents

Figures

Contributors

Les Back ~ Les Back is Professor of Sociology at Goldsmiths, University of London and Director of the Centre for Urban and Community Research (CUCR), which is located in the old bathhouse and swimming pool at Laurie Grove, London SE14. He has worked in this building for over twenty-five years and its urban history forms the basis of his contribution to this book. Les is a water lover and family legend has it that one of his ancestors was hanged for piracy on the banks of the Thames. He is an enthusiastic outdoor swimmer and a regular visitor to the lake at Beckenham Place Park, South London.

Charlotte Bates ~ Charlotte is a sociologist who enjoys dipping her toes in different waters. Both in the water and on dry land, her work explores the entanglements and connections between the body, everyday life and place, with a particular focus on belonging, wellbeing and our relationships with the natural world. She lives and works in Wales, where water drips, seeps and flows through her home and the landscape.

Emily Bates ~ Emily is a visual artist and photographer based in Amsterdam, having studied at Glasgow School of Art in the 1990s. Taught to swim as a child in the cold sea waters of a Swedish summer – waters that also became winter ice-rinks – swimming remained only an occasional leisure activity for many years. During her fieldwork travels to remote and high-altitude locations in Europe and South East Asia she has plunged the mountain streams of Hoy in the Orkney Isles, and swum before the official sea-opening ceremonies of Amami Oshima in Japan. Waters from swimming pools, city canals, ponds, lakes and seas have been plunged throughout the pandemic, in a new understanding of the Lowlands and herself.

Wayne Binitie ~ Wayne is a doctoral candidate at the Royal College of Art, London, where his contemporary fine art research explores hidden histories written in polar ice. In collaboration with the British Antarctic Survey and Arup engineers, he has developed three bodies of written and practical work: Solid Series (glass sculpture), Liquid Series (painting) and Vapour Series (sound installation). He has exhibited at the V&A Museum and the Arup Gallery. Wayne is currently Polar Zero Research Associate at the Royal College of Art and received the Arts and Humanities Research Council commission to exhibit three climate-related artworks during COP 26 at the Glasgow Science Centre.

Sans façon ~ Sans façon is an art practice that responds to the relationship between people and place. Working internationally, their approach renews awareness and tempts interaction with the surroundings, and is realised through networks of communities, organisations and individuals. They have worked with the city of Calgary's Water Services and Water Resources department and were the lead artists for Watershed+, a programme which embedded artists and art processes within the municipal department. In 2021 Sans façon and their collaborative team were the recipients of the Canadian Society of Landscape Architects' national award of excellence for *Dale Hodges Park*, a 40 hectare land artwork, park and stormwater facility.

Vanessa Daws ~ Vanessa is a visual artist and long-distance swimmer living in Dublin. Swimming, journey, encounter, conversation and Vanessa's first-hand swimming experiences are the starting points for her projects, a watery drifting and re-imagining of place. Vanessa uses film, sound, drawing, publications, sculpture and live events to create her work. In the past few years she has created art projects in watery spaces as diverse as the frozen Pirita River, Estonia; the Rideau Canal in Canada; The President's Fountain, Bulgaria; the Pacific Ocean, Santa Barbara; the M50 Aqueduct in Dublin and the Bogs of Ballycroy, County Mayo.

Lorna Flutter ~ Lorna's research attends to the kind of water that cuts, pools and flows through the city. She first researched London's boat dwellers during her undergraduate degree. Her attention then turned to Bristol's urban anglers, exploring their practice of baiting, casting, waiting and sometimes catching freshwater fish as mode of mapping 'hidden' city space. Now in the midst of her PhD and living on her narrowboat, London's boaters have been revisited as she explores the intimacies of water as it becomes part of home. Water's ability to (re)shape experiences of urban space has led, diverted and swept Lorna into many avenues of academic thought and fields of research, both situating and sustaining her interest in it as a main character in the social world.

Aurora Fredriksen ~ In diverse empirical settings, Aurora's research has explored more-than-human ways of living and making sense during social and ecological crises. Water flows through much of her writing, as storms and floods, as drained swamps and stormwater treatment facilities, as coastal tides and estuaries, and most recently as the waterlogged stillness of mires and mosses. She has conducted research in the coastal cities of New York and Halifax, the shores of Lake Geneva, the Orkney Islands, peatlands in northern Britain and the eastern US, and, of course, the extraordinary Bay of Fundy. She lives and works in Manchester, where it rains quite a lot.

Joanne Garde-Hansen ~ After being caught up in the UK summer 2007 floods, Joanne turned her attention to an arts and humanities approach to water, and co-developed a concept of sustainable flood memory. Expanding this concept into projects in Brazil she learned how local communities use protest and local action to re-develop rivers used as sewers by water agencies with good PR. She recently completed a monograph on media and water which explores the representation and cultural production of flood, drought and a watery sense of place in film, television, journalism and community media, cultural archives and national heritages. Joanne is Professor of Culture, Media and Communication at the University of Warwick.

Stephanie Krzywonos ~ Stephanie is a Mexican-American nonfiction writer and polar logistician. After growing up on the shores of North America's Great Lakes – enormous glacial footprints – ice led Stephanie to Alaska, then to Antarctica, where she has spent seven seasons living and working, surrounded by most of the world's freshwater and nearly all of its ice and snow. She thinks about glaciers as nonhumans with agency and is interested in the ways humans and ice act on each other. Stephanie is working on her debut book, a memoir about grief, descent, rebirth, and Antarctica as a living place and metaphorical woman.

Jessica J. Lee ~ Jessica is a swimmer who makes a living as an author and environmental historian. Born between two large lakes in Canada, she has sought home waters in Britain, Germany and Taiwan. Her doctoral fieldwork with winter swimmers at the Kenwood Ladies' Pond in London helped her accept a long-held fear of water and led to the writing of her first book, a memoir tracing swims in fifty-two German lakes and a period as writer-in-residence at the Leibniz Institute for Freshwater Ecology. She has since swum in high mountain waterfall pools in Taiwan, in a lake that served as outflow for a decommissioned nuclear power plant, and is now regularly found descending the banks of the River Cam.

Eva McGrath ~ Water first emerged for Eva through the study of words; semantics holding river, sea, tears, meaning spilling over. She followed these watercourses to search for what water means to people, finding creative methodologies to encourage passengers to draw, reflect, imagine, write and dream, while crossing tidal rivers on a ferry. She immerses herself in salty seas and cool rivers year-round, skin as blubber, and paints in watercolour. She searches the shoreline for seabirds and the estuary for wading birds.

Kate Moles ~ Kate has been a swimmer almost all her life, and a sociologist for some of it. Her swimming foundations were laid in the pools of competitive swimming, but the sea has offered enduring ties and possibilities. Kate's sociological imagination was turned towards swimming as it afforded a site for the exploration of themes that recur in her work: enduring practices and meaning making, everyday encounters between people and place, and the ways we do belonging and becoming in different contexts. It also meant she got to swim more and talk to people about their swimming, which was very welcome.

JLM Morton ~ JLM Morton is a poet for whom a morning well spent means sliding down a frosty bank into a clear, cold lake. In 2020 she was poet-in-residence at the Cotswold Water Park, exploring boundaries between the natural and the human. Her sense of belonging is strongly bound to water and a family history that glistens with tales of the high seas: a father swimming the Channel smeared in goose fat, granddads working the London docks, sailing the world in the merchant navy, migrating to Canada to work in fishing. In the present, water offers an ancestral connection to that past but also to the geological timescales of millennia and the future. Juliette is fascinated by that temporal simultaneity and the ritual and symbolism that surrounds our relationships with water, fresh and salt.

Rebecca Olive ~ Since her childhood, coasts and oceans have been part of Rebecca's life. Her enthusiasm for coastal cultures and relationships is clear in her research focus on surfing and ocean swimming, including the politics and ethics of access and belonging. Despite her warm water foundations, she has come to enjoy warm and cold water equally, as well as all coastlines, whether sand, rocks or cliffs. Now living and working in a river city, she is rediscovering the value of pools, and the communities of women who swim in them.

Perdita Phillips ~ Perdy lives in country where water is the focus of life above ground and below. The changeable and ephemeral nature of waterbodies in dry climates is paralleled in an art practice where she ponders small moments of entanglement with/in the world. Watching a river coming down a dry riverbed was a highlight of her previous career in environmental science, but sediment sampling and streamflow monitoring have been replaced by the uncertainty of porous repair. She has written about running out of water and worked with groundwater and stygofauna and bodies of water disappearing. One of her earliest memories was almost drowning in the Kalgan River. She returned to the same terrain in 2018 for the *Follow the water* project.

Becky Shaw ~ Becky makes live artworks that explore the frozen and mutable nature of institutions and infrastructures. Becky's dad was an industrial chemist in a plastics factory: a site of disturbing toxicity, grinding bureaucracy, and the magic of turning solids into liquids and gases. This began a curiosity transferred into artistic inquiry. Some works explore water, including making real ice diamond rings, or working with leak locators. Other works seek to generate flow to challenge spatial perimeters or to resist expectations of legibility and purpose. Becky is Reader in Fine Art and leads the art, design and media arts PhD at Sheffield Hallam University.

Alys Tomlinson ~ Alys is a photographer and anthropologist based in London. Having grown up by the sea in Brighton, her work is often connected to the power and influence of water in cultural and social settings. From empty American swimming pools to Irish holy wells, she has documented a wide range of photographic subjects. For her major project *Ex-Voto* she photographed and observed the centrality of water at the pilgrimage site of Lourdes, France. Her landscape and still-life photography are often situated within forests, rivers and rocks. For her portrait photography, the natural landscape is used to frame her subjects. In 2018 she was awarded Sony Photographer of the Year and in 2020 she won First Prize in the Taylor Wessing Photographic Portrait Prize.

Phillip Vannini and April Vannini ~ Phillip and April are ethnographers whose work has taken them to waters around the world, especially small islands and remote coastal communities. Together they have written about fossilised sea-living creatures, dammed boreal forest lakes, fjord stories and ferry boats. Their research together has taken them to the Galapagos Islands, the island of Tasmania, New Zealand's Milford Sound, the waters of Belize, the glaciers of Patagonia, the remote islands of Japan's Ogasawara Archipelago, and the fossil cliffs of Canada's Miguasha and Mistaken Point Ecological Reserve. They live on Gabriola Island, British Columbia, where they spend long summer days enjoying the waters surrounding them.

Samantha Walton ~ Samantha is a writer, academic and editor based in Bristol. She learnt to swim in Highgrove Pool in Ruislip, where an instructor accidentally sent her to a smaller kids' group and she spent a year thinking she was much more competent a swimmer than she was. Her first memory is grazing her knee at Camber Sands, East Sussex, and then dropping an ice cream down her top. She first got interested in open water swimming in France, in an artificial lake created in the 1950s through the flooding of the Maulde River. Since then, she has gravitated to cold water rivers and lakes, and has a particular affection for the free, art deco marine lake at Clevedon and high-tide, full-moon swimming along the Severn Estuary.

Sophie Watson ~ Sophie fell in love with the sea when she lived in Sydney. Having grown up in London she was thrilled to live somewhere where she could start the day with a surf before heading off to university, or swim in the magic ocean pool – Bondi Icebergs. Returning to the UK she gravitated to the Hampstead Women's Pond and lido as the only places in the city near her home where she could swim outside. Her passion for outdoor swimming represented a route into thinking about what different cultures of water meant for the city. Sophie is Professor of Sociology at the Open University.

Foreword

Jessica J. Lee

As a child, I was deeply afraid of water. All water: oceans that churned with seaweed. Rivers that squelched with muck. Worst of all were lakes that plunged everything they touched into immediate obscurity. Rising, cold and dark.

It didn't help that I grew up near the Great Lakes, during a time when pollution choked them, in a town where the river was rumoured to be toxic. Water was simply an otherworld into which I did not long to go.

This fear lingered long into adulthood, and often came coupled with a frustrating inability to be around the kinds of movement that water implied: standing still on a dock, the flicker of water beneath it made me dizzy. The slow thumping of a motorboat on waves scattered my nerves. On a particularly tumultuous express ferry crossing between Maine and Nova Scotia, I was forced to admit that I suffered brutally from seasickness.

So how then did I become a person who not only loves water, but who seeks it out in every new place I visit? A person who regularly swims in whatever body of water presents itself, whatever the weather? How did I become the sort of person who would be asked to write the foreword to a book called, of all things, *Living with water?*

It might be said that water, in slow patters, seeped into my life. First, in the years I lived by the ocean, learning to be less afraid. I swam in the North Atlantic and found in waves and tides – rhythmic, lunging and forceful – a kind of comfort in the sheer power of water. In its vastness. And then in my work as a historian, tracing the movements of a London river forced below ground and the scattered pools, popular with swimmers, where it reaches fresh air.

Slower still, the water that I least expected to love was in lakes. Over the course of many months, I willed myself to swim in German lakes as I wrote a book about them. Even when they scared me. Even in winter. Fear held, my body afloat, I learned that lakewater could be a testing ground for the senses. A way of attuning my body to the subtlety afforded by freshwater: unlike seas, lakes held hardly any movement at all, but still each was different from the last. Water held minerals, algae, life itself. It froze and melted and evaporated, and rain tugged at the surface of a quiet lake. In bounded freshwaters, my body and its borders become more apparent than ever.

Each of the pieces in this collection points to something I had to learn: that living with water is learning to live with uncertainty, with changeability and with depths unknown. We cannot know the bed of a lake perfectly and cannot measure a shoreline exactly. I could not control my fear of water but rather had to learn to notice it, then notice the water, notice the ways it held my body even when it scared me.

The essays and artworks gathered here circle a series of watery questions: What does water do when we are atop it? When we are moving with it? And when we are submerged? Falling asleep when living on the water on narrowboats points to the subtle grada-tions of sensation that water invites us to notice. The body appears throughout – gleaming with cold from a winter swim or slick with sweat in a summer heatwave. And we are, as a result, asked to inquire after the especially unique relationship of women with water. The ways something central but often perceived as peripheral is more important than arts, humanities and social science scholarship may originally have contended.

But these pieces also touch on the ways water is not a consistent medium: the ways it can shift our attention to things beyond itself and ourselves, to life forms that rely upon watery habitats – like man-groves, coral reefs, horseshoe crabs and seabirds – as well as precari-ous livelihoods, as in the case of those working in fisheries. What happens when water is inaccessible, or worse, disappearing alto-gether? Thinking about drought is a vital component in our thinking about how water shapes the world. Water and the ability to negotiate it are both deeply political. Water's presence is a marker of vitality inas-much as its absence – whether due to climate change, hot weather or our remaking of the landscape – is a cause for deep concern.

Linguistic and disciplinary boundaries are slippery things in this book. Old English and Icelandic, sociology and ethnography, visual art and poetry – all slide together here. And why shouldn't they?

Water is the slipperiest of mediums, and flowing through each of these pieces, it invites us to make connections we may not otherwise make on dry land. When thinking about water, we must contend with what Vannini and Vannini call a 'tangle of interlaced trails, currents, flows, lifelines'. As a result, this is academic writing pushed to its boundaries: dynamic, attentive to the world, to the body, and to the limits of language itself to capture the most material and elusive of focuses. Reading *Living with water* is a way of asking again and again what it means to shapeshift: solid, liquid, gas, scholarly study and swimming song.

Over the decades, I've lived and worked in countries obsessed by the weather: in Canada, by snow. In Britain, by rain. In Germany, ice. These facets of water are the subject of small-talk and the determiners of our human infrastructure. And what else could be more interesting? More indicative of how we really *live* with water in its many forms? In taking in so many perspectives, this is a collection that underscored for me the degree to which water does not hold fast to the boundaries we place upon it: whether materially, as it leaks across supposedly impervious borders, or imaginatively, as we try to catalogue all the things water could mean across cultures and lifeways. I invite you, as I have, to dwell in this indeterminate space, where word and water – traversed by bridge, by boat or by body – flow freely.

1

Living with water

Kate Moles and Charlotte Bates

Water is within us and it flows through our bodies, our worlds and our words. The liquid connections between the contributors and contributions within this collection bind us and our work together. But this book – a book about living with water – is not simply birthed from a love of water. Water gives us life, but it also troubles us. While dipping, plunging, floating and swimming bring comfort and joy to many of us, there are darker encounters with water beneath the surface too – childhood memories of almost drowning, deep and bodily fears of lakes, vast oceans that sear the eyes and heart. Relentlessly, water drips, seeps and floods our existence, reminding us of our vulnerability and our place in the world. Recognising these conflicts and connections, we acknowledge the multiple ways in which we live with water.

In this collection, we consider how living, thinking and writing with water offers ways of attending to emerging and enduring social and ecological concerns, allowing us to make sense of them in lively and creative ways. Water is the most ubiquitous material on the planet and a mundane element of our existence. Water flows through our lives in multiple and varied ways – we drink water, wash our bodies in water, exercise and play in water, make a living on the water, and even risk our lives crossing water. Yet, for those of us who have it 'on tap', it is easy to take water for granted, to overlook the ways in which water filters our existence and shapes our lives. This collection seeks to include water in the ways we make sense of the social world, to bring water into the conversations we have about life and living, and to recognise water as both a co-creator of human domains and as having agency and its own rights.

Water streams across and through different spaces, calling forth and bringing to life a wide range of situated and contextual meanings, representations and interactions, meshworks and inter-animations. In one form or another, water participates in the making and unmaking of people's lives, practices and stories across the globe. The social life of water enables and sustains the world we know, its materiality sustains and produces human life and its symbolism reaches deep into our histories and shapes our imagined and lived futures. People have made sense of these different facets of water through a range of knowledge systems, methods and narratives. The different perceptions about water that run through them are both disparate and cohesive, though water holds them together. Like all the water on our planet, these accounts are joined, run together, share life and tie faraway people and places to each other. Attending to the granular detail of water, and focusing on the ways we live with it in our everyday lives, in extraordinary moments and in different times and places, offers one particular way of unfolding entangled, more-than-human, flowing-knowing. Permeating our senses and our imaginations, infusing our lives with material realities and symbolic resonances, this collection offers valuable insights into the multiple ways in which we live with water.

Most accounts have not tried to represent water in its vast wholeness, and instead have attended to it in smaller places, through local practices and ways of knowing. These attentions have allowed us to consider the ways our lives are always related to the water around us. Academic work has invited us to consider our relations to water, with different ways of framing experiences, ontologies and materialities. As part of this work, we can explore the poetics and politics of water, of access, of ways of knowing, and being and becoming in and of water. Broadly, academic work has conceived water as a site of leisure; as a substance of scientific and industrial interest; as an environmental concern; as a part of spiritual and religious life; as a space of health and wellbeing; as a feature of everyday encounters and interactions within and between human and nonhuman participants; and, throughout and always provocatively, as a lively contributor in our ways of thinking, knowing and acting (Chen, MacLeod and Neimanis, 2013).

We can learn much from work that considers water as a site of leisure about questions of belonging, practices of inclusion and exclusion, and the ways in which gender, race, sexuality, class, and structures and relations to power are made and remade within these spaces. The embodied practices of surfing, swimming, kayaking and sailing, which bring people into close contact with different waters, enliven and provoke questions about bodies, self and identity, and attend to the ways we conceptualise ideas of wellbeing, health, risk and danger. The enduring legacies of colonialism and claims to belonging that displace or exclude Indigenous people and ways of knowing run through this work too, with the whitewashed histories of surfing and newly imposed communities along the waterside eroding existing narratives and ties to the water and the land. The ways in which people conquer, make claims to and pollute the waters of leisure and life are legacies of particular Western ways of relating to the natural world.

Questions around ways of knowing water, and the erosion of traditional ways of knowing, are also found prominently in more scientific and industrial accounts that consider water as a resource and a problem. This work seeks to control and coerce water into particular paths, manage issues of pollution, and limit access through material and economic means. Counter to these scientific accounts run Indigenous ways of making sense of water that dispel the singular positioning of water and instead recognise the spiritual and symbolic importance of waters. Environmental concerns around pollution and rights can be reframed in these ways, removing our understanding of water from neoliberal, capitalist imaginaries and instead considering waters as agentic and significant parts of the social, cultural and spiritual life of those living around them (Liboiron, 2021).

Recognition of the role that water can play in restorative and recuperative narratives has embedded it in contemporary accounts of wellbeing and health. These present the physiological and psychological benefits of water, lauding the life-changing potential immersion can offer. Samantha Walton (2021) has explored these potentials, reverberating in her poem in this collection, in relation to ideas of beauty, nature and the water cure. Often enrolled in a more general call for a 'return' to nature, it expounds the idea that the natural world can offer our bodies and minds respite from the stress and anxieties of modern life. Water is nourishing, rejuvenating, healthy and pure in these accounts; it washes away contemporary trials and traumas, while at the same time building up experience, resilience and wellbeing.

But water is also unknown and murky, hiding dangers and courting disaster. It is a site of political battles and questioned science – pollution levels in rivers are at once the highest and lowest they have ever been; beaches are the cleanest ever while also being sites of nuclear mud dumps and sewage seepages. The ways these different accounts come into contact with our practices around it draws attention to the assumptions we hold about the water that runs through our lives. The ways we know water, and the sense we make of that knowledge, are contested, debated and disputed. These processes of contestation and consideration offer insights into processes of knowing and sense making, as well as the political and economic power that flows through water. Through careful consideration of local practices, politics and poetics, we can come to understand the complexity that exists in each drop of water, and the multiple ways we can know, represent and experience it.

Water is all these things, and the ways we negotiate these complex meanings have significance for how water is encountered in the everyday. Water is embedded in social and cultural relations that can be traced through history. It is at once fluid and shifting and emplaced in local and global politics. While empires may have been built on claims to, contestations around and conquests of land, throughout history water has connected people, and the power of future economies and societies will be framed by their access to water. Ways of understanding water as a commodity to be claimed or an artefact we can own or exploit stem directly from colonial understandings and knowledge systems, and increasingly new ways of relating to the waters in our lives need to be carved out and allowed to dissipate through our everyday lives. Within this collection, we have indicated spaces of hope alongside struggle, joy alongside risk, and shown how historical and contemporary understandings can and should be woven together to produce rich meshworks of understanding and appreciation of the places of water in our lives.

Together, we ask how water is part of our everyday lives, how it gives meaning and is made meaningful to practices, encounters and understandings of place and social life, how we live with – and without – water in practical, symbolic and material ways, and how we navigate and negotiate social interactions in and around water. Throughout the contributions runs a focus on the values, beliefs, attitudes and practices that people have in relation to, and which are shaped through, their connections with water, traced through local and global cases and stories. Attending to water as a place of pleasure and joy, of risk and fear, and as a site of pollution, danger, power and conflict, this collection positions water as a material, symbolic and practical resource that seeps through our everyday lives and infuses our lived experiences with its presence, and troubles us with its absence.

Attuning to the water that flows through our bodies, homes, cities and lives, the collection shows that water is remarkable, from raindrops to rivers, and ponds to oceans. Each contribution reorients us to the water around us, raising awareness of water's presence and power. Water is hidden but hissing in underground water pipes, draining away from cities, and ebbing and flooding with the tides. In doing so, the collection takes inspiration from water instead of land, allowing water to flow through our ways of thinking and seep into our writing. At the same time, the collection is not 'all at sea' or out of sight of land. Attending to boundaries and crossings, our collective imagination stops separating land from water and instead recognises how land and water intermingle and are entangled. Rebecca Olive finds oceanic thinking in the depth and volume of trees, and Perdita Phillips sees porous repair in weedy, overgrown stormwater channels. Water is both everywhere and nowhere – in the 1976 drought or the drained Laurie Grove Baths.

On the cover the Jökulsárlón glacial lagoon, photographed by Wayne Binitie, wraps itself around the collection – made of water and sculpted by it, it is both above and below water, frozen, shapeshifting, melting and disappearing. The iceberg is a monument to many of the themes that flow through the collection. Jökulsárlón is striking, and dangerous, a structure that extends into the past and drifts perilously towards an unknown future. To interact with it and explore the sensorial, seasonal world of the ice, Wayne opened himself up to alternative forms of engagement, new risks and rewards, and different understandings of how to be present in that space, at that time. At once attending to the beauty and tragedy of these transient natural sculptures, the image of Jökulsárlón was made possible through the collaboration of Wayne's artistic sensibilities, local understandings and knowledges, and technological and material capacities. In *Living with water*, we explore new ways to engage, understand and be present with different waters to enliven our situated, contextual and universal appreciations of what water means, does and brings to life in our social worlds.

Water has a capacity to connect, and it holds this interdisciplinary collection together. As Jessica J. Lee writes in her foreword to the collection, 'disciplinary boundaries are slippery things in this book'. Slippery boundaries, disciplinary crossings and liquid connections bring us together in a confluence of waters and disciplines. Words trickle and flow, images pool and animate, ideas seep and sink. These different forms collect together in three sections – *Float*, *Flow* and *Submerge* – each showing us what water does and what bodies do in water. We offer them as a reservoir for future thinking, working and ways of living with water.

Float

Focusing on life on and around the water, *Float* considers what water can bring to the surface and how people move, love and live while staying afloat. We begin by meeting Ryan and Alfie, with photographs by Alys Tomlinson. These young fishers show us the ways they interact with the natural world through the practice of fishing and the significance water holds for them in remaining happy and healthy in the world. Fishing helps these young men to 'keep their minds straight' and to keep off the streets. The reservoir offers them a place to continue family traditions, and a way to be filled up with experience and to remain afloat in a world of pressing concerns and potential and fleeting connections. Next, Eva McGrath invites us to consider the act of floating through evocative descriptions of social life as it unfolds on ferries. Considering the passages these boats make, the meanings people ascribe to them, and the connections between the materiality of the vessels, the water and the people who travel, Eva attunes our senses to the poetry of the crossing and the act of staying afloat. We continue to think about a life unfolding on the water with Lorna Flutter's intricately crafted chapter aboard London's canal boats. Interweaving the mundane domestic rituals of life on board a narrowboat with the demands and intrusions of water on these practices, Lorna highlights the ways life on a boat is both enabled and constrained through its relationships with the water on which it floats. Les Back invites us to consider the flow of social life through the history and stories of Laurie Grove Baths. Les's beautifully detailed account of the lives, and deaths, in and around the Baths serve as a way of thinking about the tensions that run through our cities, around improvement and regulation, respectability and vibrancy, cleanliness and morality. Thinking about movement through and across the mighty Thames, Sophie Watson invites us to dwell on and in the ways in which bodies are carried through water in watercraft, below the water in tunnels and above the water on bridges. Rich in detail, Sophie retrains our eyes to the lives lived and made through crossing the city's waterways. Through the threat of living without water, Joanne Garde-Hansen turns our attention to the memories, stories and histories of water and the particular ways women feature within accounts of drought that circulate in the UK's normally wet self-narrative. Joanne shows how in a geographical and socio-political context normally dominated by maritime histories, island mentality and a watery sense of place, drought narratives work against the norms of media templates, cultural memories and gender conformity.

Flow

In *Flow*, we are confronted and challenged by water's propensity to escape, disrupt and overwhelm existing systems of infrastructure and knowledge. Becky Shaw describes the work she undertook with Calgary's leak locators, and the different instruments they drew on to make sense of the world as leaky. Rather than using visual clues that alert us to problematic results of leaks – surface water, loss of pressure, unexpected meter readings – these leak locators listen, using various instruments, to find the source of the leak. Resulting in a multiform artwork that spanned different sites and sounds, Becky invites us to consider the world of water through our ears, and attune to it afresh. San façon's *Monument to Rain* celebrates the banal and commonplace while also the galactic and prehistorical. Rain is singularly an annoyance and life, part of national identity and the birth of grunge, and in this piece we are invited to consider these water cycles and our enduring relationship with rain. The ways in which waterworlds, the environment and humans tangle together as meshworks are explored by Phillip and April Vannini through their account of ecological preservation at Laughing Bird Caye in the Belize Barrier Reef. They also surface ideas of hope in the affective ecologies they encounter, considering the ways hope flows through encounters, across species, through actions and within connections. Attending to interconnections and entanglements with water, Aurora Fredriksen takes us to the Bay of Fundy at the northern end of the Atlantic's Gulf of Maine. Her research draws out the different ways of knowing that exist together and in conflict around these waters and brings to the fore Indigenous knowledges, problematising narratives that position tidal energy development as unproblematically positive. Instead, Aurora describes how tidal energy extends terrestrial property rights and modes of authority into the sea, displacing other relations in its wake. Next, Peredita Phillips invites us to 'Follow the water', listening as it flows to the nearest waterbody and dealing with the runoff through history, the drains and the stories it brings to life (and death). Peredita invites us to be with these moments, and the pairs of photographs presented call for reflection and animation of the idea of porous repair, encouraging us to look forward rather than back, to allow risk and sharing and to occupy the uncertain state of both/and together. Weaving personal narratives with glacial progress, temporalities and geographies and insights and meanings gleaned within and across both, Stephanie Krzywonos considers the place of glacial erratics in and as her life. Tracing flows of frozen water, family and journey, Stephanie beautifully attends to the patterns, threads and ways we fit into place, water and time in her essay originally published in *The Willowherb Review*.

Submerge

Submerge immerses us in water, plunging us into its depths through the act of swimming and soaking us through. We begin in the city of Dublin, as swimmers stride through the streets barefoot. Taken from artist Vanessa Daws's booklet *17 bridges*, the drawings and accompanying text invite us to jump with them into the brown depths of the Liffey and to explore questions of ownership and trespass – questions that we return to throughout this section. Next, we accompany poet JLM Morton as she swims, walks and wades along the Churn, her home river. She shares her journey with us through a playful poem sequence from source to confluence, and from home to motherhood. We submerge deeper into cold water in our own chapter – a sequence of storied encounters with bodies of water that teach us about wild swimming and the liquid boundaries and entanglements between water, bodies, wellbeing and risk, told from the threshold and through the moment of entry. Back on dry land, Rebecca Olive swims without water under jacaranda, manuka and sequoia trees. Immersed in these new depths and comforted by the embrace of green, she challenges assumptions about our – and her own – relationships with water, and takes lessons from swimming and the water into life on land. In 'I just want an earth of cool mysteries' Samantha Walton shares the jouissance of living with water in a poem and through thinking with Nan Shepherd's writing and lessons from the Cairngorm mountains. To end the collection, artist and photographer Emily Bates takes us to the Noord Brabant province of the Netherlands, where she explores the Dutch landscape and its relationship with water, and conjures a swimming pond from brush and ink. The black ink flows, ripples and glistens, wetting the page and echoing the shape and depths of nearby bodies of water.

References

Chen, C., MacLeod, A. and Neimanis, A. (eds) (2013) *Thinking with Water.* Montreal: McGill-Queen's University Press.

Liboiron, M. (2021) *Pollution is Colonialism.* Durham: Duke University Press.

Walton, S. (2021) *Everybody Needs Beauty: In Search of the Nature Cure.* London: Bloomsbury.

2

Jökulsárlón 64°04'13"N 16°12'42"W

Wayne Binitie

The Jökulsárlón is a fast-receding glacial lagoon situated at the head of the Breiðamerkurjökull glacier in Iceland on the edge of the Atlantic Ocean. One and a half kilometres long, the lagoon covers an area of 18 square kilometres. Partly covered by volcanic ash caused by ancient eruptions, the fragile icebergs of the Jökulsárlón appear as dissolving sculptural forms that have been carved by nature. Only 20 per cent of the icebergs can be seen above the water, the remaining volume scrapes the glacier floor, reaching depths of 248 metres below the surface.

On my visit, I was immediately struck by the powerful geothermal scent pervading the lagoon and the sounds of compressed atmospheric gases being released from floating fragments of icebergs. The scale and mass of the icebergs suggested a fixed solidity that belied their extreme volatility and unpredictability; this can result in large chunks breaking away at random moments in a process called calving. Getting close enough to take audio and photographic documentation of the Jökulsárlón was a necessarily dangerous undertaking and involved negotiating with a local guide prepared to risk travelling far into the lagoon to get up alongside the icebergs in a speedboat. Once we had reached the centre of the lagoon, the guide switched the boat's engine off as planned and we fell into glacial silence. I then dropped my hydrophone over the side of the boat and began to record and listen to the depths of the lagoon.

Having studied weather patterns before my visit, I arrived at a time when the shifting Nordic light was at its most intense. I had been lent a Leica lens at the last moment with which I hoped to capture these glacial forms, held momentarily in stasis within the semi-enclosed lagoon. The intensity of colour and nuanced hues of the Jökulsárlón glacial lagoon derive from the interplay of light and air molecules within the ice crystals. Observing the lagoon from the speedboat, the icebergs stood as transient monuments, seeming to memorialise their own passing before a final dissolution takes place, as they are swept out into the violent rush of the Atlantic Ocean to vanish forever.

Float

Fishing floats, floating boats, dancing and wrestling afloat – *the contributions in Float are floating on water. Bodies are carried and cared for, transported, washed and floated away. They are both wet-and-dry, in baths, on banks, on bridges, on board and in tunnels, above and below waters that connect them with each other and with the social life of the city. While not exclusively urban, these stories are connected by waters that bear witness to intimate and domestic ways of moving, working and living with water in London and along tributaries across the UK, from the mighty Thames to the River Tamar. Together, they bring to the surface intimate grief and promises, sounds and sensations, traditions and distinctions, illuminating hidden water histories and the communities that water brings together. From the teenage fishers at Walthamstow Reservoir in North London who find refuge from the streets at the water's edge, to the limbo dancers, wrestlers and musicians who flooded Laurie Grove Baths in South London with convivial social life and broke the colour bar, each contribution highlights a different way in which water is buoyant. Elsewhere, contributors explore what happens when water finds its way in or runs away, making floating impossible – the fear of a sinking narrowboat, a drained swimming pool, the 1976 drought. Here, the presence and absence of water challenge us to think about our watery vulnerability and the connections, dissections and cuts – through our bodies, places and lives – that water both allows and demands.*

~

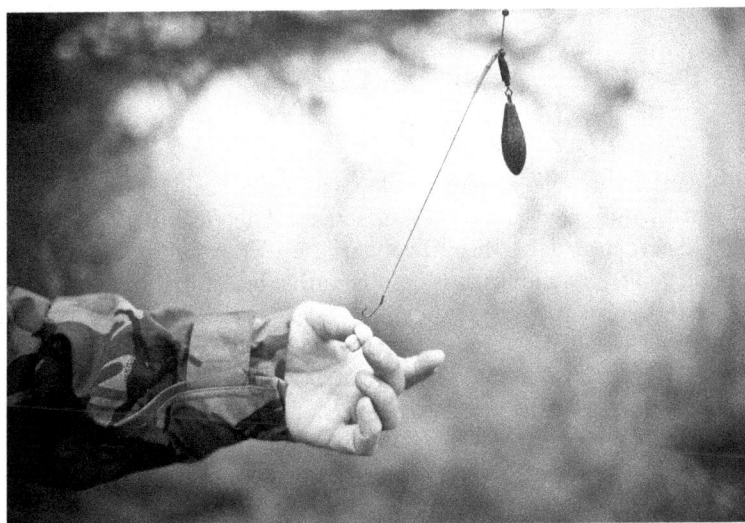

3

Ryan and Alfie: the teenage fishers

Alys Tomlinson

sounds of birds and ducks

Ryan: Like, some people sit indoors and play their Playstations or XBoxes ... and they get glued to the screen. Whereas this, this is fun.

Alfie: Yeah. I don't think I've played an XBox or Playstation for about, yeah, about four years now. I'd rather be fishing.

birds tweeting

Ryan: I first went fishing when I was sort of like a baby, cos my Dad used to take me when I was small and he sort of, cos he used to do it, and his Dad used to do it, it goes throughout the family and it sort of ... for me, my Dad brung me into it. But nobody else.

birds tweeting

Ryan: What I love about fishing is, like, nature, and it's just getting out and it keeps you from sitting indoors ... and, it's just nice, it's nice to go outside sometimes and it's just fun. It's like, when you're fishing there and you've got your rods out, it's just fun for you ... and it's like, you get to see all the birds and different things ... the rats and everything.

Alfie: It's just, like, it's tranquil. You can get out of the house. Places like here in London it's very rare to have somewhere you can come and sort of ... free your mind a bit, get away from, like, the city and ... keeps me off the streets, to be honest. I could be doing a lot worser stuff than fishing, do you know what I mean? So, it's good, keeps my mind straight. If you like it, it's something that you will always have there for life, it's not like football where you can get injured and like your career's over or you can't play again ... it's like the lakes are never gonna run away, kind of thing, and you'll always be able to go fishing, so ... and there's not many other places we can go. So, it's good.

birds tweeting and ducks splashing

Ryan: My life, if it didn't have fishing involved ... I don't know where I'd sort of be in life. I'd just be empty and I'd be sitting indoors, like, just sitting there. And then, er, like, it's sort of ... fishing ... I don't know how to explain it, but if it weren't in your life it's just boring. It's just boring, you're not getting out and you're not seeing stuff. Like, certain things you can see anywhere else. Like if you go down the high street, or round the city, you won't see all the ... you might see a few seagulls and that, but you won't see what you're seeing at a reservoir. So it sort of would kill me if I didn't have fishing in my whole life.

I can't imagine my life without fishing.

4

Fereð ofer flodas: floating on a ferry

Eva McGrath

fereð ofer flodas[1]

ofer, over, offer to float.

Flo–, flow, slo–w,

fɛri

faerigan, fergan, feran, ferian, ferigan, ferigean, fyrigan,
ferigen, farjan, fähren, uere, uerie, fere, fare, ferie, verie, very,
verye, ferh, fery, fére, ferrye, ferynge, ferrie, ferring, ferre, fery[2]

ferry

Shifts of these words over time, lost in translation, changing
meaning crossing

river, sea, ria, estuary floating,

flowing, flowering, flowing bloating language:

---

[1] Riddle 14. In Muir (1994).
[2] Etymology of 'ferry': source Oxford English Dictionary (2021a, 2021b).

To ferry, to be ferried faery, ferry, ferrian, fereð, flodaas, float,

Float: /f l / fluvial boat, I wrote

Umbilical chord, toward: we board.

The word 'ferry' holds as both a noun and a verb. As a noun, it is ety-mologically entangled with a river, as a

> crossing over a river or other stretch of water which is served by a ferry boat. Also: a place at which a ferry boat departs or lands. Now some-what rare. (*Oxford English Dictionary*, 2021a)

Movement across water is therefore folded into the meaning and memory of the word itself: a description of a transactional, diago-nal movement, a 'crossing over', a floating over, a buoyant tug to shift from one side of the river to the other, 'fery over a watyr' (*Promptorium parvulorum sive clericorum*, ca. 1440). Mark the place the ferry boat 'departs' or 'lands', as that is the location where this river will be crossed over, floated over, navigated across. Wait for the ferry. The final tentative phrase, 'now somewhat rare' alerts us to the fragility of this mode of transport: routes washed by the tide as the suspension bridge is built up-river, diverting passengers away from this floating ferry place, a distance from the water.

'Ferry' is also a transitive verb, a direct action: 'to convey or transport (people, goods, etc.) over water; *specifically*, to convey by ferry boat. Frequently with *across, over*' (*Oxford English Dictionary*, 2021b). As a verb, 'to ferry' is a dynamic action, where 'people' or 'goods', belongings and bags, words, bodies, buggies, bicycles, muddy puddles, litter-wrappers, keys, phones, wallets, jokes, memories and pieces of paper float. Temporarily suspended: held by boards atop the buoyant salty waves, steered by the ferry operator's silent command. A route settled by historic legal deeds; marked on a map by a dotted line; navigated through a three-dimensional understanding of the river, calculating tide and water level, wind, weather, current and the movement of other vessels. Back and forth, forth and back. Where strangers slowly shift towards the slip and step onto the side of a boat: take a seat. Low above water, to ferry and be ferried. To float.

That a ferry is both noun and verb draws attention to what is acted and enacted through the ferry, crossing the river. Nouns draw our attention to the people, places, things or ideas that are performing the action of the sentence, or receiving the action of the sentence. Note the landscape, the river, the distance between the two shores, the shape and size of the ferry boat, the rights to offer a timetabled service and to charge a fee for its use; oh ferry passenger, ferry place, ferry way, ferry wharf, ferry boat. Verbs indicate the action of a sentence, to board a ferry, to travel, to ferry and be ferried; ferry me, telling you what the noun does. Shifting from one side of the river to the other, to ferry and be ferried. Ferry: thing and action, double-crossed strand intertwined as ferry means floating, and floating shifts us towards water.

This chapter is a reflection upon the act of floating across water, and the different meanings that emerge while crossing a river, on a ferry. Geographically, the river at the centre of this chapter is the River Tamar, a waterway forming the regional border between Devon and Cornwall, in the South West of England. The ferry of focus is the Cremyll Ferry that carries passengers between Admirals Hard in Plymouth (Devon) and Cremyll (Cornwall), a river crossing first recorded after the Norman Conquest, although it has been suggested that there has been a ferry crossing at this site since the first century (cf. Sharman, 2003). The time it takes to cross the river on today's ferry is around ten minutes in length. Imaginatively, the river crossing discussed in this chapter also holds a wider ethnographic research project, Across the River (2017–2021). Passengers on the Cremyll Ferry (River Tamar), Appledore–Instow Ferry (River Torridge) and the Helford Ferry (River Helford) were invited to reflect upon their thoughts, emotions and experiences while on the water. Some of those cards created on the river are incorporated into this chapter, referred to as 'reflection card responses', and quotes from three interviewees (Rita, Simon, Ruth) used as a dialogue for poetic reflection. Floating, in this chapter, therefore bridges my own, personal experiences of crossing over the River Tamar, and situates these reflections in relation to the recorded voices of those who have previously crossed this river, as well as other rivers between places. The flexibility of such a positioning is required to question what it means to float on water, and to encapsulate the movement between arrival and departure. Three central sections, 'floating waters', 'floating with others' and 'floating as exchange', give attention to the meeting point of the ferry, where people and things, ideas and imaginations are held together, for a few minutes in the crossing from one side of the river to the other. The transverse movement that people find themselves within, floating above the river's current, pushing and pulling, and the engine's motor whirring and rumbling, lifts attention to the present; a movement at the junction between here and there, this side of the river and that side; a pause between past and future.

Floating waters

Floating is crossing water: the desire to move from one side of the river to the other. I cannot safely float across myself: I have my body, but the water is too wide to swim and the cold might course through my veins. Besides, I would have to navigate the current, choppiness of the water and dodge other boats, bigger than me. I have no boat of my own, to move in my own lines of direction. So I wait, for a ferry. Check the times, 30 minute cycles, there and back again, on a historic boat taking me back in time, taking me into time, suspending me over time on the water, moving me to a different land; to over there, to where I want to go, to where I move in the leap of my imagination, where I would like to be. Is this river a border, a barrier, an obstacle to movement? To some extent: but the ferry is like an accordion, pulling and tugging and stretching in the reverberations of time and tide and melody and musicality; a tension tug, glug, mug, floating over. Trusting in this ancient boat, in its mechanics and maps and signals in the control room located above, the driver steering. Trusting in the staff who unravel the rope and unloop the boat from the buoy. Look around, at the others in this sphere-shaped floating vessel, with anoraks and walking boots, binoculars and waterproofs. Corduroy jeans and striped shoes. Others have walked through into the interior section, sheltering from the rain now pelting at the window, as the chug chug chug of the ferry reverses, spluttering noises, sprinkling foam, outward ripples. The reverberations jitter through my bones, I smile, open out wide as the landscape unfolds, as we float, soar, move across this water, river, ria, fluid interchange, place of exchange. Gulls cry kra—ws and as they fly, we float; as we float, they fly. What does this journey feel like, floating, fl-o-a-t ing, floating in thought, memory, imagination, possibility ...? fl-oat.

Floating, on a ferry, is a choice made by individuals who want to move from one side of the river to the other. 'You don't happen to be on a ferry for no reason', an interviewee told me: 'you do it because you want to get to another point' (Rita, ferry passenger, River Tamar). It is, as I write in the vignette above, this 'desire' to move between land, across water, that spurs individuals to 'wait for' and board a ferry. A transition between terra firma, the firm land, land locked, landed-ness (Peters, Steinberg and Stratford, 2018) towards a tidal river, which is never the same twice, a watery passage characterised by current, tide, flow, weather and movement (cf. Bowles, Kaaristo and Rogelja Caf, 2019). Above, the body is initially considered through the act of swimming, an embodiment of energy to submerge beneath these waters, yet the limitations of the body soon become apparent, in relation to cold, wet, distance, and of forces and currents too powerful. An independent boat is dismissed from a practical perspective as I do not have the skillset required to know and navigate these tides. Stepping onto a ferry, and floating across these waters, is, therefore, required for those who need a 'guide' (Rita, ferry passenger, River Tamar), to direct them across the river, and also requires a certain level of 'trust' in those guiding (Rita, ferry passenger, River Tamar), reassurance for the passengers that float atop these waters.

My line, 'there and back again, on a historic boat taking me back in time, taking me into time, suspending me over time on the water' echoes Walt Whitman's phrase 'suspend here and everywhere, eternal float of solution' (line 107), in his poem, 'Crossing Brooklyn Ferry' ([1856] 1881). Tying together the literary and the literal is the phrase 'suspend', a perplexing and puzzling phrase which can be defined in multiple ways: 'to bring a stop to for a time; to prolong a phrase (as in music), to keep from falling or sinking, and to be kept in a state of expectation or suspense' (*Collins English Dictionary*, 2014). Such etymological flexibility is apt for a ferry, which has been used by writers across time to symbolise and draw together transitional worlds between landscapes: from the Greek mythology of Charon, transporting souls between the land of the living and of the dead across the River Styx (Sullivan, 1950); to the imagined speed of the ferry in Shakespeare's Merchant of Venice (1600) or Edmund Spenser's (1509) knight, who crosses a ferry before arriving on a 'floating island'.

Macfarlane and Flynn's (2021) song 'Ferryman', on an album inspired by the Epic of Gilgamesh, depicts a ferryman called upon to 'carry my memory on / out to the island / on the horizon / following the path to the sun'. The term 'suspend' seems to hold these layers of meaning together, where the ferry is both a physical connective point transporting people between places, and also layered in symbolism and possibility. It is as if the movement, from one side of the river to the other, opens up possibilities of thought in an imaginative pull. The ferry's double movement from here to there, there to here: suspended matter crossing water makes routine and rhythmical an age-old question of how and why we float upon water.

Returning to Whitman's poetic line, 'suspend here and every-where, eternal float of solution', floating is both a 'solution' for mobility, creating movement from one side of the river to the other and also an act of 'suspension'. Passengers are required to remain still, allowing the ferry operator to guide their movement across the 'crested and scallop-edg'd waves' (line 102). And yet, in the poet's imagination, time onboard this floating ferry offers both an opening towards and proximity in relation to the river, as seen out from beyond the hand-'rail' (line 25) towards wind, sky and seabirds; moving between the 'flood-tide and ebb' (line 101). The poet is also drawn to the 'crowds' (line 3) of people onboard, both 'of the past and those of the future' (line 8), who may be 'returning home' (line 4) and whose thoughts are 'more curious to me than you suppose' (line 4). Reflecting this poetic structure, the next section of this chapter considers the river itself, and the unique sensations of floating across the river, and there-after, considers floating as an exchange. To conclude, I share reflections upon the act of floating, on a ferry, over water.

To begin, an account of floating on a ferry is narrated through fragments of conversation, overheard, and exchanged between two young children and their parents while crossing the river on the Cremyll Ferry (July 2021). Thereafter, I use these words to weave my own reflections, while echoing that journey.

Seaweed steps

Look, you can see the water,

– Watch the rope –

Are we going?

No, they are still loading people onto the ferry

Ice cream

Water

   Boat

      – I'll get you a drink

We're on a boat daddy, that's why we're on the water.

Is he starting up the engine?

One at a time *(eating popcorn)*

Seagull cry

See, look!

We are still not moving yet

Yay, no we are moving

Ruuuuuuummmm (engine)

We're not going that fast

   We're leaving the land – wow!

Don't fall in

Parent and child, reversed on the seat take a photo

We're turning around!

   Why are we going round again?

That's better, we are facing the right way now

   We're going pretty fast!

Ripple eases behind us

Waves bounce

You're dropping it *(to the child eating popcorn)*

Child on phone, recording the journey, child poses for a photo

We're on the water – wow!

Dad, are we going to turn that way

I've never seen a –

Sound of engine drowning sound

Why have we stopped moving?

Because we're nearly at the other side now

Nearly

Yeah, look there's the beach on the other side

Fire on the boat

Why do we have to cross the river?

When we see granny, we go over the bridge

Now, we are going over on a boat –

You have popcorn everywhere!

Ruuummmmm, ruuuuummmm

What are we doing?

We are mooring: you moor a boat, you park a car

You'll have to jump off and wade to shore

You can't see the bottom here.

No, it's deeper here than on the other side

Will we come back?

Yes, we have to return home on the ferry

I can see the bottom

Look, we're in Cornwall now

Why are we not where we were?

The experience of crossing the river churns up immediate questions about the present: where are we going, what is happening, how am I being moved? This water, interacting with the side of the boat, is also disruptive. 'Waves bounce', a ripple eases behind the boat, and the water shapes the direction of the boat, but leaves the child passengers in a sense of disorientation with questions arising in the unfolding journey punctuating the account. The water is before and to the side and, while on the ferry, all around. Shifting speeds, from pause, to acceleration, reversing to rotation, impact the experience of the passengers, as the child attempts to pre-empt the direction that the skipper will steer the boat, 'are we going to turn that way?', 'Why are we going round again?' Noise, difficult to capture through written language and record in the ever-changing space of water, is the characteristic of this ferry crossing, the sound of the engine overpowering the spoken voice, 'drowning sound'. The engine's sound is more widely characterised as a 'hum', sometimes 'gentle' and at other times 'chugging' and 'noisy' (reflection card responses). The sound of the engine is a constant undertone, and punctuates particular points, decibels of sound rising higher as the speed increases, then lowering as it slows, before a releasing and fizzling noise and gurgle, corresponding with the ferry swinging round and shifting its position on the river.

The very first line, 'Seaweed steps', is an alert to the sensation of the river's rise and fall, as seaweed, carried by the motion of the river, floats up to the slip at high tide, and leaves its cloak as a strand line to step over. The seaweed is a reminder of the 'interchangeability of land and sea in this marginal world of the shore' (Carson and Hines, 1955: 6) as steps, usually conflated with the concrete ground, are covered by a thin, micro-film layer of algae. A sensory signal to passengers of the watery environment they are just about to float upon. 'For life to flourish, there must be gaps or fissures that allow a passage between the two' (Ingold, 2021: 101). The stranded seaweed, lining the edge of the slip brings attention to this 'transitional zone between terrestrial and

aquatic ecosystems' (Chen, 2013: 274). Smell of the river's depths, as
the seaweed curls, knots and intertwines in a pattern bulged by the
force of the tide, meeting footsteps and street debris. Step over seaweed.
Passage between the terrestrial and aquatic. The directive, 'Look, you
can see the water' shifts the visual gaze upwards, towards the water,
as passengers queue, shuffling slowly towards the ferry, now momentarily linked to the edge of the land by the material fibres of rope.
Rope has always been a fundamental part of a boat's itinerary
(Barnes, 1996). The rope is a stable, weaved material connected to the
internal space of the ferry, which ties and holds the floating vessel to
the stable structure of land, if only for a temporary time as passengers
board. A tight rope held to a fastened loophole on the adjacent slip
has the material capacity and stretch to resist the moving buoyancy
of the river's waves beneath the bow of the boat, and is a key piece
of equipment. Without a tightly held rope, the ferry may drift in the
current, meaning that the gap between the edge of the slip and side of
the ferry may widen, thus creating a possible hazard for members of
the public, so it is important to 'watch the rope'. The rope is looped and
hooped through a metal ring, arching up and drilled down to the side
of the slip, providing a link for people to 'load onto the ferry'.

The two phrases, 'we're leaving the land – wow!' and 'we're on
the water – wow!' parallel and complement each other, in the shift
from land to water and from water to land, that the ferry crossing
tugs and pulls and achieves. Yet, despite the excitement and anticipation that being on the water clearly affords, there is a subtle and
slight tension that emerges, that can be traced through the warnings
and concern scattering these fragments of exchange: 'don't fall in',
'fire on the boat', 'you can't see the bottom here'. Chen reminds us
that 'watery places are not always comfortable, or even familiar. They
can be uncanny – a place of others, or an *other place*' (2013: 281). 'We
like this boat because it can float', one person writes on their reflection
card (reflection card Torridge 46), the simple rhyme seemingly craft-
ing an innocent poem, but which draws attention to the individual's
ultimate dependence on the boat's function 'to float'.

Onboard, I see two signs, large stickers containing information
within the interior space of this ferry, that alert my attention to the
fact that we are floating across water. 'LIFE JACKETS', with an arrow
pointing down. I realise that I am sitting on top of these life jackets,
stored beneath my seat. My eyes turn within the boat and I note a
drawing of a silhouetted passenger demonstrating how to put on a

flotation device. 'FERRY PASSENGER: 100N BUOYANCY AID', the capitalised text alerts me, and the drawing motions how there are three intended stages to putting this life jacket on. Pull overhead; fasten; adjust. Advance warning of a hypothetical scenario I am now drifting towards in my imagination where this ferry collides, crashes, breaks down while we are crossing the thalweg line of this river. At the deepest navigable point, inflate flotation device. Remain still; float. The words of a ferry passenger come to mind, as he admits, 'you're also thinking about what happens if it sinks' (Simon, ferry passenger, River Tamar). Sinking is the elephant in the room, the unspoken subject onboard, 'the thing everyone's thinking but no-one's saying' (Simon, ferry passenger, River Tamar). That reminder of our vulnerability, of our instability on this changing tidal, weather-beaten, surface-depth, churn of water as,

> There are some days ... when you're getting exceedingly thrown about, the boat is keeling over, both left and right, waves are splashing right over the front of you and you're very glad to get to the other side. And at that point you understand nature and vulnerability. You mentally look to where the lifejackets should be. You think, are there any lifejackets in there? (Simon, ferry passenger, River Tamar)

'I can't swim', she jokes, as she boards the ferry. A warning passed from father to son, 'don't fall in', the caution evoking a subtle fear we all might have of drowning. 'fǽmig; foaming waters' (Bosworth, 2014a). 'Ðæt ceól scyle fǽmig rídan ýða hrycgum; that the foamy vessel shall ride on the waves' (Bosworth, 2014a); that the vessel may not be turned to foam. Misty, murky, fǽmig, foaming, flodas, l/ost through translation. Keep afloat. A reminder that crossing water is not the same as crossing land. Mentally note where the life jackets should be. Flotation device, floating alongside us, a reminder that,

> Travelling on the water is not the safest thing humans can do and we are not actually built to be on the water so we kind of are working against what we are supposed to do in a way, working on the land just enjoying ourselves. Humans are not normally built to get on ferries and get to other parts of land. So energy meant, for me, in that moment, to be brave and to ignore the very subtle fear you might have of being surrounded just literally by water. (Rita, ferry passenger, River Tamar)

I have heard it said that early flotation devices were inspired by the natural world. Look closely at bladder wrack, a common seaweed found between the high and low water mark on the shore, and see its embedded round air bladders, that enable the seaweed to float upright in the water. Rise to the surface.

Are we grounded

/or/

are we afloat?' Ingold (2021: 104) asks.

As we exchange the ground for the planks and boards of the ferry, take a seat, make space, move around, do we become aware of this subtle, semantic, surface shift? Floating is reliant upon the water levels, low tide, high tide, water is needed here to keep this ferry afloat. Continuous stretch of ground between these two landscapes on either side of this river would negate the need for this ferry. Structural passage of a bridge not practical here. The ground gives way to the river, and the river provides a medium through which this ferry can float. Passengers step across ground, onto the shaky board, and find common ground with those onboard. Boards form part of the structure of this wooden passenger ferry, a material held together with iron and nails, engine and motor, wooden beams and soft furnishings, words imprinted onto signs, crossing these waters. Does being afloat alert us to the ground? Does the ground shift into possibilities of being afloat? Not a permanent state of floating, but a crossing that takes us across this watery ground, that is what I have found.

Why are we not where we were? A question left, floating in the air, soaring in the imagination of a child processing the movement from one side of the river to the other. A journey, a route decided on their behalf, where floating feels like you are not moving at all. And yet, being aware of the subtle distinctions and differences on the other side of the water, changes of shapes, of patterns and people, the beach here, the quay there, the greenery here, the urban place there. Why is it that we cannot straddle two places at once? Why can we not simultaneously be on this side of the river, and that side of the river? Why cross the river at all?

Words float above this floating structure, are related to and entangled with the route of the river, suspended in time and space, just as this ferry moves across time and space, from one side of the river to the other.

Floating with others

Floating on a ferry cannot be distinguished from the other passengers who board the boat with you, those sheltering in the bus stop until the last drizzle of rain flutters away, those with their walking gear, oil-streaked boots tightly laced, waterproof trousers. Those carrying a bike, a wheelchair, a buggy, those tugging the hand of their child, children jumping, dancing in a fit of excitement at this boat to board, an adventure to be had, caught in the transitional tension that awaits towards the other side. People carry with them their ideas, worries, hopes, fears: review the day. Discuss house inflation, the garden project where the wild flowers are assigned to the edges. That man sits, replacing trainers with smart shoes, revealing water-stains dripping like ripples into his dark socks. Some sit in silence, absorbed by their own thoughts, concerns, imaginations. Regular passengers may exchange small-talk among familiar faces, friendships built up over time in this shared experience of floating, of movement, of crossing. For some, these minutes are sacred, as work starts on the other side. Hold on to this buffer zone between your own time and work time. For others, this space is a hands-free opportunity to catch up on texts, emails, messages; to share a photo, take a selfie, ping across these invisible infrastructural lines of communication that hold us together. The journey dependent upon those that board the boat with you, snatched moments of connection, shared temporary experience, a willingness to open up. Ferry: floating over.

Chen observes that boats are an 'apparatus with which to know a watery place' (Chen, 2013: 281). A ferry, by extension, is both an apparatus for which to know a watery place and a place where people can get to know each other. To know and be known. The distinction being that a boat lends itself towards being a private space; a ferry is a public space. And those that board the boat with you, who sit next to you, talk next to you, stroke your dog, share a smile, look away, look up, reach out in small-talk, turn towards deep conversation, watch the water, enter into their own thoughts and imagination, are an entangled and central part of this river-crossing experience. The ferry crossing is an example of how,

> places are continually (re)produced through the mobile flows which course through and around them, bringing together ephemeral, contingent and relatively stable arrangements of people, energy and matter. (Edensor, 2011: 190)

People arrive, queue, board, float, depart. That is the fundamental shape of this crossing point, the energy of this river crossing, demand creating daily cycles, rhythms, timetables shifting people from one side of the river to the other, and repeat. A 'beginning, as well as an end, but also duration in the unfolding of spatio-temporal processes' (Andrews and Roberts, 2012: 1), in the shift from land to water, and returning back to land.

In this in-between watery space, there is a meeting of bodies, as individuals cross this body of water. Old, young, 'we are all bodies of water' (Neimanis, 2017: 96), and we remember our wateriness, in this act of stepping off land onto water, recalling how,

> We're born in water, we're literally shaped by water. So our human form is shaped by water and we have come to the edges to remember that; and re-engaging with the simplicity of sharing our space with gulls and fish and crabs. And retired river boatmen who take us across a river. We re-engage with that simplicity of ropes and catches. (Ruth, ferry passenger, River Torridge)

For Ruth, the act of stepping off land, onto water, is a reminder of her watery connections, the proximity towards 'gulls and fish and crabs', connected with the marine environment both above and below water, and finding herself shifting towards those who can 'take us across a river'. This is a floating with others that is conscious of the exterior, the sounds of water, movement and activity of people, ever shifting towards the other side.

Boarding a boat is a social experience, '– fére; a companion' (Bosworth, 2014b). Ferry-fére; a 'meeting place, a place to talk, a place to get advice' (reflection card, Helford 132). And meanings are created in this space, in this meeting of bodies, these companions, being in company, crossing water, crossing over, body of water. Aware of space and distance, molecules and bodies. Drifting and letting each other drift on these waters, this changing river body. Has this river changed, or have I changed through this river, on this river, crossing this river? Landscape to move towards, landscape to move away from, this river straddled at every crossing. I shuffle to my seat and try to keep space. People are seated, watching water. Will I ever see these people again? Might I recognise them? These minutes of chance encounters, these strangers that shape this journey with me, the sound of conversation drifting, dragging, lifting, shifting, rising, meeting, entering my ears, my eyes. Sensory overload. That feeling of floating across water. Not quite floating, as there is a friction here, there is an intention, a pushing forwards towards movement, effort, churn of the engine, accelerate. Unlikely I will remember these faces of those who float with me.

'My desire

    to move

        from one place to another,

                is in water'

        he turned

      and said to me,

a phrase that introduced stories of swimming across water, distance, channel, across river, lake and fjord. Somewhat disgruntled that he is floating on a vessel this time, rather than choosing his own bodily movement through water. Perhaps. We board, we are held, there is an opportunity for connection, for those that choose to lift their eyes to the passengers sitting opposite, or who are squeezed beside them. Small-talk about the weather, birds, the shape of the day, that boat, that building, return to the weather, oscillating sky, cloud formations, sun-shine, strike out a flattering comment complimenting your outfit, stroke your dog. Listen to the sound of water, mixed with engine noise, churned up by current, wind, rain. Enter into that space of pause as we cross these waters. Before we go our separate ways.

...

So the birthing process is to find oneself on another piece of land and then the ferry is the umbilical cord. The ferry is the umbilical cord. That transitioning, that kind of breathing, that allowing you to breathe. All that dive apparatus. The ferry is that dive apparatus where you have the two tubes, one for oxygen, one for carbon monoxide allowing you to breathe. (Ruth, ferry passenger, River Torridge)

...

Breathe in, breathe out

...

Breathe in, board the boat, breathe out, sit down.

...

Breathe in look around, breathe out that tension you are
floating on water.

...

Breathe in smile at that passenger, breathe out, look down.

...

Breathe in, breathe out

...

Hear the sound surrounding the water punctuated by
rhythmic intervals of seagull cries, catch the sporadic melody
of oyster-catcher calls. Distant, echoey sounds float over
the river from the boatyard, a dung-dung-dung rhythm, as
if someone is tapping a chamber of sound, long, vibrating
rhythms. Wavelengths.

...

Breathe in, breathe out

...

Flitting in and around the water are people in conversation,
shouting, nattering, lifting their voices with syllabic aahes and
maams and whiiiyyziis – look across the water. Sounds of feet
on gravel, scraping against pebbles.

...

Breathe in, breathe out

...

Breathe in, water is the magnet pull, bringing us together here.
Breathe

out, water draws us together, as we are being pulled across this
water.

...

Breathe

...

Umbilical chord, chord of connection.

Breathe in ... breathe out ...

I have heard stories of proposals positioned on these waters;
heard stories of ashes being scattered, mingling with the tide, as
the ferry reaches the mid-point of this river. River holding intimate grief, intimate promises. 'We carry the river, its body of
water, in our body' (Diaz, 2020: 51), these waters holding layers
of symbol stretching into meaning, river-deity, water-spirit, gift
of life, cleansing power, the shifting tide a resting place for the
soul. Be mesmerised by water. 'Hí ofer sǽ ferdon; they went over
the sea' (Bosworth, 2014c); let that journey take you inwards,
outwards, inwards. Breathe in. Breathe out. A joining together, a
letting go, ebb and flow. 'Ealne wídan ferh' (Bosworth, 2014d); ferh
means life.

This membrane

is not a divisive barrier,

but an interval of passage:

solid enough

to differentiate,

facilitate change.

but permeable enough to

(Neimanis, 2016: 21)

Interchange, exchange, to be changed. Reach for the spare change.

Floating as exchange

Floating on a ferry is a chargeable fare, £2 to cross one way, £2 to cross back again. 'Don't pay the ferryman until he gets you to the other side', de Burgh (1982) warns, the song surfacing in my memory. It used to be that the fare was collected on the river, but that has shifted now, so that the ferry fare is paid at the other side. Land is the payment line, where coins and notes are exchanged, passed over from one to another. Alternatively, an encoded plastic card floats in front of a screen – beep. Transfer, a crossing over of money from one material object towards the other. I give a £10 note, receive a return ticket, bearing,

No 15130 Cremyll Ferry (Return Crossing) ADULT Ticket must be retained and shown on the return journey. Weather, Tide & Circumstances permitting.

Alongside, she drops a £1 coin into my hand as change, and places a waxy, blue sheet into my palm, its width wider than my hand, a five-pound note. I look at it. Shades of blue, white, yellow and green, echoing the colour of the river today, ripples reflecting the cloudless blue sky, with streaks of the golden sun. The note is partly crumpled, folds of past passengers, who have tucked this note into pockets, into purses. I search the note for a sign of the river. It is there, but hidden, flowing beneath Westminster Bridge, written over and under with the repeating letters,

BOEBOEBOEBOEBOEBOEBOEBOE,
ten layers separating the south from the north shore.
Current into currency.

It is said that 'water no longer flows downhill, it flows towards money' (Syngedouw, 2007: 195). Yet, what about when water is enfolded into the illustrated fabric of money? Look closely at a £5 note and you will see a river just about visible, running beneath the structural width of Westminster Bridge, London, its waters running into words – BOE – Bank of England, Bank of England, Bank of England. Repetition is a form of change. Change is a form of repetition. Fortunes lying beneath this river, treasures found at low tide by the mudlarks (Maiklem, 2019). Bear, in describing the Hooghly River (Ganges), that borders India and Bangladesh, writes how the river and its workers are visible in local posters, on the 'back of buses, majhis – *boatmen* and their boats appear bearing the Indian flag' (2015: 21). A parallel, of sorts in this £5 note, although the River Thames' ferry operators that offered a 'passage to and fro across the Thames' (Roberts and Godfrey, 1951) before the construction of Westminster Bridge are not remembered on this note. There is something here that I hold onto. In order to cross this ferry, I exchange a £10 note and in return receive a £5 note illustrating this shifting river story. I have to look closely, unpick the words that have become water. Look down from the bridge, scan south to north, find the gap where the Thames ferry would have been. The note exchanged for the River Tamar ferry leads towards the lost Thames ferry, now replaced by a bridge. Bridge representing and becoming symbol of constant connection, a permanent structure over two previously separated places. Cross the river at any time, no need to wait to float across on a ferry.

Bridges are also visible on one side of a Euro bank note, as symbols of connection between two shores. A German interviewee told me, just before crossing the River Tamar on the ferry, 'as far as I know, these bridges don't really exist, but they exert this European idea of connecting countries' (Rita, ferry passenger, River Tamar). Bridging as metaphor: to bridge two shores, two people, countries, cultures, across this river. Ideal of connection.

> In separating two objects,
>
> we underline their connectedness
>
> and in connecting two objectives, we simultaneously
>
> acknowledge and
>
> underscore what separates them. (Baldacchino, 2007: 4)

Bridge over river; remove the temporary ferry, replace with permanent structure, cement ideals of connection. Ferry too complex, with the shifting tides, current, weather, wind, potential to drift off-course. Bridge deep-set lines within the landscape, spanning landscape, creating height and distance away from the surface of water – suspension bridge. Remove the feeling of floating, create 'sensations of flying, falling, calmness, spirituality and vertigo, before reaching land on the other side' (Irving, 2015: 145). Floating a feeling of embodied transience, change dependent on atmosphere, weather, tidal current; on those others that float across with you, in – fére, company. Water flows towards money, money flows as water. Yet erases ferry, sketches bridge, idealistic connection – bringing a bridging of shores. Passenger ferries remembered and forgotten, forgotten and remembered while I cross this river, on this ferry, exchange money, receive a pink ticket, with a slight tear to show that I have been there.

Floating reflections

Words within this chapter record and draw attention towards a temporary act of travel, departure, movement, landing: floating, suspension, friction; movement from land to water to land and back again, the ferry a connective structure creating routes across water. Out of operation hours, when the ferry is not there and you look at the river, the only sign of movement is through the written signs displayed on either bankside. A timetable setting out regularity, promising transportation across water. The river itself shows little sign of this floating structure, in the rise and fall of the tide, the multi-directionality of the wind, flying of seabirds and undulation of seaweed, alongside whatever else these waters carry, not quite possible to see from the surface. 'The water is wide, I cannot cross o'er, and neither have two wings to fly. Fetch me a boat, that will carry two, and it shall row, my love and I', writes a passenger, travelling on a ferry (reflection card Helford 121), a quotation from the traditional ballad, 'The Water is Wide' (Sharp and Marson, 1906), but with a small memory slip, where the meaning is subtly changed. Rather than the individual taking the action of rowing, as in 'I shall row', this reflection transfers agency to the boat, where 'it shall row', the floating object itself, seemingly effortlessly ferrying the passengers, enwrapped in 'love'. Floating is a letting go, but also an act of pure determination. To cross over is a conscious act, and allowing yourself to cross over is often a retracing of footsteps, of routes, routines.

Why is it that we want to float? What draws us to the water? What propels us to step onto the side of a boat, to depart land, and to float? Is it an ancient memory, stirring up from within us, reminding us of who we are, of our water-borne origins, where fluid moves within us as channels, arteries, capillaries, buoyant that we are? Remain still in the water for a fraction of time and you will float to the surface. We have turned our backs on water, to carve structures on-land, forged straight edges in materials of earth and ore, rock and stone. Returning to the water stirs up a deep sensation from within, that stepping off of land into, onto a colourless, rippling salty liquid. Raft, boat, ferry, floating structure. Hold on tight. Observe the leaf, the twig, the reed; watch out for the stone, the sand, the sediment weighed down at the bottom while water ripples over. Learn to float. Lean in to float, stroke of water, casting ripple, churning foam, forging friction. Move across water. Join the poets of the past in this transitional space between life and death, past and future, possibility and creativity. Cross the river to be refreshed, cross the river to see land anew, cross the river to understand your place in relation to these elemental forces that shape the places we move through and bodies we inhabit. See the river reflecting and refracting; holding and resisting being held, in constant, changing movement: sound, water, ripple. Drink water, think with water, float across water. That pull of gravity, tug of an oar, pull of engine, transforming us, shifting us, lifting us. Float.

References

(2014) Suspend. *Collins English Dictionary*. 12th edition. London: HarperCollins Publishers.

(2021a) Ferry, n.1. *Oxford English Dictionary*. Online: Oxford University Press.

(2021b) Ferry, v. *Oxford English Dictionary*. Online: Oxford University Press.

Andrews, H. and Roberts, L. (2012) *Liminal Landscapes: Travel, Experience and Spaces In-Between*. London: Routledge.

Baldacchino, G. (2007) Introduction: bridges & islands: a strained relationship. In G. Baldacchino (ed.) *Bridging Islands: The Impact of Fixed Links*. Charlottetown: Acorn Press, pp. 1–14.

Barnes, R. H. (1996) *Sea Hunters of Indonesia: Fishers and Weavers of Lamalera*. Oxford: Clarendon Press.

Bear, L. (2015) *Navigating Austerity: Currents of Debt Along a South Asian River*. Stanford: Stanford University Press.

Bosworth, J. (2014a) Fǽmig. In T. Northcote Toller, C. Sean and O. Tichy (eds) *An Anglo-Saxon Dictionary Online*. Prague: Charles University.

Bosworth, J. (2014b) – fére. In T. Northcote Toller, C. Sean and O. Tichy (eds) *An Anglo-Saxon Dictionary Online*. Prague: Charles University.

Bosworth, J. (2014c) Feran. In T. Northcote Toller, C. Sean and O. Tichy (eds) *An Anglo-Saxon Dictionary Online*. Prague: Charles University.

Bosworth, J. (2014d) Ferh. In T. Northcote Toller, C. Sean and O. Tichy (eds) *An Anglo-Saxon Dictionary Online*. Prague: Charles University.

Bowles, B., Kaaristo, M. and Rogelja Caf, N. (2019) Dwelling on and with water – materialities, (im)mobilities and meanings: introduction to the special issue. *Anthropological Notebooks*, 25(5), 5–12.

Carson, R. and Hines, B. (1955) *The Edge of the Sea*. Boston: Houghton Mifflin.

Chen, C. (2013) Mapping waters: thinking with watery place. In C. Chen, J. MacLeod and A. Neimanis (eds) *Thinking with Water*. Montreal: McGill-Queen's University Press, pp. 274–294.

De Burgh, C. (1982) Don't pay the ferryman. *The Getaway*. London: A&M Records Ltd.

Diaz, N. (2020) The first water is the body. In *Postcolonial Love Poem*. London: Faber & Faber Ltd, pp. 49–58.

Edensor, T. (2011) Commuter: mobility, rhythm and commuting. In T. Cresswell and P. Merriman (eds) *Geographies of Mobilities: Practices, Spaces, Subjects*. Farnham: Ashgate Publishing Ltd, pp. 189–204.

Ingold, T. (2021) *Correspondences*. Cambridge: Polity Press.

Irving, A. (2015) Granite and steel. In M. Harris and N. Rapport (eds) *Reflections on Imagination: Human Capacity and Ethnographic Method*. London: Routledge, pp. 135–160.

Macfarlane, R. and Flynn, J. (2021) Ferryman. In *Lost in the Cedar Wood*. London: Transgressive Records.

Maiklem, L. (2019) *Mudlarking: Lost and Found on the River Thames*. London: Bloomsbury Publishing.

Muir, B. J. (1994) Riddle 14. In B. J. Muir (ed.) *The Exeter Anthology of Old English Poetry*. Exeter: Exeter University Press.

Neimanis, A. (2017) Thinking with matter, rethinking Irigaray: a 'liquid ground' for a planetary feminism. In C. Taylor and H. Sharp (eds) *Feminist Philosophies of Life*. Montreal: McGill-Queen's University Press, pp. 42–67.

Peters, K., Steinberg, P. and Stratford, E. (2018) *Territory beyond Terra*. London: Rowman & Littlefield International.

Roberts, H. and Godfrey, W. H. (1951) Lambeth Bridge and its predecessor the Horseferry. In *Survey of London: Lambeth South Bank and Vauxhall*. London: British History Online, pp. 118–121.

Shakespeare, W. (1600) The merchant of Venice. In S. Greenblatt, W. Cohen, J. E. Howard and K. Eisaman Maus (eds) *The Norton Shakespeare based on the Oxford Edition*. London: W. W. Norton & Company.

Sharman, J. (2003) Tamar ferries: part I, the lower reaches. *Tamar: Journal of the Friends of Morwellham*, 25(1), 1–10.

Sharp, C. and Marson, C. (1906) The water is wide. In C. Sharp and C. Marson (eds) *Folk Songs from Somerset*. Third Series, No. LXVI. Online: Traditional Tune Archive, pp. 32–33.

Spenser, E. (1590 [2007]) *The Faerie Queene*, ed. A. C. Hamilton, book II, canto VI, stanza 4 and stanza 11. Harlow: Pearson Education Limited.

Sullivan, F. A. (1950) Charon, the ferryman of the dead. *Classic Journal*, 46(1), 11–17.

Swyngedouw, E. (2007) Water, money, power. In L. Patitch and C. Leys (eds) *Socialist Register: Coming to Terms with Nature*. volume 43. London: The Merlin Press, pp. 195–212.

Way, A. (ed.) (1843–1865) *Promptorium parvulorum sive clericorum*. Camden Society edition, 3 vols. London: Camden Society, 25, 54, 89.

Whitman, W. (1856) [1881] Crossing Brooklyn ferry. In M. Ferguson, M. J. Salter and J. Stallworthy (eds) *The Norton Anthology of Poetry*. New York: W. W. Norton & Company, pp. 1066–1071.

5

Homes, happenings and everyday lives: afloat on London's waterways

Lorna Flutter

Although somewhat concealed and secretive, the domestic and mundane is afloat on London's inland waterways. The majority of boats found along the public towpaths take on some kind of domestic arrangement and provide their occupants year-round residency. Boat dwellers, however, are well used to being asked, by those passing them on the towpath, 'Do you actually live in there, all of the time?' Despite the frequency of these questions, there are clues that boats are homes. In the colder months, bags of coal are piled up on roofs, often set down in between solar panels, plant pots and a combination of other essential and rejected items. Smoke rises from little chimneys and lit-up windows bring a comforting glow to otherwise darkened towpaths.

The boats moored along the city's canal- and riversides form awkward residential patchworks that, due to their requirement to complete a fortnightly move, are continually undone and re-sewn. The continuous cruiser licence, which mobile boaters on the UK's (Canal and River Trust managed) inland waterways are required to hold, stipulates that boats should 'not stay moored in the same neighbourhood or locality for more than 14 days' and should cover at a minimum, 20 canal miles over the year in one continuous direction (Canal and River Trust, 2021; for extended take see Malkogeorgou, 2019: 222). Thus, boat dwellers are placed in perpetual navigation of, and in negotiation with, broad stretches of inland waterways.

London's waterways form a 'linear village' that many continuous cruisers frequent (for analysis of the 'linear village' see

Malkogeorgou, 2019 and Bowles, 2015). It stretches through industrial outskirts, along the edges of parks, under roads, train lines and a portion of lower Islington, through central city space and between residential streets. Boaters' route in, through and out of the city is led by this embedded network of canals and navigations (canalised rivers). These waterways are terrestrially contained, bound by concrete edges and muddy banksides. However, they are mobile and materially transformative spaces. The water's levels, contents, inhabitants, seasons and the surrounding environment shift and change continually. Consequently, the waterways both encourage and require an intimate attentiveness from those who live on them.

Boat dwellers' pursuit of living with water, at its most fundamental, is to float on it; thus ensuring the stability and most basic liveability of their homes. However, while their relationship with the water represents a precariousness, it also provides a playful and joyful way of living differently in the city, disrupting the foundations of dwelling and weaving water into the meaning, practices and embodiment of home.

The interests of this chapter lie in how water, both literally and figuratively, seeps into and shapes boat dwellers' experience of everyday life, considering its role as a joy and a threat, a substance that offers both support and conflict. Viewing water as it is framed through boaters' homes is intended to draw out its capacity to inform practices of home making and sustaining, while exploring its potential to both enable and constrain domestic life.

The ability of public city water to inform the everyday experience, and particularly its positive association with wellbeing, has become increasingly acknowledged (see, for example, Buser et al., 2020; De Bell et al., 2017; Foley and Kistemann, 2015; Voelker and Kistemann, 2013). This body of research has brought attention to the notable health benefits and social value in access to, and engagement with, bodies of urban water and waterways. More recently, however, theorists have begun to draw out the multiplicities of urban water, presented by its role in entangling bodies, socialities, politics and cultures within the city (Watson, 2019a, 2019b), while considering its ability to inform disparate emotional and embodied experiences (Pitt, 2018). In refreshing and exciting ways, city water is being presented through its pluralities, pointing to the meaning it takes on and makes within the city (particularly relevant to Watson, 2019a).

London's navigable waterways are simultaneously cut into and set back from the surrounding city, shaping a unique residential experience and informing particular spatial practices, socialities and politics (see Bowles, 2015, 2019; Malkogeorgou, 2019; Roberts, 2019). This has been explored by Ben Bowles (2019) in terms of how living on London's inland waterways reshapes social connectivity and 'flattens' organisational structures. Here Bowles is highlighting the metaphorical potential of the waterways' material and geographic qualities, which he considers to be 'free flowing' and 'flat' in a 'Deluzian sense' (2019: 51). Bowles, Kaaristo and Caf (2019: 5) further encourage water to be taken seriously as a source of 'political, socio-cultural and metaphorical meanings', revealing its ability to enable and constrain mobilities, shaping new meanings while it 'muddies' terrestrial certainties (Bowles, Kaaristo and Caf, 2019: 8).

Boat dwellers' homes are precariously positioned on the water, bringing its varied potentialities into the realities of their everyday lives. This encourages us to consider not only how water shapes public and collective experiences within the city, but also how it informs the lived experience of home, its making and embodiment. Sarah Pink (2006) explores the kind of practices undertaken within, and meanings made out of, the sensory experience of domestic settings. Through these, the intimate sensory observations, temporalities, material transformations and home making that occur each day within our living spaces are sensitively drawn out. An increased need to observe, negotiate with and maintain the home environment can be demonstrated by those living 'off-grid' (Vannini and Taggart, 2015), inviting us to consider the unique relationships people hold with their home environments, particularly when geographically isolated, self-sufficient and environmentally dependent.

This chapter will offer a sensitive and ethnographically informed account of how living on canal boats informs multiple, conflictual relationships with water as it enters into and shapes boat dwellers' experience of home. It will explore how water is mediated and imagined, situating it as an active part of the domestic environment and recognising the way it can inform practices of home making, sustaining and everyday life. Doing so will extend on work that has explored the process of becoming accustomed to narrowboats as confined spaces that move, moor and float (Kaaristo, 2018; Kaaristo and Rhoden, 2017; Roberts, 2019) and how waterways and scapes are experienced through the confines of the craft that situate you within them (Malkogeorgou, 2019; Vannini, 2012).

The experience of living with water is explored through ethnographic accounts of 'Bed', 'The space under the floor', 'The window' and 'The ropes'. Each part gives a sense of what it is like to spend everyday life afloat, illustrating the different ways water is considered and interacted with through particular parts of boat dwellers' homes. Taking water's many sensory, material and imagined qualities seriously draws out varied and conflictual experiences of living on and with it. Framing the chapter through individual components of residential canal boats is an attempt to draw out the sensitivities of everyday life as it is shaped by, and situated in, domestic space (as seen in Bates, 2019; Miller, 2008; Pink, 2006; for a methodological take, see Lenhard and Samanani, 2020). Thus, water is attended to as a joyful, unruly and 'risky' substance within the context of the domestic and mundane (Watson, 2019b).

Floating through the field

In October 2020, I bought and moved onto a 47.6ft narrowboat and have been living on it as a continuous cruiser and navigating London's waterways ever since. I have met, shared locks, lockdowns, moored alongside and befriended many of London's mobile boaters. There are people I have met once, some I see now and then, and others with whom I share fond friendships. During the 2020/21 winter Covid-19 lockdowns I met and became friends with five other boaters new to the water. The shared experience of being confined to and dependent on our newly acquired canal boats led the interests of my research towards the intimacy of boaters' relationships with their boats. A focus on home provided a lens through which the ever-changing and dynamic qualities of living on the waterways came through more significantly than that of the participants' temporary social isolation or immobility. Therefore, this chapter does not focus on themes of isolation, but instead presents living with water in its enduring unpredictability, mobility and shift.

Social-distancing restrictions and the limitations to participant observation informed a heavier reliance on interview and video methods. Therefore, supporting my own observations of home, the stories boat dwellers have shared in interviews, video tours of their boats and chats on the towpath shape and appear in each 'part' of home the chapter presents. The majority of the boat dwellers within this research, including myself, live on narrowboats, which are the traditionally shaped long and thin boats that are found, typically in the highest numbers, on London's canals. These boats have provided both myself and my participants an autonomously chosen, and relatively adequate, standard of living, despite periods spent quite normally without electricity, running water, a working engine or heating.

Bed

Weary bodies clamber over one another, tired from the demands of the city and home in equal measure. Their resting spots are often found in the recesses of boats, in a windowless stern, tucked into the point of the bow, or assembled from sofas and tables that sit below the window line. Time spent lying in bed might be when you become most aware of being afloat, or at least, the sensory experience of being afloat becomes more intimate and delicate. Slack ropes let the boat pull away from the bank and fenders pad each return. Bodies mirror the restful position of their craft in the water, merging together softly. A cradle-like comfort capable of lulling on sleep. 'Have you had a dream that you're sinking yet?' is a question frequently posed to those new to the cut, perhaps considered a necessary reminder that one's new and precarious relationship with water does not relent during unconscious states.

In bed you will likely not be able to look over the flattened waterscape, but in return, its sounds and sensations become acute. Darkened cabins draw imaginations outward while letting in the finer qualities of living on the water, easily missed when entangled in the day. Canal birds can be heard foraging the weedy greenery growing on hull sides, detected from the inside by delicate taps. Rain sounds tinny as it hits the roof but slick as it slips down the sides into the cut (the canal). Boats unexpectedly whir past in the small hours, their headlights merging with the moon or city's midnight gleam on the water. The stillness of some nights contrasts sharply with the jolting and thudding of others, and attempts to sleep can be easily distracted by the collaboration between craft, water and wind. A sometimes frustratingly elemental battle of bedding down for the night.

Ill-arranged ropes and fenders creak and groan, not that you would have noticed their irksome whines in the day, and warm bodies are pulled outside to adjust them. Tuning out these noises can be more effort than a dark and cold re-negotiation with their source. Abstracted by darkness and periodic sleep, you feel the weather weaving its way through the waterway and the patchwork of boats stitched to its sides. The wind is funnelled through gaps in buildings that line the canal, exaggerating its strength. The water, wind-whipped, lets boats test the slack in their ropes, which respond by tugging them, frustrated, back to the bankside. Bed is brought into 'the open' as the water laps around the edges of home (Ingold, 2000).

On calmer nights, when water and weather combine in a state of stillness, the city is more likely to take its turn in bed with you. Groups gather on darkened stretches of the towpath, taking their turn to look over the reflective recess, giving sanctuary from mundanely matte and more scrutinised city spaces. Passing trains on nearby lines are felt through sensations that can only be noticed in bed. Although, only on nights when bed is suspended in stillness. In central portions of the city, the towpath ticks over with visitors. A cyclist slicks pain- lessly past in direct contrast to a loud drunken pair that come slowly in and out of range. Lying in whatever you wear to bed, the city feels as though it might come stumbling through the door, catching you in a state of homely vulnerability.

> It took Laura a while to get used to sleeping on her boat. At first she had felt as though she was sleeping 'basically in a ditch in a public space and it was a bit like in a shed in the middle of London'. Semi-naked and half asleep, a strong sense of being both in and out of place is brought on. One is at home and in bed, eyes are closed and your head is on the pillow. The covers are pulled over, the curtains are drawn and the doors are locked but the sense of being adrift in the city, exposed for those stumbling past to stop and peer in, is there too. Amy describes that at night her boat feels like an 'embryonic sack', in which she is suspended in protective fluids but at the mercy of being pierced at any moment from the outside. The delicacy of this arrangement makes her feel oddly more vulnerable inside than when she steps out into the realities of the night. It is from the inside that 'cosy confronts the edge of menace', a conflictual duality of an urban life afloat.

Even from bed, London's 'waterways can be simultaneously a homely and inhospitable place' (see Roberts, 2019: 62). The comfort of containing walls is questioned; they are seemingly more porous and pierceable than the superstructures that in reality encase. The vulnerability of attempted sleep sees the imagination transform the material structures of home, beds tucked into 'a sort of half-box, part walls, part door' (Bachelard, 1969: 137). Eyes close and the walls thin, passers by peer in, light licks the ceiling and the water laps at the floor. The waterway comes in, as imaginations reach out, both nightmare-ish and dream like. Sheds and embryonic sacks start to better reflect home as the waterway seeps into the imagination and shapes material bounds of oneiric space.

Although boat dwellers take to a new place every two weeks, they remain in their 'corner of the world', wrapped within home, rather than routed by it (Bachelard, 2014: 26). Being in bed constitutes a large part of being at home in each temporary place, thus the observations made from it become part of boat dwellers' imaginaries of both home and place. The closeness of the waterway on one side is matched by the closeness of the wayward city on the other. The vulnerability of losing waking consciousness exaggerates the need to imagine the edges of home. The sounds and sensations of the city's waters are heightened, imagined, dreamt about and abstracted. The waterway sneaks in easily through the senses. However, to sleep, trust must be placed in the superstructures that separate you from it and the ropes and pins that attach you to its sides.

The space under the floor

Unlike other recesses of boats, such as beds, cupboards, draws and wardrobes, the space under the floor is mostly unseen, ignored and casually walked over. It is not somewhere boat dwellers would choose to go, casually route around or spend any unnecessary time in. It isn't a living space but a problem space, a fixing space. A bit of home not filled with clothes, blankets, tools or food, but instead only with pipes, ballast and portions of empty space. Here, the water is brought into a sharper reality; its presence zoned in on rather than out of, it is accounted for and dealt with. This is a part of home that is not 'embracing and embraced', but test and chase, loose ends and ticking time bombs, frustration and chore (Bachelard, 1969: 8). Boat dwellers have variable relations with this part of home, referred to technically as the cabin bilge, and varying frequency with which they visit it. However, it is perhaps the site of boaters' most fraught and contentious relations with water, serving as a barometer of imminent danger or the slower brewing of less threatening tensions.

On narrowboats and their wider counterparts steel base plates are either flat or v-shaped and form the bottom of the boat. On the internal side, wooden or steel slats are laid across the boat's beam (width), measuring around six inches high. On top of the slats is the under-flooring, leaving a gap in between the floor that is walked over and the very bottom of the boat. Portions of these underfloor spaces are occupied by ballast, the name given to materials used to offset the weight of parts of the household that often line one side, such as stoves, sinks, beds and the bodies that lie in them. Lifting up the floorboards can reveal an interesting selection of dead-weight items, such as remaining steel from the boat's build or assorted concrete paving slabs.

The under-flooring is followed possibly by a layer of insulation but often not, then carpets, lino, floorboards or whatever else is deemed sole worthy. The solidity and spread of each material layer makes getting to the space under the floor more difficult. Although access to the cabin bilge may be essential in establishing where water is getting in and how to stop it, boats often have very limited 'inspection hatches'. These are essentially removable floor panels that expose compartments of the cabin bilge, allowing checks for the presence of water. However, it is often found that the ease of simple flooring installations and domestic comfort are prioritised over the ability to inspect this lowest layer of home.

The space under the floor is designed to allow water either internally escaped or been taken on to gather. Thus, it is built in the knowledge that unruly water will, one way or another, eventually find its way there. Cabin bilges are typically slanted towards the stern (back of the boat) with small holes connecting the compartments, allowing water to gather at the rear of the boat where it can be found and removed. Water found under the floor can be a sign of something serious, a hull breach (hole in the hull), water coming in from a submerged outlet pipe or vent, or rainwater that has found its way through unsealed gaps. However, water found there is often much more mundane. The water that is collected, contained and carried rather than floated upon. The drinking water, washing up water and shower water. The water that doesn't collaborate with silt, weeds, rubbish and birds. The kind of water that flows, often without conscious measure or limit, into kitchen sinks of the houses that line the canal.

Late on a January night, Maria and Steven noticed their boat was silling (leaning) sharply to one side, having been silling to the other side just the day before. They pondered the severity of their tilt, confused as they had not moved their boat off their winter mooring or moved anything heavy around inside. The lack of change to their observable living space led their concern quickly to the more concealed happenings of space under the floor. Their access to it was limited to one inspection hatch, positioned directly underneath their bed in the stern of their boat. Therefore, instead of getting into bed as planned, Maria pulled it apart, removing their pillows, duvet and mattress as fast as she could. They opened their inspection hatch to find the cabin bilge full to the brim with water. The nightmare about sinking, unfortunately not experienced through the medium of sleep.

Maria grabbed the bathroom bin, being the closest thing to a bucket she could find, and bailed out the water for four hours, one slow scoop at a time. As the amount of water gradually reduced, so did her panic and Maria began to look closely at the water she was removing. It was clear, not murky. The side of the coin you would hope to toss when finding water there. It was water of the more forgiving variety, once contained now on the loose. There was, however, a huge amount of it. Almost the entire contents of their water tank had been leaking, undetected and running down the length of their boat. Not directly handing them this information, their boat had lent uncomfortably under the strain of its uneven load and although usually steadfast in ensuring the balance of bodies, books, beds and furniture, the ballast became unable to offset the unruly and mobile liquid mass.

Maria and Steven's late-night rodeo with the space under the floor was an extreme one, one where their boat had felt under imminent threat. They were shaken, understandably. However, when I caught up with Maria six months later, they hadn't managed to find or fix the leak. They both work long hours; Maria is a catering manager and Steven a chef who has recently opened a couple of restaurants in the city. Without the time to find or fix the leak, they manage it. Every week or so they remove their bedding, lift their mattress, propping it up in the corridor, and bail out the water that has gathered under the floor. The life of their leak is now learnt and traced and its management has become a mundane and repeated aspect of their everyday life.

James, a mechanic on the cut, takes the opinion that all boats are sinking, just at different rates and 'if you leave any boat indefinitely, it will eventually sink. It is just that the better boats take a lot of a longer time than others'. As water is always 'trying to get in somehow or other', it is the management of our inevitable sinking that really matters, thus making it important not to ignore weeps, seeps, drips or their gathering in space under the floor. Boats' weaknesses are to be learnt, sensed, observed and catered for. Leaks are expected and waited for. Unexplained sideways leans investigated and unruly water is negotiated with. The material qualities of each boat shapes its occupants' conflicts with water, forcing them to let go of preconceived ideas that their boats will hold perfect separatism, both internally and with their watery surroundings.

Each boat holds its own set of problems and through the originality and the intimacy of their occupants' caring practices, boats become needy and bodily (see Jalas, 2006 and Kaaristo, 2018). Dealing with water out-of-place is a part of home's sustaining, a project forever materially incomplete, but held together by a 'repetitive performance of tasks that aim to maintain a result or equilibrium' (Pink, 2006: 41). Rainwater, canal water or shower water can find its way in quickly or very gradually, overpowering the stability of home. The space under the floor becomes contentious, shaping individually experienced conflicts with water that are potentially threatening or mundane, sudden or ongoing.

The window

The sun shines down on the cut and the water in its reflective form appears on the ceiling, bathing fleetingly in the upper reaches of home. The window lets the reflections in and they dance, flicker, wobble and writhe in a restless combination of liquid and light. Len says he could look at them for hours, although they don't usually stay that long. Watching them dance on his ceiling is one of his favourite things about living on his boat. He is a fretter and gets easily caught up in the stresses of daily life. The reflections 'mellow him out', as he sits inside transfixed by the water's movements presented above him. The reflections bring Len a sense of being 'at one' with his surroundings, a result of water's '"boundary-less-ness", vibrancy and transparency' (Watson, 2019b: 18). In this performative form, the water is joyful and welcomed in. The windows bring the water into the inner bounds of home, despite their required separatism.

Looking outwardly, boaters make daily observations of their liquid surroundings. Coconuts float past boats in the West and oil spills slick across the surface, curling around the curved edges of bows and sterns. In mid-winter, coots fight for food and drag half-submerged plastic bags into patches of scrubby offside (opposite side to the towpath) to build their nests. In the warmer months, duckweed blankets the water's surface, transforming it momentarily into a long bowling green, before being carved apart by boats and birds on the move. The coal boat comes past every couple of weeks, the comforting clunk of its one-cylinder engine conveniently heard long before it stretches past the window. Banksides, overhanging trees and buildings temporarily suspend their bodies onto the water before retracting back to shadow on the street. Sometimes, the water is clear but more often it is murky. Regardless, the course of the day is always reflected on its surface.

Emma used to live in a high-rise flat that looked down onto the canal from above. But now, living on her boat, she is sunken down, in eyeline with it. This new perspective has made her feel a little more 'immersed in the landscape'. With her partner, Fin, she used to spend a lot of time walking along East London's towpaths, taking in the shifting scenery as they made their way around its bends and along its pathed edges. Emma explains that she 'used the canal just as walkways before, they are really nice routes just to get to places. But yeah living on it, it feels more stationary.' Despite the fortnightly move, daily observations of the waterway bring her a sense of embeddedness, rather than perpetual uprooting and passing through. A unique opportunity for stillness within a city space defined for most as a route.

Through drawn-out national and local lockdowns, continuous cruisers were able to moor for months in the same spot, allowing them to develop unusually intimate understandings of the happenings of their stretch. While boats unusually stayed in place, the seasons shifted and windows provided front row seats to the waterworld around them. The social lives of the waterway's nonhuman residents continued on and their daily routines could be studied over time. For some, these daily window observations became both comforting and addictive, resulting in unique observations such as that of Phillip's, that passing cormorants would fly over the blue footbridge at Little Venice by day and under it by night. Isolation wore on and moving boats were longingly watched going past, their names and paintwork mentally noted if not already known. Perhaps heading off for work, topping up water or off to find a new place to see out their remaining isolation.

The lifting of social distancing and travel restrictions saw the return of the fortnightly move. The view from the window came back into shift, the water coming nearer and further, defined by the arrangement of each mooring. In the central portions of London, the treasured view out onto water is often under threat. When your boat is double moored against, meaning it is sandwiched in between the public towpath and another boat, the entertainment of the reflective and transformative waterway that was there only moments before is replaced by uneventful sheets of steel, wood, fibreglass or plastic. The odd glimpse into the neighbour's living space, allowed only when windows awkwardly align and curtains aren't fully drawn, is all that is offered in return. In this position, the city seems immediately closer and the relentlessness of the towpath's footfall can slowly wear. Most hope to find themselves on the outside of a double mooring, extended out into the waterway and able to enjoy observing, both inwardly and outwardly, its reflections and happenings. A temporary calm until the next re-arranging.

The ropes

Home clings, by string and pin, to the land. It's not built into it, dug down and cemented, not walled, fenced or gated. Simply strung to it, stitched temporarily to the city's sides. The arrangement is not always secure, the land limply letting mooring pins slip out when the displaced water of a fast-passing boat draws home outwardly in its course. Sometimes, boats come loose and float free, their occupants sleeping soundly inside. The waterway is where home rests. It is what supports it and guides its route through the city. But the ropes stop it straying too far, they limit the liberties a boat alone on water can take. They are the occupants' stamp of a somewhat limited authority. Tying the boat to bankside instils a desire to protect, secure and control. You want to know that home will be where you left it. It makes you want to tie the ropes tight and not give it any slack, making it heel to the city and not the will of the water. Bringing the land closer, however, can hand the water more control.

Water levels can change suddenly and without any warning, a fairly regular occurrence on both navigations and canals. The levels can quickly swell with heavy rainfall or be drained as a result of a lock paddle being left up. When support from the water slips a foot hold lower, tight ropes dangle boats at precarious angles. Part of the boat's undercarriage becomes exposed on the side of the bank, and the opposite, now precariously low in the water, risks the intake of water through outlet pipes, skin fittings and vents. Unable to retract with the water from the canal's shallow sides, hulls get stuck on ledges, sometimes immovable until the water returns. Learning to keep the ropes loose is a lesson in living with water. It has to be worked with and not against. Its fluctuations and forces cannot be controlled by an anxious knotting to the land, but rather, by handing home the ability to ebb and flow with its liquid surroundings.

Boat dwellers learn how to secure their pins and ropes to weather the tug of a dangerously fast passing boat, the hull hitting the bottom following a water-level drop or the rocking of a returning neighbour, crossing over your bow to get to their own. Through the structural confines and materialities of home, they sense shifts in the surrounding environment, and in response, attend to the altered needs of their boats. Being away from the boat with no way to sense these shifts can consequently become a source of anxiety, something that when left, is left with a sense of guilt and uncertainty. Even tying your ropes loosely is not enough to reduce anxiety of home being left alone on the water, its constant happenings challenging home's precarious fastenings. Many only leave their boat alone for a couple of days at a time and text a friend moored nearby, 'if you happen to walk past could you have a quick look at my ropes?'

As I pass through central London for the first time, the muddy banks of the Western stretches are replaced by less forgiving concrete edges. Choosing a mooring is no longer based on appealing bends, trees or grassy patches but for signs in the cement that the ropes welcome. If time allows, a land-based recce of mooring fixtures lying ahead is done on foot or push bike, which makes for an easier and finer reading of the canalside. Finding a space with well-positioned fastenings can be tricky and, as a result, there are varying opinions of what constitutes a securely fastened boat. On busier stretches, boats double moor, or sometimes even triple. Boaters adopt variable methods of tying the ropes when double mooring, influenced by the shape and size of the boat they are mooring against, the fastenings afforded by the canalside and the ability of their ropes to reach them. Some boaters have particular expectations regarding their entanglement with others' ropes, and might request, via handwritten signs placed in windows, that neighbouring ropes are not tied directly onto their boat. Fear incited by the possibility that a neighbour could pull you out or down with them.

The regulations continuous cruisers live under signal their ropes undoing, forcing home placements within the city to be perpetually temporary. Always, however, with the ability for home and city to come back together, pass each other by and reconnect in a different season. The freedom afforded by this temporary attachment defines favourite, well known and avoided places. Jasmin and Seb's five years spent on the cut has resulted in well-rehearsed mooring patterns, sometimes shared with other boats that contain their friends, but while retaining their ability to deviate from them. In the summer, they take trips up Grand Union or the Thames, leaving the city behind them for a while. However, not everyone can just untie and take off, it is an intimate battle of confidence, practice and reliance on others. Untying the ropes brings on a sense of freedom but is not something experienced, or perhaps even wanted, equally.

The ropes draw together a complex entanglement of freedom, regulation, (im)mobility and a perpetually transient relationship with the city. The personal demands of living on and with the water are intimately translated through them, experienced as a need to be there, observing and negotiating. Tying the ropes indicates boat dwellers need not only to observe, but also imagine the capabilities and unpredictabilities of the waterway, accounting for its potential to shift and change. The experience of living with water, in both practised and imagined ways, becomes a mundane and usual part of boat dwellers' everyday lives.

Water as part of home and everyday life

Water, as it works its way into boat dwellers' homes and everyday lives, brings with it a conflictual set of experiences, feelings and practices. Bed, the space under the floor, the window and the ropes each inform a different experience of living with water, illustrating the conflictual realities of occupying and navigating a home that relies precariously on it. Ethnographically exploring the intimate qualities of life afloat reveals the agency of water, finding it to seep into and shape experiences of home and home-making practices in unexpected and complicated ways. Consequently, it is situated as a main character, its agency vibrant within mundane and domestic happenings.

Living on London's waterways offers many pleasurable moments and meaningful encounters, evoking 'passions, attachments and a sense of connection' between boaters and their surroundings (Watson, 2019a: 135; also see Djohari, Brown and Stolk, 2017). Boat dwellers' embeddedness in the water, the lower portions of their boats literally sitting a few feet below its surface, informs intimate sensory and embodied experiences as it supports and flows around hull edges. The reflections give a sense that the water not only surrounds home but also finds its way in. They embody the comforting qualities of the water and its potential for peacefulness, gently bringing it into the interior. In these moments, the water offers the kind of joy, comfort and sense of belonging that the collection and display of material things have been considered to afford people within their living spaces (as explored by Hurdley, 2013; Miller, 2008; Rose, 2010). However, with this comes an understanding that experiences made with water are often only fleeting, slipping through your fingers or disappearing from the ceiling.

Boat dwellers' rootedness within the waterway allows for close observation of its transformations, noting their encounters with the water's many sensory and material forms. As a result, boaters create meaningful connections to their surroundings. The transient qualities of the waterway are reflected more broadly in continuous cruisers' experience of living on it, defined by their residential mobility, chance friendships, unexpected stoppages, returns and new discoveries (Bowles, 2019). Although the mobility of continuous cruisers is regulated, it brings with it a sense of chance and autonomy not afforded by most terrestrial living situations. This is demonstrated by boaters' ability to transition from central city space into wilder surroundings, off-setting London's relentlessness and bringing a sense of looseness and rural connectivity.

However, even from within the city, the water can be understood as 'a space of redemption and immersion away from the messiness and tensions of the everyday, and as a space of connection with the sublime and with tranquility' (Watson, 2019a: 154; Watson, 2019b). The waterways' reflective, calming and wilder qualities contrast sharply with the city spaces they cut through. For many, this aspect of living on the water makes living in the city far more tolerable. However, the joyful and carefree feelings that living on the water can elicit, such as observing rippled reflections on the ceiling, bumping into friends and watching birds out of the kitchen window, are tempered by the demands of dwelling on it. Rather than the water providing an escape from boat dwellers' everyday lives, it is fundamentally embroiled within it, as a supporting but simultaneously threatening presence that to live with, demands attention and practice.

As Hannah Pitt explores, relationships with urban waterways are not always straightforward or positive. The demands of boat dwelling point to 'the need to acknowledge the diversity, ambiguity and complexity of water experiences in relation to wellbeing' (Pitt, 2018: 161). Pitt's leisure-based assertions can be extended upon when considering residential relations with urban water. Boat dwellers' interactions with the water are shaped intimately through their homes. As residential and domestic spaces, boats on London's waterways carry a sense of fragility, informed by their varied material qualities, self-sufficient domestic systems, regulated mobility, the way some people are forced onto boats purely by necessity, and the anxieties of keeping boats functioning and afloat. Therefore, the problems water can cause boat dwellers are certainly capable of overpowering its 'positive potential', presented most clearly when it challenges, submerges and damages their homes (Pitt, 2018: 164).

The water's ability to transition from supporting to destabilising substance situates it as 'risky matter' (Watson, 2019b). Though, as Watson notes, its potential to overpower and 'cause destruction' is often not realised but 'imagined' (Watson, 2019b: 18). For boat dwellers, however, the vulnerability of their domestic arrangement finds that the overpowering potential of the water is dreamt about and abstracted when lying in bed, but also informs their purposeful everyday actions, exampled by checking under the floor for leaks and the tying of loose ropes to account for sudden water-level changes. Therefore, despite the dangerous capabilities of the water often only being imagined, they manifest in the realities of boaters' experiences of home, both in a form of abstraction and everyday practices.

The sensory and embodied experience of living in something floating, wobbly and bodily shifts the perception of home from something materially stable and fixed, to something lived and negotiated with, through its continual and unpredictable 'process of the transformation' (Hodder, 2012: 5; for a domestic contextualisation see Pink, 2006). There is a gradual undoing of the material expectations of home forged when living on land as the unpredictable presence of water becomes an accepted part of living on it. This is illustrated by Maria and Steven's leaking water tank, which saw water sensed initially as an imminent threat transition into a routine part of their home (un)making and sustaining. The water is intimately engaged with and translated through parts of the boat, its presence familiarised by mundane practices of 'moving about' in, 'exploring' and 'attending' to home in everyday life (Ingold, 2000: 55; also see Malkogeorgou, 2019).

For new boaters, there is a process of coming to learn the sensory qualities of their homes. Each sound and sensation within its vocabulary is slowly identified and mentally catalogued, either as an inconsequential watery happening, a demand or a warning signal. Boat dwellers embody and imagine change, they attend to groans and leans, readjust paddings and fastenings and treat rusty surfaces, learning systematic weaknesses and negotiating with their liquid surroundings. The learning boaters undertake and the attention they pay to the bodies of their boats sustain a home environment that can provide for the needs of their own (for bodily needs and domesticity see Bates, 2019 and Imrie, 2004; for boats thought of as alive see Jalas, 2006 and Kaaristo, 2018).

This process reflects Kaaristo's exploration of the 'boat–human assemblage' that occurs between bodies as they learn to navigate canal boats both as domestic spaces and as craft, that moor and move through the canalscape (Kaaristo, 2018: 174). Through this 'expertise and knowledge develop through practice and in interaction' between bodies, boats and boats' bodily (dis)functions (Kaaristo, 2018: 182; Jalas, 2006). These are the kinds of observations, understandings and negotiations that are intensified by boat dwellers' reliance on self-sufficient and disconnected domestic systems.

Continuous cruisers' need to produce heat and power, to collect water from canalside taps, contain it in tanks and deliver it to their sinks can throw up all kinds of problems. It brings domesticity away from the obscurity of convenience and into the often harsh reality of life 'off-grid' (see Vannini and Taggart, 2015). For many boaters, to pursue a life on the water, for all its pleasures and benefits, is to accept a fair amount of inconvenience. This reflects Vannini and Taggart's findings that those disconnected from conventional domestic systems and resources take on a 'unique set of material practices' that represent an intimate understanding of and negotiation with their domestic systems, structures, resources and surroundings (Vannini and Taggart, 2015: 16).

As for many 'off-gridders' spoken to by Vannini and Taggart (2015), the project of self-sufficient living can be personally rewarding and motivating. Many boaters accept but also find purpose and satisfaction from the work associated with maintaining their home environments. However, for some the challenges of living aboard can be an unwanted component of their living arrangement and over time can become extremely demoralising. The problematic potential of the water accompanies the more general demands of work, social lives, domestic labour, responsibilities and needs. Therefore, boat dwellers' homes and their reliance upon them take on a sensed and lived precariousness. Within this, the specific structural, material, mechanical and domestic qualities of each boat each defines a different experience and precarity, informing disparate financial expenses, work, discomfort and anxiety.

Through boat dwellers' experiences, we are invited to consider that as urban water brings 'new publics into being', so it informs extremely varied experiences of private space, home making, home owning and everyday life (Watson, 2019b: 3; sentiment echoed in Watson, 2019a: chapter five). The uncertain qualities of living on the water means that beyond being a space of autonomy, ownership, rest and comfort, home is something to be looked after, planned for and negotiated with. In turn, the water cannot be separated from the domestic spaces through which boat dwellers encounter it. Its presence is embodied, sensed and imagined through the materialities of home but also through the disjointed and mundane practices of living that occur within, like lying in bed, getting ready to leave for the weekend or brushing your teeth as you look from the window. Consequently, water is shaped by, and experienced through, the vulnerabilities of domestic experience.

To draw from experiences of dwelling means to attend to water as a publicly situated and entangling substance, but also as something that can be intimately encountered and privately experienced. The conflictual qualities of water absorb into the practices, imaginaries and embodiment of home, situating it as something that both comforts and threatens, bringing on many joyful moments while informing responsibility, anxiety and labour. Home, therefore, serves as 'a hearth, and an anchoring point' but is also something anchored, illustrated by boaters' navigation of mundane happenings, practices of home making and everyday life (Blunt and Dowling, 2006: 11).

Living on London's waterways is found to shape many realities, temporalities, feelings and practices. It is observing fleeting reflections on the ceiling, a friend's boat passing by the window, the anxiety of leaving the boat alone for the weekend, battles with condensation, seeing an abandoned boat slowly sinking, losing the view to a new neighbour and moving every two weeks to find a new mooring. Living with water, in this context, does not relate to water in a singular form or one kind of interaction. Relationships with it are subconscious and active, detached and negotiated. Simply, water is a main character and material substance that is observed through both pleasure and necessity, shaping mundane and extreme relations with it as a part of home and everyday life.

References

Bachelard, G. (1969) *The Poetics of Space*. Boston: Beacon Press.
Bachelard, G. (2014) *The Poetics of Space*. New York: Penguin Books.
Bates, C. (2019) *Vital Bodies: Living with Illness*. Bristol: Policy Press.
Blunt, A. and Dowling, R. (2006) *Home*. London and New York: Routledge.
Bowles, B. (2015) *Waterways: Becoming an Itinerant Boat-Dweller on the Canals and Rivers of South East England*. PhD Thesis, Division of Anthropology, Brunel University.
Bowles, B. (2019) 'This squiggly wiggly, not quite democratic thing': a Deluzian frame for boaters' political (dis)organisation on the waterways of London. *Anthropological Notebooks*, 25(2), 35–55.
Bowles, B., Kaaristo, M. and Caf, M. (2019) Dwelling on and with water – materialities, (im)mobilities and meanings: introduction to the special issue. *Anthropological Notebooks*, 25(2), 5–12.
Buser, M., Payne, T., Edizel, Ö. and Dudley, L. (2020) Blue space as caring space – water and the cultivation of care in social and environmental practice. *Social & Cultural Geography*, 21(8), 1039–1059.
Canal and River Trust (2021) Continuous cruising. Available at: https://canalrivertrust.org.uk/enjoy-the-waterways/boating/buy-your-boat-licence/continuous-cruising (accessed 19 December 2021).
De Bell, S., Graham, H., Jarvis, S. and White, P. (2017) The importance of nature in mediating social and psychological benefits associated with visits to freshwater blue space. *Landscape and Urban Planning*, 167, 118–127.
Djohari, N., Brown, A. and Stolk, P. (2017) The comfort of the river: understanding the affective geographies of angling waterscapes in young people's coping practices. *Children's Geographies*, 16(4), 356–367.
Foley, R. and Kistemann, T. (2015) Blue space geographies: enabling health in place. *Health & Place*, 35, 157–165.
Hodder, I. (2012) *Entangled: An Archaeology of the Relationships Between Humans and Things*. Malden: Wiley-Blackwell.
Hurdley, R. (2013) *Home, Materiality, Memory and Belonging: Keeping Culture*. New York: Palgrave and Macmillan.
Imrie, R. (2004) Disability, embodiment and the meaning of home. *Housing Studies*, 19(5), 745–763.
Ingold, T. (2000) *Perception of the Environment: Essays on Livelihood, Dwelling and Skill*. Abingdon: Routledge.
Jalas, M. (2006) Making time: the art of loving wooden boats. *Time & Society*, 15, 343–363.

Kaaristo, M. (2018) *Mundane Tourism Mobilities on a Watery Leisurescape: Canal Boating in North West England.* PhD Thesis, Manchester Metropolitan University.

Kaaristo, M. and Rhoden, S. (2017) Everyday life and water tourism mobilities: mundane aspects of canal travel. *Tourism Geographies: An International Journal of Tourism, Place and Environment,* 19(1), 78–95.

Lenhard, J. and Samanani, F. (2020) *Home: Ethnographic Encounters.* London and New York: Routledge.

Malkogeorgou, T. (2019) The linear village: experience of continuous cruising on the London waterways. In C. Tilley (ed.) *London's Urban Landscape: Another Way of Telling.* London: UCL Press, ch. 5.

Miller, D. (2008) *The Comfort of Things.* Cambridge: Polity Press.

Pink, S. (2006) *Home Truths: Gender, Domestic Objects and Everyday Life.* New York: Berg.

Pitt, H. (2018) Muddying the waters: what urban waterways reveal about blue spaces and well being. *Geoforum,* 92, 161–170.

Roberts, L. (2019) Taking up space: community, belonging and gender among itinerant boat-dwellers on London's waterways. *Anthropological Notebooks,* 25(2), 57–70.

Rose, G. (2010) *Doing Family Photography: The Domestic, the Public and the Politics of Sentiment.* Farnham: Ashgate.

Vannini, P. (2012) *Ferry Tales: Mobility, Place and Time on Canada's West Coast.* New York and Abingdon: Routledge.

Vannini, P. and Taggart, J. (2015) *Off the Grid: Re-assembling Domestic Life.* New York and London: Routledge.

Voelker, S. and Kistemann, T. (2013) Reprint of: 'I'm always entirely happy when I'm here!' Urban blue enhancing human health and well-being in Cologne and Düsseldorf, Germany. *Social Science & Medicine,* 91, 141–152.

Watson, S. (2019a) *City Water Matters: Cultures, Practices and Entanglements of Urban Water.* London: Palgrave and Macmillan.

Watson, S. (2019b) Liquid passions: bodies, politics and city waters. *Social and Cultural Geography,* 20(7), 960–980.

6

Bathed in feeling: water cultures and city life

Les Back

Introduction: water and city life

Understanding the place of water within social life makes us ask different questions about cities. Thinking about water puts sensation to the fore in how we understand urban culture and the body bathed in history. Cultures of water can focus on containment, regulation and civilisation. The pandemics of the industrial age – like cholera and tuberculosis – generated public concern about cleanliness and hygiene. The industrial poor were a particular focus of concern and the disciplining of their habits a site of the exercise of power in the creation of what Michel Foucault called 'docile bodies' (1975: 136). These disciplinary forms of power exercised through maintaining hygiene and 'good water' aimed to inhibit forms of social contagion.

In Liverpool during a cholera epidemic in 1832, Kitty Wilkinson, an Irish immigrant, used her own house and yard to wash her neighbours' clothes. Kitty, who became known as the 'saint of the slums', used chloride lime (bleach) to rid the rags of disease for a penny (Kelly, 2000). The smell of bleach still has a particular classed affordance for many even now. Clean water and clothes washing was a way to combat the spread of lethal disease, particularly among the urban poor. Ten years later the first warm freshwater public washhouse in Britain was opened on Frederick Street, Liverpool.

The washhouse was a tool for social improvement, a place for the industrial poor to get clean. In working-class life it was a huge achievement to heat enough water in a tin bath to bathe. Once a week – Friday night most often – water was heated in coppers in the scullery behind the front and back room. But washing was also a way to manage the population and regulate the behaviour of city dwellers. I think this establishes a tension between *regulation* and *improvement* that is so often mediated through ideas of moral behaviour and respectability (Dazey, 2021; Skeggs, 1997). Keeping yourself clean is a distinguishing moral act, a kind of baptism in values that distinguishes the deserving from the undeserving. A Lewisham resident told me that in the early days of council housing in the 1950s and 1960s potential tenants were sometimes visited in their home by housing officers to see if their homes were well kept – that is, spotless and tidy – and if their net curtains were clean (Back, 1996). Cleanliness is a weapon in classed and gendered judgements and struggles for value. As Sophie Watson argues in her cultural history of laundry in London and New York, 'dirty washing' and soiled bodies summon 'social-spatial assembles' that mark cultural and moral distinction within city life (2015: 888).

Baths and bathhouses were also places for public life and association. They could be places where an alternative sense of being together in public could be contested. While they were workshops for classed and gendered judgements, as public spaces they could be less prone to the brutal informalities of racism and the colour bar. In the winter the pool was covered with boards and converted into a dance hall for reverie from swing to rhythm and blues, and provided a place for racial integration in 1950s London, a period when an intense colour bar was enforced in local pubs and other leisure spaces. A different sense of convivial social life could be floated – sometimes literally – on the still waters of the swimming pool.

Bathhouses also hosted the spectacle of all-in wrestling matches where it was the men who were on display for audiences of predominantly working-class women. These examples of watery and slippery cultural practices are rich sociologically because here the body moves between nudity and the clothes of culture and history, enabling us to think anew about the sensuous and olfactory experience of life in the bathtub, inside our clothes both fresh and soiled, in motion on the dancefloor, or sitting excitedly ringside at the wrestling match. Traces of those histories and their ghosts are socially alive in our present if we are willing to offer them the hospitality of consideration.

In this chapter I want to use this kind of approach with one example, namely Laurie Grove Baths in New Cross, South East London.

Today, this former bathhouse and swimming pool has been annexed by Goldsmiths, University of London. Its ancient pool accommodates artist studios for students, and the Goldsmiths Centre for Contemporary Art, known as Goldsmiths CCA, is in the former boiler house and public laundry of Laurie Grove Baths. It is also where the Centre for Urban and Community Research is based, where I am the Director; indeed my office is one of the converted bedrooms of the bathhouse manager's flat. My affection for this building has been driven by a fascination with its social history. This chapter is based on archival research, oral histories and written reminiscences that have been collected over twenty years through living and working in this place. I want to show the paradoxes of city life, like the unresolved tensions between regulation and resistance, through documenting the history of this grand old building and the forms of social life housed there.

The remarkable history of Laurie Grove Baths

The baths opened on 20 April 1898, as part of a municipal drive to improve the plight of the industrial working class of South London. Jess Steele, in her wonderful book *Turning the Tide*, quotes a letter to the *Kentish Mercury* from E. Dudley Ward on 2 April 1889. 'There is always a disagreeable smell, more or less, at Deptford, of what appears to be sewage, and now it seems we are to have it extended to Greenwich. If private residents are not to be driven away, it is time the local authorities bestirred themselves' (Steele, 1993: 95). Richard Hoggart described the struggle against dirt within working-class life and how the burden of this often fell to women. 'It's a hard life. ... Curtains can hardly be kept "good colour" even with frequent washing in dolly blue or cream; the fireplace range may need black-leading and hard "nursing". Everywhere the smoke and soot from the nearby factories and railway lines creep in, and most women "can't abide the thought of dirt getting a hold"' (Hoggart, 1957: 42).

Riverside industries flourished in this part of London, including metal industries, rope making, timber and foodstuffs, processed in places like the Foreign Cattle Market – opened in the 1870s – where legions of young women called the 'Gut Girls' worked. They did filthy work gutting the carcasses of the livestock that were slaughtered in the market. They earned good money but liked to spend it on ostentatious multi-coloured Ostrich feathers. The Duchess of Albany Institute, which established a Girls Club, was set up in large part to try to keep them in line, and personal hygiene – like stitching undergarments – was one of the markers of their moral improvement (see Steele, 1993: 145–147).

Architect Thomas Dinwiddy designed Laurie Grove Baths, which cost £48,695, and also designed local hospitals, schools and workhouses (Rimel, 1994). The impetus to build public baths and washhouses was primarily a bid to improve social conditions among the labouring poor. The construction of Laurie Grove was authorised under the Public Baths and Washhouses Act of 1846, which allowed borough councils to raise funds for social improvement through hygiene and cleanliness. And people welcomed these developments.

The Laurie Grove building consisted of three swimming pools: Large, Small and 'South pool', which was separate, accessed from the main building by underground passages. It also included baths for washing and getting clean, but this was a profoundly segregated social affair. There were separate baths for men and women, and the trace of this is still carved in the physical structure of the two entrances of the building, which are titled 'Men' and 'Women' respectively. Bathers had a choice between '1st and 2nd Class' baths, the former being more luxurious and three times as expensive (Crook, 2018). The local *Kentish Mercury* newspaper would publish weekly statistical breakdowns of who was using Laurie Grove. On 22 July 1898 it reported that nearly 6,000 men swam that week and only 318 women. It reported that week that 39 people took a bath, while in other weeks this figure sometimes reached 300.

At the rear of the building was a laundry for washing and drying the bath-towels. This was largely a female working-class public sphere. The Deptford Official Borough guide of 1910 announced 'a large laundry containing accommodation for 35 washers, of whom there were nearly 10,000 in a single year'. Laurie Grove was designed to be the hub for all the other washhouses in South East London, including Clyde Street, Forest Hill, Bellingham and Downham. The cost of using the laundry in 1936 was 'one and a half pennies per hour inclusive'. The use of the baths revealed the gendered divisions in urban culture, with men accessing swimming and physical activity, while women were assigned the domestic responsibilities of cloth washing.

The laundry was a public arena particularly for working-class women. Clothes would be loaded in baby prams often wrapped in a bedsheet and pushed to the baths to be washed and dried in one day. The laundry was washed by hand in iron tubs and then dried using large drying frames heated by steam and hot air generated from the bathhouse boiler. Throughout, the bathhouse provided a space for public sociability for women. They could be fractious places as well as providing forms of community solidarity. In Scotland the bathhouses were referred to as 'steamies'. Paula Larkin, archivist at the Govanhill Baths Community Trusts in Glasgow, told the *Scotsman* newspaper: 'The washhouses were really important places for women to get together. ... Every time you mention the word steamie, people light up. They want to tell you about it' (*The Scotsman*, 3 September 2018).

This is no less true of public laundries throughout England. Miriam Glucksmann, in her insightful study of the changing relationship between gender, labour and time, points out that working-class women had 'enthusiasm for the municipal wash-house. They did not want to give it up until forced to by its closure' (Glucksmann, 2000: 144). They were beloved places because of the ways in which they could be a place to 'clean up' city dwellers but also as a place of shared community experiences that were controlled by women.

Getting clean at the washhouse could be the last form of dignity left to those who had fallen into destitution. George Orwell explained brilliantly how the working-class fear of institutions like hospitals could be explained by their connection to bourgeois discipline and regulation (Orwell [1946] 1968). By contrast, bathhouses were often beloved places within working-class communities. Peter Powers grew up in Laurie Grove Baths; his father was the last official manager, and he lived in a small flat in the building between 1969 and 1987. Now living in the Basque country in northern Spain, Peter got in touch with me via email in 2000 on hearing of the work being done on the history of the baths. One of Peter's most lasting memories of living in the baths was the penniless old men who visited Laurie Grove: 'They came to the slipper baths in order to die with dignity. Destitute men who died washed and clean-shaven, and as my father always said 'that were taken away as naked as the next man' without embarrassment of being found wrapped in rags' (Personal Communication, 12 March 2000). Getting clean washed off social stigma and the grime of destitution in a final act of resistance and restitution.

Women's experience of washing in the public baths is no less vivid. Martin Johnson shared with me an exert from his grandmother Lille Smith's unpublished memoir. Lille, who was born in 1916 in Plumstead, South East London, described visiting the Plumstead bathhouse:

It was a penny to have a bath and we went every Saturday morning. There were about 20 bathrooms upstairs and fewer downstairs. On Saturday mornings there were always a lot of children upstairs and we had to sit in a waiting room until one of the bathrooms was free. Then the attendant would call 'Next' and she carried a large key which turned the taps on from outside the room. We had to put our hand in the water and tell her when we thought the water was the right temperature. If when you had undressed, you found the water was too hot or too cold you rang a bell and asked for more hot or cold water. Going every week, we got to know which attendants were more amiable than the others. If the one on duty was unfriendly the water had to be very, very hot or cold before we dared ring the bell as we knew she would be very grudging about turning on the tap for us. When we left school and were earning money we used the First Class and seldom had to wait! (Personal communication, 12 January 2022)

The 'slipper' baths were so called because of the Victorian sense of modesty in draping bath-towels over the lower half of the bath to conceal their bodies and by doing so making the bath look like a huge slipper. According to an advertisement that appeared in the local *Kentish Mercury* newspaper in 1962 there were sixty slipper baths still in operation and you could have a bath-towel included for thruppence (3*d*). The vast numbers of towels were washed and dried on huge racks built on a pull-out roller system at the rear of the main bath.

The cult youth subculture movie *Quadrophenia* (1979) contains perhaps one of the most ribald portrayals of male proletarian life and the pleasure of the slipper baths. The film, based on The Who's 1973 album of the same name, documented the youth subcultural rivalries between Mods and Rockers during the 1960s. It features an encounter between the two characters played by a youthful Phil Daniels (Jimmy – The Mod) and Ray Winstone (Kevin – The Rocker) each naked in a slipper bath stripped of the trappings of style. Neither of the characters can see the other because they are in separate but adjacent cubicles. As Lille described, water is provided by an attendant that used a crank handle to add hot and cold water from outside. Ray Winstone's character, Kevin, starts to sing the Gene Vincent greaser anthem 'Be-Bop-a-Lu-La'. Jimmy, the Mod character, complains and shouts to his neighbour telling him to 'shut up'. This makes Kevin sing even louder. Unable to get him to stop, Jimmy simply retaliates by singing The Kinks's Mod anthem 'You Really Got Me'. The youths play out their subcultural rivalry still submerged in the bath water singing noisily into their respective scrubbing brush 'microphone'. Jimmy peeps over the cubicle and sees that Kevin is an old school friend, only to realise that they've fallen on opposite sides of the Mod–Rocker divide when they come to get dressed. Filmed in the public baths of Porchester Hall, Porchester Centre, Queensway, West London that was still active at the time, the scene captures the playful aspects of bathhouse life in male working-class London culture. Baths are also beloved because they evoke a sensation of place. Water makes us think about the body as inscribed socially with value and distinction but it also invites us to think about the sensuous aspects of culture or structures of feeling, as Raymond Williams once put it. Going to the bathhouses was a sensuous experience, from the smell of the carbolic soap to the sound of voices reverberating on watery surfaces and through cavernous, tiled walls. These are felt outside and embodied what Williams called aptly 'social experiences in *solution*' (Williams, 1977: 133). Williams also argued that the appreciation of the importance of tacit patterns of culture is often revealed only at the point when this social world is dying or coming to an end. It is perhaps for this reason that the affection for the bathhouse, as what Williams would call a *residual* aspect of this structure of feeling, is so vivid even now when most London homes have a bathroom and washing machines and where public bathing and laundry are no longer necessary or valued.

George Orwell noted this in his wartime study *The Lion and the Unicorn*: 'the old pattern is gradually changing into something new', he wrote in 1941. In the improved conditions of the council estates the distinctions between classes were being culturally blurred: 'There are wide gradations of income, but it's the same kind of life that is being lived at different levels, in the labour-saving flats or council estates, along the concrete roads and in the naked democracy of the swimming-pools' (Orwell, [1941] 1970: 98). It is within the bathhouses and swimming pools that we can see the interplay between the residue of old aspects of class culture coexisting with an emerging 'naked democracy' in which distinctions between classes are blurred within everyday life.

Swimmers, wrestlers and limbo dancers

Learning to swim was a special form of practical knowledge. Thousands of South Londoners learned to swim at Laurie Grove

Baths. It was a place where childhood memories were made. I received a letter from a former Lewisham resident in 2000 who said that he'd 'learned' to swim here in the 1930s. The master would hold a rod in the pool and walk slowly to the deep end. The boys would have to hold the rod – then the master would pull the rod away. They would learn by ordeal – literally sink or swim! This fable is a reminder of the kind of discipline that is enforced through swimming in the baths. Regardless, he told me that learning to swim saved his life when, during the Second World War, he was on a ship in the North Atlantic that was torpedoed by a German U-boat.

Susie Scott has written insightfully about how within swimming pools there are accepted rules and interactions that performatively regulate the swimmer's body. She writes: 'The pool is a self-contained, institutional organization with its own rules, schedules and hierarchical structure, and this formal exercise of power governs the swimmers *en masse*, as a social body' (Scott, 2010: 163). For Scott, social regulation in the baths is achieved through pool etiquette and social interaction that result in a negotiated order (Scott, 2009). The naked body is desexualised in this regulated order and its movement is regulated in lanes and any rebellious splashing outlawed. Anyone who has been thrown out of a swimming pool will recognise the power of Scott's analysis. However, the meaning of swimming and the complexities of bathhouse culture are much more than the interactions happening in the pool.

Bathhouses were places where rules could be broken and the moral order could be transgressed. For example, Kay wrote this reflection in an article posted on the Transpontine Southeast London blogzine about how she learned to swim at Laurie Grove in the 1960s: 'My little brother swam his first length there in 1968/9 at the Deptford Festival'. Kay was taught by volunteers at Laurie Grove Baths. Swimming shaped her life and she ended up spending over thirty years training swimmers, specialising in teaching people with disabilities to swim. 'My parents would have never paid for my lesson', so being taught by Laurie Grove volunteers transformed her life: 'without their help I would never have enjoyed a lifetime of swimming and been able to pass it on. Laurie Grove holds a special place in my heart' (Transpontine, 2011: 2). Like other forms of body culture, swimming is both disciplined and governed by rules, but it is also an expressive way of achieving individual mastery over one's own body. Breaking the rules of the 'negotiated order' of the pool can be dangerous too.

The Transpontine Blogzine documented a tragic case that took place in November 1952 when Arthur William Burgess, of Biggin Hill, Kent, dived off the top diving board in six feet of water, struck his head on the bottom and died from his injuries (Transpontine, 2017). In the winter, the main pool at Laurie Grove was boarded over and turned into one of South East London's finest dance halls with a capacity for eight hundred dancers. In 1936 it provided the venue for the South East London Dance Band Championships with black American swing musician Benny Carter present as the judge, although he declined to take the bandstand himself (*Melody Maker*, 11 April 1936).

US rock 'n' roll pioneers played concerts at the baths in the 1960s, although the sprung floor suspended over the water posed problems, with exuberant jiving Teddy Boys and Girls spilling their drinks and covering the floor with beer. One of my favourite stories of gigs from this time is when the rhythm and blues legend Jimmy Reed played at Laurie Grove in early 1964. I think of the image of him, walking through the doors of the baths with his signature Kay guitar with its tiger-stripe tortoise-shell pick guard, every time I enter the building. Sadly, he played to just a few people because the promoters misspelled his name Reid. The considerable numbers of rhythm and blues fans just didn't realise that one of the people who had inspired the British blues boom – including the Rolling Stones and the Animals – was performing in New Cross, and he played his signature blues shuffles to an almost empty dancefloor. Still, like other bathhouses in the area, Laurie Grove became an important venue. Many British rock bands performed there, from the Spencer Davis Group to Manfred Mann. The Who performed their own high-volume 'Maximum R&B', destroying their instruments floating above the waters of the swimming pool.

The baths were also a female public sphere but not just for washing clothes. Audiences at the wrestling matches during the 1960s and 1970s were largely working-class women. Sarah Cox (2019) has documented how this part of London had a particularly rich history of wrestling in the nineteenth century, producing wrestlers like Jack Wannop who wrestled in local pubs. By the mid-twentieth century Laurie Grove was part of a network of commercial wrestling venues. I received numerous accounts from local women of the bawdy fun had, sometimes at the expense of male wrestlers in the ring. The wrestlers included Americans like 'Rebel' Ray Hunter and 'Ski Hi' Lee, the giant cowboy from El Paso, Texas. Acting out on Saturday night pushed the boundaries of femininity in these alternative public spheres – where gendered norms of working-class respectability could be stretched, carnivalised and even transgressed. My argument here is that Laurie Grove Baths provided a context for forms of self-expression and cultural resistance, and played an important part in creating racially integrated forms of association in public.

In 1954 Deptford Borough offered the Committee Room in Laurie Grove Baths to the Anglo-Caribbean Club – established in 1953 – as a meeting place. George Brown, the organisation's leading figure, pioneered the struggle for equal rights and opposition to racism. He commented in his memoir: 'I discovered that there were a few pubs in South East London who deliberately refused to serve coloured people. Some were rudely abused by customers of these pubs. ... In some cases it was so bad that on many occasions the coloured man could only ask someone inside the pub to purchase drinks for him. That person would hand the drinks to him outside the door' (Brown, 1999: 82). In 1961 the baths offered the venue for the Miss Brockley contest, a black beauty pageant that was won by student nurse, Yvonne Rosario. Some five hundred people attended the event and partygoers converged on Laurie Grove from all corners of London. In a time when many of the pubs in South East London excluded black people overtly, the meetings and dances that were held in the baths were at the forefront of integration and breaking the colour bar (see also Anim-Addo, 1995).

In March 1971 limbo dancers Joyce Hutchinson and Kevin Livingston were flown in from Trinidad to perform at a dance held in Laurie Grove. Two bands performed for the dancers and the *Lewisham Borough News* reported: 'The baths were filled with almost equal proportions of Lewisham's coloured and white community'. While there is little evidence that the public laundry and slipper baths were used by the local Caribbean community, the baths could be used as a less racially coded public space. The pool was a place that young black Londoners felt was open to them. William 'Lez' Henry, who grew up in Lewisham in these years, remembered: 'Laurie Grove ... absolutely used to go there after school and during holidays. It was a welcoming place for black and white working-class youth. I'm sure they had a little canteen where we could chill if we didn't swim and it was in many ways a neutral space as the racist boys from Cold Blow Lane [where Millwall football club was located] never seemed bothered with it' (Personal Communication, 12 January 2022).

Draining watery public spheres and the 'knowledge pool'

Given its remarkable history it might be of no surprise that the building is said to be haunted. The large crack running up the wall at the end of the main pool was caused by a Nazi V2 rocket that killed 168 people, including 33 children and babies in prams, shopping in the Woolworths store on New Cross Road at 12.26 pm on 25 November 1944. These tragic events form the basis of Francis Spufford's novel *Light Perpetual* (2021). Laurie Grove Baths was used as a mortuary during this period. It was also a billet for Canadian troops before they left for the Normandy invasion. Peter Powers remembers the suite of rooms where my office is being guarded by Gurkha sentries when the First Earl Mountbatten and his generals visited troops at the baths for tea.

Peter told me that during the eighteen years that his father managed the baths numerous members of the public – even several police officers – witnessed strange phenomena. Almost always at night, these included lights coming on suddenly, and doors opening or slamming for no reason. The said 'poltergeist' was affectionately known as 'Charlie' because he was given to whistling the tune 'Charleston'. Three members of staff left because of Charlie's antics, two without giving notice. We've not seen anything of Charlie but as Peter has told us his antics were usually confined to night time and Sundays.

In the last quarter of the twentieth century Laurie Grove Baths and the watery cultures that flourished there were drained of life. Richard Hoggart, who became Warden of Goldsmiths College in 1976, enjoyed an early morning swim in what he described as a 'grotty local swimming baths', as did many other faculty members of the college (Hoggart, 1992: 182). Hoggart's enjoyment is fitting, as his book *The Uses of Literacy* (1957), based on his experience of growing up in Hunslet, Leeds, is arguably the best document of working-class community. However, the bathhouse was dying and the bracing cold waters unpopular with schoolchildren who favoured the newer heated swimming pools at Ladywell and elsewhere.

A series of industrial disputes at neighbouring Deptford Townhall during 1977–1978 was the final death knell. The townhall received its heating from the baths, which meant that in spite of the manager's guarantee that the offending pipes had been isolated, the baths continued to be picketed twenty-four hours a day – ironically enough by politically active students from Goldsmiths College – and this prevented any fuel-oil from entering the building, causing the pools to go cold. This cooling effect led to substantial structural damage, breaking the small pool's back and rendering it useless for almost five years and totally destroying the South pool, which was demolished to become a car park. In addition to this, the plant equipment and ancillaries, most of which had been using the original Victorian pipework, suffered irreparable damage.

Unlike many people who have been Warden of Goldsmiths College, Richard Hoggart lived locally with his wife in New Cross. In his memoir *An Imagined Life* (1992), he writes affectionately about this period of his life and saw his time at Goldsmiths as connected to his commitment to community education. It was more than merely offering educational opportunity, for Hoggart felt the task of the university was, as he put it, to 'intellectualise its neighbourhood' (Hoggart, 1992: 180).

The pools were finally closed in 1991 and taken over and renovated by Goldsmiths College. In 1994 the building became the home of the CUCR and also converted into art studios. The floor of the main swimming pool is divided into a grid of studios in which young artists work. Much of the research work conducted at CUCR through its twenty-five-year history is in tune with the history of Laurie Grove, including studies of bowling alleys, gentrification, football and working-class life, food and multiculture, and popular music and reggae. Alongside this work, staff at CUCR have conducted applied policy evaluations of the Deptford City Challenge, a mortality audit for the Lambeth Drug Reference Group, and the Heritage Lottery-funded renovation of the Fellowship Inn by Phoenix Community Housing. Staff and graduate students at the Centre include a variety of internationally renowned urban studies scholars, photographers and artists, including Michael Keith, Caroline Knowles, Emma Jackson, Marj Mayo, Lez Henry, Alex Rhys-Taylor, Paul Halliday, Alison Rooke, Anamik Saha, Charlotte Bates, Monica Figuero-Moreno, Anita Strasser, and many more.

CUCR's research has done a good job of realising Hoggart's vision of turning the local district into an intellectual project. There is a further paradox here and a last trick that the Old Bathhouse has played on us all. Our desire to honour this past and its culture – like writing this chapter – is at the same time tied complicitly with the University's role in gentrifying and remaking the local landscape (see Strasser, 2020). The public cultures of the baths have been drained of their water and life, and all that is left is a dry ruin of their memory. In 2000 I wrote an article about the work of CUCR for a local magazine called *Lewisham Life*; they ran it with the title 'Knowledge Pool'. It is a poignant reminder that our desire to know and value community, culture and history can also go hand in hand with institutional forces and University interests that are simultaneously causing its destruction and erasure.

Conclusion: the paradoxes of water

Water is implicated in the baptism of the body with patterns of culture and structures of feeling, and it can also create a form of social buoyancy that creates links between people who may have little in common. As Sophie Watson argues: 'The very substance of water has the capacity to evoke a sense of attachment and belonging, which generates new connections and politics' (Watson, 2019: 163). Here the public bath is implicated in the paradoxes within city life. There is the tension between improvement and regulation, the ordering of people in terms of respectability, cleanliness and moral probity and the unwashed and disreputable. For many poor Londoners having a bathroom and not having to resort to the public bath or the tin bath were signs of postwar progress and social improvement. So, in a way the baths are crucially implicated in the history of postwar culture, both a site of nostalgia and something to be happy about not having to use anymore.

Then there is also the sense of the body as part of the care of the self, maintaining personal dignity even when the social circumstances seem stacked against this possibility. Movement and embodiment within popular culture – be it dancing above the waterline or swimming below it – is about being the owners of our own bodies in motion. Alex Rhys-Taylor captures this so vividly when he writes: 'The senses are revealed as the cement binding social strata together, as well as the solvents evaporating the boundaries between hitherto distinct life worlds' (Rhys-Taylor, 2017: 22). From the smell of chlorine to the feel of carbolic soap, the sensations of a shared working-class culture were felt, if not in solution, then certainly when wet. More convivial ways of being together across the colour bar in public were also floated above the watery pools. At ringside female audiences watched the pinfalls and submissions of male wrestling matches and turned gendered norms upside down and stretched them irreverently, and as result expanded the terms of how women could be together in public. Perhaps, it is for these reasons – among potentially many others – that a place like Laurie Grove Baths remains so beloved.

Acknowledgements

I would really like to thank everyone who generously shared their time, tips, memories and experiences to help complete this chapter, including Peter Powers, Professor William Henry, Sarah Elizabeth Cox, Bruce Downie, Lisa McKenzie, Jacqueline Springer, Teresa Piacentini, Rebecca Taylor, Antonia Lucia Dawes, Ronnie Hughes, Lyndsey Stonebridge, Rosaleen O'Brien and Martin Johnson.

References

Anim-Addo, J. (1995) *Longest Journey: A History of Black Lewisham*. London: Deptford Forum Publishing Limited.

Back, L. (1996) *New Ethnicities and Urban Culture: Racisms and Multiculture in Young Lives*. London: UCL Press.

Brown, W. G. (1999) *Windrush to Lewisham: Memoirs of 'Uncle George'*. London: Mango Publishing.

Cox, S. (2019) Without doubt Jack is the most popular man in New Cross. *Grappling with History*. Available at: https://grapplingwithhistory.com/2021/04/21/the-most-popular-man-in-new-cross-2/ (accessed 14 January 2022).

Crook, T. (2018) 'The Artesian well of contemporary art – Laurie Grove Baths. Available at: https://sites.gold.ac.uk/goldsmithshistory/the-artesian-well-of-contemporary-art-laurie-grove-baths/ (accessed 20 January 2022).

Dazey, M. (2021) Rethinking respectability politics. *British Journal of Sociology*, 72(3), 580–593.

Foucault, M. (1975) *Discipline and Punish*. London: Allen Lane.

Glucksmann, M. (2000) *Cottons and Casuals: The Gendered Organisation of Labour in Time and Space*. London and New York: Routledge.

Hoggart, R. (1957) *The Uses of Literacy: Aspects of Working Class Life*. London: Pelican Books.

Hoggart, R. (1992) *An Imagined Life: Life and Times 1959–91*. London: Chatto & Windus.

Kelly, M. (2000) *The Life and Times of Kitty Wilkinson*. Liverpool: The Liver Press.

Orwell, G. [1941] (1970) The lion and the unicorn. In S. Orwell and I. Angus (eds) *The Collected Essays, Journalism and Letters: Volume 2*. London: Penguin Books, pp. 74–134.

Orwell, G. [1946] (1968) How the poor die. In In S. Orwell and I. Angus (eds) *The Collected Essays, Journalism and Letters: Volume 4.* London: Penguin Books, pp. 261–271.

Rhys-Taylor, A. (2017) *Food and Multiculture: A Sensory Ethnography of East.* London: Bloomsbury Academic.

Rimel, D. (1994) *Thomas Dinwiddy: A Forgotten Architect.* London: Lewisham Local History Society.

Scott, S. (2009) Reclothing the emperor: the swimming pool as negotiated order. *Symbolic Interaction,* 32(2), 123–145.

Scott, S. (2010) How to look good (nearly) naked: the performative regulation of the swimmer's body. *Body & Society,* 16(2), 143–168.

Skeggs, B. (1997) *Formations of Class and Gender: Becoming Respectable.* London: Sage.

Spufford, F. (2021) *Light Perpetual.* London: Faber & Faber.

Steele, J. (1993) *Turning the Tide: The History of Everyday Deptford from the Romans to the Present.* London: Deptford Forum Publishing Limited.

Strasser, A. (2020) *Deptford is Changing: A Creative Exploration of the Impact of Gentrification.* London: Anita Strasser.

The Who (1979) *Quadrophenia.* Directed by Franc Roddam, The Who Films Ltd.

Transpontine (2011) The history and future of Laurie Grove Baths. Transpontine blogzine, 26 July 2011. Available at: http://transpont.blogspot.com/2011/07/laurie-grove-baths.html (accessed 12 January 2022).

Transpontine (2017) Laurie Grove Baths event at Goldsmiths. Transpontine blogzine, 14 June 2011. Available at: http://transpont.blogspot.com/2017/06/laurie-grove-baths-event-at-goldsmiths.html (accessed 12 January 2022).

Watson, S. (2015) Mundane objects in the city: laundry practices and the making and remaking of public/private sociality and space in London and New York. *Urban Studies,* 52(5), 876–890.

Watson, S. (2019) *City Water Matters: Cultures, Practices and Entanglements of Urban Water.* Singapore: Palgrave Macmillan.

Williams, R. (1977) *Marxism and Literature.* Oxford and New York: Oxford University Press.

7

River crossings: the mighty London Thames

Sophie Watson

Taking the Thames in London as its focus, this chapter considers the movements through and across rivers and the different ways water in cities is traversed, and what is made and unmade in the process. The chapter delves into the ways bodies are carried through water in watercraft, below the water in tunnels or above the water on bridges. Each of these material artefacts speaks to different cultural interpretations of water and the objects with which it connects bodies to each other and across space. Bridges are more than roads across the river; they convey different understandings of city spaces and cross social and cultural boundaries in their construction and use. Water enables objects to float and move, enacting different forms of mobility. Thus, watercraft are also embedded in complex cultural, social and economic relations which are differentiated both in terms of use and in the meanings attributed to them. Drawing on stories of the wherry (and later the ferry) and the barge in London, this chapter unpacks their associated mobilities, uses and meanings. A selection of bridges and tunnels represent another matter of concern – how and why they were built, in what location and by what means – in order to reveal the complexities of river crossings in any city. I look specifically at the Thames, a waterway that exists as the life blood of this global city, whose role in the building of the British Empire, as the waterway from which ships departed and to which the multiple goods from distant territories returned, was vital. Though not the focus of my writing here, this is a dark side of this history too, where the river played a part in the transportation of slaves and the subjugation of people across the world. The selection of a city as the site of major river crossings was one of the determinants of their growth. A cursory glance at any atlas reveals the significance of rivers to the construction of many of the world's capital, and subsidiary, cities, many of which are also close to the sea. Most capital cities are situated on rivers or harbours, and are central to the city's identity and image. Rivers enable commerce, trading, industry, irrigation and food production, produce water to drink, and for many centuries have represented the life blood of the city, quite literally its major artery. At the same time rivers dissect city spaces. They must be crossed. River technologies, boats, craft, docks and wharves similarly produce, and are produced by, shifts in everyday cultural practices and technical – more recently digital – knowledges and economic imperatives.

Reading a city through the river and its crossings reveals new understandings and tells different stories. Among others, Lichenstein (2017) describes the haunting landscape of the Thames estuary where the tides of history of trade, tradition, war and piracy have left different traces on the river and surrounding topography. Ackroyd (2008) explores the history of the river as a site of the sacred, pleasure, nature, trade and art, as well as its materialities in the form of locks, weirs, docks and palaces. In his *Illustrated* book of London, Henry Mayhew (1861: 93) began his account of the river:

> by enumerating the numerous classes of labourers, amounting to many thousands, who get their living by plying their respective avocations on the river, and who constitute the customers of these men. These are first the sailors on board the corn, coal, and timber ships; the 'stevedores', or those engaged in stowing craft; and the 'riggers', or those engaged in rigging them; the ballast-heavers, ballast-getters, corn-porters, coal-whippers, watermen and lightermen, and coal-porters.

This description evokes the crowded and animated life of the Thames at the time, when some forty thousand men worked on or near the river. This was a material culture of boats and other water related infrastructures such as piers, where 'steamers pass and repass, twisting and wriggling their way through craft of every description, the unskilful adventurer would run into continual danger of having his boat crushed like a shell' (Mayhew, 1861: 93). The river was so full of boats that at certain moments a foolhardy youth could cross from one side to the other hopping from deck to deck without falling in. In contemporary photographs and paintings the river is an empty space by comparison.

Watermen and watercraft

The major form of crossing the river until the bridges and later tunnels were constructed was by using watercraft – different artefacts which could float on the river's surface. In what follows, we briefly look at two of these and some of the men – as ever a gendered world – who work(ed) on them. Over time all material objects change, adapt and are reconfigured according to different technologies and different social relations. Some of these watercraft have found new forms or been re-versioned in recent years.

First, the men who worked on the Thames enabling the cross-ing of people and goods, connecting disconnected spaces from one side of the river to the other. Men on the river were categorised as either lightermen or watermen – the former carrying cargo on their boats, the latter carrying passengers. These men joined together in 1700 to form the Company of Watermen and Lightermen. Most of the city companies developed from religious fraternities in the Middle Ages, whereas the Company of Watermen was created by an Act of Parliament in 1514 to regulate and control watercraft on the river, and as such had a strong craftsman ethos, rather like the later hackney cab and taxi operators. This rather august institution still exists in a splendid building in the city, where I conducted inter-views (Watson, 2019). The walls are adorned with portraits of former masters of the company, the prestigious red coats, oars, cups and the Doggett's badge, which is discussed later. These are men who typi-cally came from long-established East End families, whose grandfa-thers and fathers had worked on the river before them. As Dean, a lighterman put it:

> It was always families so it was always passed down and passed down, so anyone you ever work with you knew their family, they knew your family, so it was ... You didn't really mess around too much, do you know what I mean?
>
> In the rules it says you shall not waste the goods, cards, dice, tables or any unlawful games the master may have lost, so it's all very olde worlde. ... And ye shall not commit fornication ... Ye shall not haunt

taverns nor playhouses is my particular favourite, considering my grandfather spent most of his life in the pub.

To become a lighterman or waterman is a complex matter involving a five-year apprenticeship and education. Learning the ins and outs of the tides, the bridges, the eddies and flows, the access points to the banks and all the other complexities of the river requires following a process of learning examination much like that of Black cab drivers in London doing the 'knowledge'.

Dean described the process and how embedded it is in family tradition:

Yeah, it's very scary and all the while you've got your grandfather standing behind ya, with a hand on your shoulder and they're asking questions. So your provisional licence is not really ... it's quite easy, as long as you've been doing the work it's not really a major thing. So then you get your provisional licence.

So then you go back to work, carry on learning, your granddad's still your master, you are then a ... you're still an apprentice but you're like a young freeman they call it then. So you do another three years then you go back to the sea school, it's in Gravesend, Kent and you do some more training with the PLA [Port of London Authority]. They teach you chart work, seamanship, throwing ropes and all that, navigating, radars, this sort of stuff.

Then you get a letter through the post ... so they invite you to go to the Watermen's Hall and be examined to become a freeman of the company.

The complexity of the knowledge required is breathtaking, as Dean describes:

So that's where these licences took us from, from Lower Hope to I think it's Teddington Lock or something, so they can ask you anywhere within that and it's a bit like, you know the taxi knowledge, every stretch of river has a name, every bend's got a name, so every wharf's got a name and they ask you anything. So I think ... they'd ask say, from Tilbury Docks up, and then so you say, 'I leave Tilbury Docks ...' and then there's all the radio channels and everything like that, you have to talk them up.

You just tell them everything you can see and everything that's around you. They said to me, 'Your vessel's now on fire, what are you going to do?' Now, the problem with Long Reach is as you look over Dartford Bridge when you drive over there, along the Essex coast there is all Essos ...

The process ends with ritual, as is so often the case in particularly male craft industries (Cockburn, 1983) – a strategy which acts, by default or more knowingly, to exclude women:

> So you have your special little drink, then you go into the Freeman's Room and you get all your … you get your certificate. … It's like a big FA Cup thing, they fill it up with beer, so then you get presented with this, which is you're now Freeman's Company.

Another part of their tradition is rowing for the Doggett's Coat and Badge, which is the oldest rowing race in the world. The story goes that one Thomas Doggett – an actor and manager of the Drury Lane Theatre, who was ferried by the watermen regularly from his home in Chelsea to the city – was one day rescued by a waterman after falling into the Thames. In gratitude he offered a rowing wager for the fastest waterman on the river, where the prize was to be the traditional waterman's red coat with a silver badge representing liberty. Starting in 1715 the race has continued and the men who win are highly celebrated in the company, acting as the Queen's watermen on the Royal Barge. These highly ritualised and valued traditions, prevalent across many of the craft trades also, historically have perpetuated men's participation in spaces from which women, until very recently, have been excluded.

Wherries/ferries and barges

There are, and were, many forms of watercraft which could float on the Thames, of which we will briefly look at two. Until the bridges were constructed across the river at regular intervals, the main form of river crossing was the 'wherries'. Wherries were rather like the Venetian gondola, with long overhanging bows so that patrons could step ashore with dry feet before landing stages were built along the river. Wherries were the taxis of the Elizabethan period rowed by two men with long oars or a single waterman with short oars, carrying up to five passengers. Shakespeare's Globe theatre stood on the bank across the river from the theatre district, so they were frequently used by theatre goers at the time with figures of two thousand wherries being reported as going back and forth in one evening. Not only did they cross the river; like the ferries which succeeded them, they operated a service connecting places along the river with circuitous routes from point to point along the river.

Wherries witnessed a rapid decline from the early 1820s to the end of the decade with the construction of new bridges and the rise of cheap steamboats. There are no traces of the wherries in contemporary London – only in the name of the ferry boats, which have recently become a feature of Transport for London (TFL). Sean, Chief Executive of the Clippers Company and another lighterman from a river family, told me how Clippers' passenger boats were launched and flourished in less than twenty years:

> We started in 1999 with one boat. We had a competitor at the time, White Horse Ferries, so we couldn't stop at any of the London river services, TFL piers, we had to stop at purely private piers. So the private piers that we very first started off on was Greenham Pier, Canary Wharf, London Bridge and Savoy. ... It was full up from the first week that we started up, with commuters. And then we got the opportunity to have the second and third boat.

The changing residential structure of the river, where more and more areas were developed for housing and employment, provided a further boost to the business, augmented by collaborating with an Australian shipbuilder which developed new craft:

> We had a lot of cross-river business between Surrey Quays and Canary Wharf, because there was a lot of locals that live there that just wanted to get across the river to Canary Wharf. ... And so the Hurricane Clipper was developed, which was the first of our 220-seater boats. And that created an amazing wow factor, it gave us the carrying capacity on those main runs in the morning and the main runs in the evening to deliver a service and not disappoint anybody, because we was constantly leaving people behind. And it grew from there ... to carrying 2.7 million passengers by 2008.

What is described here is the very rapid expansion of water-based mobility by the end of the first decade of the twenty-first century.

Barges weighing about 120 tons were used to move large cargo on the Thames and its estuaries. The barges were flat bottomed to enable movement across the shallow waters of the river, with large canvas sails that could be lowered to go under a bridge. Peter, the barge master of the Thames Sailing Barge Trust, described the structures:

> If you're talking about back in the late 1700s, early 1800s they didn't have engines and it's pretty hard to row a great big barge full of whatever on a river. So somebody started to put a mast on it and a sail, and they'd go with the tide and it would just move a little bit and they'd have

an oar and they'd poke it around, and it just developed over years and
the rig has got all sorts of influences, there's a lot of influences from the
Dutch barges that sail round the lowlands but it's a unique rig that's
developed. If you look at a square rig or an old trade boat, they had big
square sails and a big mast and it'd have a crew of tens, maybe twenty or
thirty. But they couldn't afford to do that, they didn't have the money,
so they developed the rig in such a way that it could be handled by a
man and horse. And you might have four-and-a-half thousand square
feet of sail up, which on a yacht would take twenty people; on a barge it
takes two. It's all in the design. The design is absolutely brilliant.

This was a highly masculinised world where the lowering of the
mast needed strong men, known as the 'huffers', and where the
bargemen were referred to as the truckers of the river. Unlike the lightermen who drove the wherries these men were disconnected from the
community – peripatetic and lone boatmen, who often slept on their
barges at night, who were not members of the Company of Watermen
and Lightermen, or the old river communities. But, as Peter pointed
out, managing these barges was a real skill:

They're just literally a tank that you put things in and it's a real skill to
be able to manoeuvre them around, you've got no engine, no means of
propulsion ... but in those days they didn't have those big tugs necessarily to move them around; they literally drifted them around on the
tide, they put things in them, shifted them, they might go up with the
tide, whatever. Missing the bridges was a skill.

Much of the cargo that was brought into London was carried on
the barges. Peter again:

The barges were used to transport agricultural matter such as grain
(from the port of London) and straw and hay (which was much needed
since all transport was horse drawn) which they would take from
London to the mills in Essex, Suffolk or Kent. Or they might do what
they call 'the rough stuff' which would be the rubbish from the streets
of London, the horse muck and the straw and stuff. They'd pick that
up in London and take it out to the brickworks in Kent, and the brickworks would put it into the clay mix and when they fired it it burnt in
the brick, which if you look in London on a red brick building you'll
find flecks of black, sort of ash in the brick and that's what that is, it's
the rough stuff that they took out of London, put into the mix, fired
the brick ... it makes it stronger, makes it fire better. And the bricks
would be then transported back on the barges back into London from
the brickworks.

This was not an easy job, and required strength and resilience from the men who worked there:

> They would take clay, they would dig the clay out and move it to one of the brickworks ... because they're shallow and flat they can go very shallow and they'd take them into what you might think is just a muddy creek and they would literally have great big spade-type things and there would be several boats digging and throwing the mud or the clay out of the ground straight into the barge and fill it straight up. Horrendous job, absolutely horrendous job!

Like the transformation of the wherries into a new form – the passenger ferries –, so too the old working sailing barges have been revived to enact new socio-cultural practices. The Thames Sailing Barge Trust was formed in 1948 to preserve two Thames barges in sailing condition. Their aim was to improve public understanding of the historical role of the barges, and to promote and teach the practice, traditions and skills of seamanship involved in the handling and maintaining of the craft by taking people sailing in the waters the craft traditionally sailed. The Trust thus bought, and restored, two barges – *Pudge* and *Centaur* – which are now crewed and maintained by volunteers. At the same time, the old barge races were revived and a new generation of semi-amateurs replaced the old skippers of the earlier competitions. Yet, like so many other aspects of water connections, even the new volunteers sailing the barges are men, with women involved in more 'feminised cultural practices'. As Peter pointed out:

> I don't think we've got any female skippers at the moment. But on the maintenance side we do, we have all sorts of people, only a month or so ago we had a lady turned up ... 'cause we have working parties every other weekend on one barge. She turned up from San Francisco, she'd been working, volunteered on a similar sort of barge in San Francisco Bay. ... We have a lady who's an artist, a painter, every working weekend she's there, she does general work but she also does all the nice detailed bits at the end, when we're ready to go out she'll paint the name and things like that.

Thames tunnel

In what follows, I turn to different river crossings by foot or vehicle. The story of the Thames tunnel between Wapping and Rotherhithe is a story of incredible engineering, terrible working conditions, and extraordinary spectacle. At the start of its construction there were thirteen thousand ships on the river in any one day. The tunnel was the first to be constructed beneath a navigable river and was designed in 1843 by Marc and Isambard Brunel to meet an urgent need to connect the North and South sides of the Thames and the docks that were expanding on each side. According to the Director of the Brunel Museum, 'they used to say it took longer to get stuff across the Thames than to get stuff across the Atlantic' (Brown, 2010). The project was made possible by the new technology developed by Marc Brunel called the tunnelling shield, which acted as a support structure against falling materials or the roof caving in. An example of nature/technology connections was the way in which Brunel's design was inspired by the shell of a shipworm which he had watched burrowing through timber when he was working in the shipyard. With this new method the construction of tunnels was revolutionised. The *Illustrated London News* of 25 March 1843 described the shield as: 'consisting of twelve great frames, lying close to each other like as many volumes on the shelf of a book-case, and divided into three stages or storeys, thus presenting 36 chambers of cells, each for one workman, and open to the rear, but closed in the front with moveable boards'. Not only were father and son great engineers, but in a classic erasure of women's potential, Sophia Brunel, Marc's wife, was also fascinated by and knowledgeable about engineering. But in the disregard of women's talents that was prevalent at the time, she was denied any major input and referred to as 'Brunel in petticoats'. In a talk at the Brunel Museum for Women's History month, Sarah Kuklewicz (2021) describes Sophia Brunel's life subordinated to her husband, where even when Marc Brunel was consigned to the debtor's prison for a couple of months she shared the sentence with him.

The conditions of the work were perilous, with men working with spades in cages and breathing in air and moisture in what was effectively an open sewer. Not only were the polluted air and sewage-laden water dangerous and productive of diseases such as cholera, causing illness among the miners as well as Isambard Brunel, but the tunnel was also a site of floods and drownings. In one incident Isambard Brunel was swept along the length of the tunnel by a flood wave and had to be carried out on a stretcher. During the tunnel's construction six men drowned, as the water broke through. After the flooding of the tunnel on 18 May 1827 Brunel lowered a diving bell from a boat to repair the hole at the bottom of the river, throwing bags filled with clay into the breach in the tunnel's roof. In what seems like an act of defiance to boost confidence, following the repairs and the drainage of the tunnel, he held a banquet inside it. Such was the excitement on the opening of the tunnel in 1843 that fifty thousand people visited it on the first day, a figure which increased to 1 million by the end of the month. As a tunnel for pedestrians and horses and carriages, it became a major tourist attraction. In 1852 a spectacular fair was held in the tunnel, with a large ballroom where dancers were serenaded by steam-powered musical organs, and performing horses, fire eaters, acrobats and sword swallowers entertained the crowds (Brown, 2010). It is hard to imagine such glamour and glitter on a visit to this grimy and noisy tunnel at the present day. In 1869 the tunnel was converted into a railway tunnel as a vibrant space of pedestrian or carriage mobility came to an end.

Bridges

Walk along the Thames today and you will see many bridges, all delightful in their different ways. My heart always misses a beat as I go over Waterloo Bridge and look either way over the London panorama, an evocative vista to many who cross there. Bridges have been represented in countless songs and poems, often in a whimsical or nostalgic voice. In the 1960s a rock band, the Kinks, were moved to write a song from the bridge ('Waterloo Sunset'):

> Dirty old river
> Must you keep rolling
> Flowing into the night
> People so busy
> Make me feel dizzy
> Taxi light shines so bright

Further west from Waterloo Bridge, which has been the focus of many such imaginaries, there is the Albert Bridge opened in 1873 which is a form of cable-stayed bridge and covered with some four thousand lights which twinkle in the night sky. Many of the bridges are on the sites of earlier fords, ferries and wooden structures. The earliest known major crossings of the Thames by the Romans were at London Bridge and Staines Bridge. Earlier proposals to build bridges across the Thames at Lambeth and Putney were defeated by the Company of Watermen and Lightermen, since they were seen to threaten the employment of the wherry men on the river. The eighteenth century saw the construction of many stone and brick road bridges, both new and to replace existing structures, which profoundly altered the urban development of London, opening up new areas of expansion across the river. For example, Kingston's growth is believed to stem from its having the only crossing between London Bridge and Staines until the beginning of the eighteenth century. Several more bridges were built in the nineteenth century, including Tower Bridge, which we discuss shortly. Simultaneously, the development of the railways resulted in a spate of bridge building in the nineteenth century, including Blackfriars Railway Bridge and Charing Cross (Hungerford) Railway Bridge in Central London.

These artefacts have both symbolic and material significance. Crossing the river engenders a sense of moving into alien territory – Londoners frequently refer to their disdain for the other side of the river – a place which they rarely visit. While their material presence connects industries, residence, places of employment which may be symbiotically related, bridges represent a space of transition and ambivalence. There is something compelling about standing on a bridge over the Thames watching the tides swirl below. On the darker side, a dozen or so people each year throw themselves off a bridge in London, and rarely survive. So too Westminster Bridge became the site of a terrorist attack in the spring of 2017, killing five people and injuring many more.

Timber bridges across the Thames were constructed, and re-built as they rotted, from Roman times. Richmond Bridge is the oldest existing bridge crossing the river, built from stone between 1774 and 1777 and funded by tolls, which was constructed as a replacement for a ferry crossing connecting Richmond town centre on the East bank with its neighbouring district of East Twickenham to the West. Many foot crossings were established across the weirs that were built on the non-tidal river, and some of these remained when the locks were built – for example at Benson Lock. Others were replaced by a foot-bridge when the weir was removed, as at Hart's Weir Footbridge. Since the turn of the twenty-first century, several footbridges have been added, either as part of the Thames Path or in commemoration of the Millennium. The last bridge to be completed across the Thames was the Millennium Bridge connecting St Paul's to the Tate Modern and initially a site of contestation and panic, as its original design left it vulnerable to swaying in the winds.

Material and human connections are nowhere more apparent on the river than in the construction of bridges, as the watermen were quick to see. Three brief vignettes of London bridges tell different stories which illustrate how the very matter of bridges embeds and constitutes different publics between the banks.

On a journey down the Thames on a tour boat, you might well hear the operators refer in passing to Waterloo Bridge (originally built in 1811–1817 and designed by John Rennie) as Ladies Bridge. This is a hidden gendered history illustrating one aspect of women's work during the war when in 1941 women were called upon by Ernest Bevin, the Minister of Labour and National Service, to alleviate an acute manpower crisis on the home front.

One film that caught the public imagination and inspired many second-wave feminists of the 1970s was *Rosie the Riveter*. Made in 1944 the film, inspired by a song of that name, was a cultural icon representing women who had worked in the shipyards and factories making munitions and war supplies while the men went off to fight at the front. The film portrays images of women workers, who were displayed at the time on government posters and in commercial advertising to encourage women to volunteer for wartime service in factories. Later feminists saw the film as a graphic representation of how active women had been in traditionally male-defined employment and argued that it suited governments to bring women into the workforce when needed, only to push them back into the domestic sphere when men were available to fill the jobs. The 1950s were seen as a period when women, especially middle-class women, were 'encouraged' to stay at home and tend to the needs of their husbands and children. Many sectors, including teaching and the civil service, even refused to allow women to continue in their posts once they were married.

Less well known, however, are the women who were involved in engineering and construction, who numbered twenty-five thousand by 1944, filling jobs that were vacated by male volunteers and conscripts. Most of these jobs were temporary and low paid, but many included skilled jobs that were previously inaccessible to women. One of the biggest such projects in London was the reconstruction of Waterloo Bridge, which had fallen into disrepair after more than a hundred years. A new bridge was designed by Gilbert Scott – also known for his St Pancras Station – since the government saw it as essential for the movement of troops. Working as stonemasons, welders and labourers from 1939–1944 the women played a key role. So great was the ignorance (or disavowal) of their contribution to the reconstruction of the bridge, that in 1945 Herbert Morrison – the then leader of London County Council – on opening the bridge said:

> The men who built Waterloo Bridge are fortunate men. They know that, although their names may be forgotten, their work will be a pride and use to London for many generations to come. To the hundreds of workers in stone, in steel, in timber, in concrete the new bridge is a monument to their skill and craftsmanship.

As war ended their contribution was quickly forgotten and women were cajoled back into domestic life. The story of the women construction workers on Waterloo Bridge was unearthed from the archives in the early 2000s by Christine Wall, who was joined by film-maker Karen Livesey to pursue the story through oral history. The Ladies Bridge documentary explores why these bridge builders and twenty-five thousand other female construction workers have been written out of history. As the son of a crane driver on the bridge explained in the film:

> I can remember seeing ladies here. ... I think there was quite a few hundred ladies up here they did the less technical jobs, the lifting and the tugging where the men done the crane work and the technical type of work. And the ladies were in two grades of ladies. The ladies with the turbans and the dungarees you know with the bib up – there was more of them – but the ladies which were like the senior lady that could drive and could undertake a more of a technical job like, they wore an all in one overall a bit similar to the men. ... They probably didn't remember the women working on the bridge because they didn't look like women, you know if you have a flat cap on and an overall all in one, even today I have a lot of trouble to see who's a man and who's a lady. My father he used to love the ladies ...

The Ladies Bridge film, screened first in 2006, raised the women's invisibility as a matter of concern and mobilised a multiplicity of publics, to press for the women's work on the bridge to be articulated and recognised. In 2009 the Women's Engineering group, ARUP and Women in Property started the Purple Boots and Decent Wear for Work campaign to raise the profile of women workers on the bridge. By 2015 Historic England had amended its history of Waterloo Bridge to include the participation of women in the workforce, and in 2016 the bridge was lit up with a human chain crossing the bridge in celebration. The bridge of women had won its battle.

The Old London Bridge is differently embedded in gendered relations which are long forgotten. Built in 1209, houses were built across the length of the bridge (282 metres), reaching a maximum of 140 by the late fourteenth century. Typically, they were two to four storeys high with shops at the street level. The bridge was one of the City of London's four or five main shopping streets, including haberdashers, glovers, cutlers, textile makers and other traders. There was also a chapel on the bridge. The bridge was iconic to locals and visitors alike. Not just a way of crossing the river, it was also an important part of London's identity. It dominated the view of anyone approaching London along the Thames and was a constant presence to people on the river or the waterfront. It was a place for pageants and for ceremonial entrances to the city. Its maintenance was the largest single collective endeavour of London's citizens, many of whom made bequests towards it in their wills, and it symbolised their wealth and corporate identity (Gerhold, 2019: 7–8). According to a Frenchman, in 1578 it was 'a great and powerful bridge, the most magnificent that exists in the whole of Europe. It is ... completely covered with houses which are all like big castles. And the shops are great storehouses full of all sorts of opulent merchandise' (Gerhold, 2019: 8).

Innumerable people lived on the bridge, including many women: Isabella Barnaby, trading as a silkwoman, Alice Ulfe, widow, Isabella Walle, widow, Isabella Frecock, widow of a fletcher, Agnes Basse, a widow, Alice Sauston, widow of a cutler, and the widow of Parys a tailor (Gerhold, 2019: 63). There were always some female tenants on the bridge and probably most of these were widows continuing their husbands' trades, although women in the fifteenth century acquired a lease for themselves rather than taking it over from a dead husband. The most notable example was Isabella Barnaby, who was a silkwoman from 1430 until her death in 1478. According to Gerhold (2019: 80) there were almost equal numbers of men and women on the bridge: 51 per cent and 49 per cent, respectively in 1678, and 47 per cent and 53 per cent in 1695. This, then, was a feminised space where women were engaged in commerce and shops, an arena of life that has continued to be gendered until the present day.

Tower Bridge tells a different story, one which foregrounds technology, tourism and a different kind of involvement of multiple publics. This is a bridge which stands in for London, arguably its most potent icon represented in films, objects and postcards, and visited by thousands of tourists a year. No artefact except perhaps Big Ben is more emblematic of London, symbolising both empire and nation. So important is it in the global imagination of London that Arizona bought the bridge to be shipped and reassembled there. The irony, however, was that they bought the London Bridge built in the 1830s, having confused the two.

Peter, a senior technician on the bridge, put it this way:

> It's very iconic, Tower Bridge. Seen everywhere, isn't it? You go any-where in the world and you'll see Tower Bridge wherever you go. First year I was here I got put on TV in a programme called *What's Your Job, Bob?* with the *Breakfast* show, can't remember what it was called now, but I was on that, which I thought I was coming here just for mainte-nance and whatnot and that got dumped on me, this television show! And then me brother-in-law, he went to America that year and the screen in front of him, he was flicking through the channels and all of a sudden I popped up on this documentary.

The bridge is operated on a twenty-four hour basis and, in the twenty-three years of Peter's stewardship, lifts have increased from four hundred a year to a thousand in 2000. He attributes this to the growth in pleasure craft on the river, such as cruise liners and the sailing barges, that have replaced the old cargo-carrying boats that were headed for the docks, before containerisation led to their rapid demise in the 1980s. Thus, the shift from a commercial purpose based on trade to one based on tourism has refigured the bridge's purpose over recent decades.

This is a combined bascule and suspension bridge built in 1886–1894 and copied from a Dutch design. It is one of five of the London bridges owned and maintained by a charitable trust – Bridge House Estates – and overseen by the Corporation of London. The bridge consists of two towers joined by two horizontal walkways, designed to withstand the horizontal tension forces exerted by the suspended sections of the bridge on the landward sides of the towers. The objective of its innovative design was to enable the access of sailing ships along the Thames at the same time as allowing traffic to cross the river through the capacity to raise the lower level. Peter described its workings:

> Bascule – it's French for seesaw. And a bascule bridge, you've got the long lever, which is the road, and on the back end you've got the short

part which is counterweight, and it's balanced, so that's 12 tons. So when we're talking about two bridge drivers and separate bascules, the bascules in those days were operated independently so you had two bridge drivers, one north, one south, and in those days you would have always seen the south side bascule rising first, so they'd have always been out of step, 'cause basically the south side bridge driver had control of the nose bolts which locked the two halves together. So the north side driver couldn't start lifting until he saw the south side go, because he wouldn't know whether the bridge was unlocked or not. So that's why that was.

The original mechanism was based on water hydraulics developed in the nineteenth century, which in 1974 were replaced by a new electro-hydraulic drive system to raise the lower-level bridge. Digitalisation of the bridge in 2000 enabled the installation of a computer system (programmable logic control) to control the raising and lowering of the bascules remotely. Three senior technical officers and six (so-called) bridge drivers operate the bridge during the day and at night-time. Bridge statistics recording bridge lifts provide a lens to the wider socio-cultural and economic context. Peter explained the changing profile of the bridge over the last couple of decades this way:

> The amount of pleasure craft on the river, you've got all the cruise liners coming up, war ships coming up, and during the summer months you have a lot of sailing barges up and down, they do trips up and down. ... Some of them are privately owned and some are companies like Tate & Lyle and people like that, and Allied Mills, they've got their own sailing barge and they use it for corporate clients and trips up and down the river, and of course a big part of that is coming through Tower Bridge.

This, then, is a story of the river playing a growing part in global corporate life, new forms of tourism, and pleasure craft and leisure practices. Peter:

> Also you've got the *Dixie Queen*.[1] And of course part of the package for all their clients is see Tower Bridge lift as it goes up and down the river. So a lot of bridge lifts are done for her, especially weekends and during the evening. So that was a significant increase, for her. But basically it's all tourism.

---

[1] The *Dixie Queen* is a paddle steamer which is London's largest luxury boat which is available for hire and able to host any event with a flexible capacity for up to 620 guests.

Conclusion

These meanderings through different ways of crossing the river over several centuries illustrate the entangled histories of culture, social life and technology which have produced different forms of river crossings. This is a history steeped in traditions and rituals, some of which remain in a reconfigured way until the present day. It is also a highly gendered history, where women are largely absent from the stories. Crossing a river is both an economic and a commercial necessity as well as often a moment of reflection and imagination. Rivers are powerful forces that sever and connect a city in mysterious and complex ways. In this brief excursion we have seen how the different ways of crossing a river, sometimes floating on the surface of the water, sometimes passing above or below the water's surface, produce different socio-cultural contexts, rituals, traditions and customs. Casting a lens onto river crossings in any city will open interesting questions and new insights that extend beyond the forms of mobility that we encounter in place.

Hopefully, this brief excursion will inspire further explorations of river crossings across the many water-based cities of the world. Taking the river as a lens for understanding cities can shed light on larger questions of the interconnections between different cities, through trade and the building of empires, for example. Or it can expose the multiple ways in which bodies are immersed in water, through sanitation practices, or ritual practices such as the cremation of bodies on the Ghats of the Ganges which are central to the lives of many Hindus who make long pilgrimages to the holy city of Varanasi. Rivers are also the sites most affected by shifting patterns of rainfall, such as drought or flooding, offering potential insights into the effects of climate change on urban populations. Though taken for granted sometimes as a city's artery or as a focal point for tourists, rivers and river crossings can open our eyes to new connections, mobilities and the materialities of water in unexpected ways.

References

Ackroyd, P. (2008) *Thames: Sacred River*. London: Vintage.
Brown, M. (2010) Deep beneath London's streets, visitors revisit eighth wonder of the world. *The Guardian*, 12 March.

Cockburn, C. (1983) *Brothers: Male Dominance and Technical Change*. London: Pluto Press.

Gerhold, D. (2019) *London Bridge and Its Houses, c. 1209–1761*. London: London Topographical Society.

Kuklewicz, S. (2021) *Womens History Month: Who was Lady Sophia Brunel?*, 14 March. London: Brunel Museum.

Lichtenstein, R. (2017) *Estuary*. London: Penguin.

Mayhew, H. [1861] (1986) *The Illustrated Mayhew's London*. London: Weidenfeld & Nicolson.

Watson, S. (2019) *City Water Matters: Cultures, Practices and Entanglements of Urban Water*. London: Routledge.

8

Living with/out water: media, memory and gender

Joanne Garde-Hansen

There is nothing new about the fight for better British waterways or the need for improved water knowledge in the UK context, a topic largely ignored by arts and humanities researchers until recently, with many water histories still to be unearthed. Like many living with water (seas, rivers, canals) I am struck by how little I know of the histories, memories and stories of these watery places and spaces. I live in Stratford-upon-Avon, UK, where the South Stratford Canal meets in a basin with the River Avon in the centre of the town. The canal which I run along every day, as well as further afield up to its joining with the Grand Union Canal, was saved from draining in the 1950s and 1960s by volunteer effort that restored it for new uses (liveaboard narrow-boats, cruisers, paddle boards, canoes, hiking, running, cycling). We have this canal today because local people protested its closure and laboured to keep it in operation through the help of hundreds of volunteers, boy scouts, the army and even local prisoners. In the face of the district council's application for an Act of Abandonment in 1958, the threat of living without water in this canal led to the creative use of a canoeist to produce toll receipts as evidence of continued use: a triumph of mobilising bureaucracy for public good. Slowness, deliberation and the persistence of this collective through the 1960s, as well as the role of the BBC in featuring the campaign on the *Tonight* programme, secured a watercourse for my neighbourhood and I am grateful for their determination and collaboration. This history is accessible online, maintained by a local organisation, and must be sought out; it is not widely known by the canal's many users, and one would be forgiven for thinking that contemporary social media campaigns to clean up rivers and canals are a new phenomenon when such histories are not widely shared in a digital media culture.

The new and expanded role of social media in documenting water events, environmental disasters, shaming water misusers, and celebrating clean and accessible waterways has been an important part of my own research for the book *Media and Water* (Garde-Hansen, 2021). The whole field of media and communication studies has hardly concerned itself with water and water issues, even though the field is replete with liquid metaphors (channels, storms and immersive experiences). The UK flood of 2007 was the starting point for my research on mediating water.[1] The flood seemed to come out of nowhere at the wrong time of year and in the wrong place, but then such a perception reveals weak ties to environmental histories and community knowledge, and the overriding economic imperative to move on quickly and get back to 'business as usual'. The saturation of the media landscape with flood images (just as Facebook and Twitter were emerging) and the continued focus on floods as events to be memorialised meant water scarcity hardly seemed possible, never mind imaginable. How can an island, with such a wet climate be in drought? In this chapter, I precede a focus on drought media and water scarcity culture by beginning with the research on flood media templates as the key to understanding how a cultural *watery sense of place* currently displaces an understanding of a UK flood–drought continuum. I position media, communication and digital cultures as key infrastructural requirements for water research and new appreciations of water's cultural values.

Living with (too much) water

The media representation of the 2007 Summer Floods that deluged South West England repeated a national televisual template of biblical

---

[1] One could trace the focus on the power of water within the contemporary British cultural imaginary as equally attributable to the 2007 Summer Floods (the worst peace-time disaster since the Second World War) and to the Great Swim in Lake Windermere of 2008 (with over three thousand participants). Both water events became 'mass' and 'connected' around the same time through their social mediation. Twitter was in its infancy in 2007 and the general public was setting up Facebook groups from 2006.

inundation, dramatic rescues and talking heads of experts and government spokespeople versus local residents; while local radio performed civic roles in disaster response and community reporting. What was striking was the nascent role of social media. Facebook groups were created, active and supportive, and early-adopting Twitter users were posting and tagging incidents, demonstrating the demand of citizens for sharing knowledge, feelings and practices during the flood event. As we noted:

> Remembered claims on the land (this is my flooded house, my flooded street, my flooded town) are made mobile through bodies (by walking and filming around the territory). The mobile sharing of personal accounts and perspectives through available media forms means that citizens can be seen to participate in creating common or customary – if often conflicting – narratives and memories. (Krause, Garde-Hansen and Whyte, 2012: 138)

This community process of remembering directly after a flood and commemoration at anniversaries was highly mediatised considering that the last massive flood in the region had been the Winter Floods of 1947. As a group of researchers interested in bringing expertise in social sciences and arts and humanities together, we saw a gap in flood knowledge, one that focused on storytelling, memories and histories. How were memories of floods produced and practised by individuals and communities in different settings; how were these memories and lay knowledges stored, accessed, shared? Were communities with accessible and shareable past flood histories more resilient to future floods and how might researchers, media organisations and local archives create informal social learning to strengthen community flood resilience? This research led to numerous successfully funded collaborations and publications with the Centre for Floods, Communities and Resilience at the University of the West of England and with the Centre for Disaster Risk Management (CEMADEN) in Brazil. What became clear after the 2007 UK floods was that a retreat of the state from flood risk management was reframed as or rebalanced by a need for more 'lay knowledge' and 'lay expertise' (and social media takes on a new and important role in sharing flood culture):

> Experts involved in emergency response should not ignore the skills, energy and ingenuity ... latent in most communities; in preparing for an emergency, communities have important shared local knowledge and can harness local resources and expertise. (Cabinet Office, 2008: 350)

Yet, as my ongoing research in Brazil has shown, one cannot assume hydro-citizenship straightforwardly turns water story into water action if the underlying citizenship and lay knowledge are contested and cultures of water are politicised. Sarmiento, Landström and Whatmore (2019) framed the notion of hydro-citizenship as bringing democracy and participation together. For them, the prefix 'hydro signals the idea that the material, cultural, and political-economic specificities of water make it a particularly important realm through which to study emerging understandings and practices of citizenship, democratic life, and efforts to manage human/environment relations' (2019: 361). In their exploration of environmental citizenship through drought management and water governance they determined two imaginaries of hydro-citizens: people as customers who manage water resources in response to industries, and people's emotional engagements with hydrosocial spaces, where 'particular kinds of water subjects are called into being through the deployments of various techniques and technologies' (2019: 372). Living without water or living with bad water conjoins both of these forms of citizenship but is especially challenging to engage with in contexts where the notion of citizenship itself is precarious.

Protesting, campaigning and restoring watery places is much harder to achieve in the Global South and is largely hidden from view in the Global North. Yet, in both spaces it has been going on in hyperlocal ways for quite some time and has mostly been researched in the sciences and social sciences. What has changed is the reach, participation and social mediation of water issues globally that have become connective to wider cultures, multitudinous, involving diverse audiences and creative in their communication practices through social mediation. As each generation discovers anew the pollution and propaganda, the privatisation of water, and the flood and drought risk of their community, they discover that art, culture and media are more deeply connected to geography, water science and engineering. Likewise, water organisations (companies, campaign groups and communication action groups) as well as environmental agencies and risk managers are all now using the same media and communication platforms to broadcast, narrowcast and mycast their messages and experiences of living with water. The transformation of the individual into a water consumer is not entirely complete as water users demand spiritual, cultural and creative access to water and its histories and memories. Therefore, we need to be far more connective with our

media and cultural research of archives for sensing and representing water (from hydrological repositories to television dramas) if we
are to understand the social and cultural values that flow from water
memories that (re)circulate around rivers, canals and coasts. We need
more studies of the cultural, social and digital mediations of water,
such as Alexander Hall's (2018) analysis of local and regional newspapers in exploring the 1953 East Coast Flood or Ruth Morgan's (2018)
use of newspapers to reinterpret the cultural memory of the 1914
Australian drought.

Massive floods (particularly flashy and pluvial floods) in urban and
suburban spaces bring old and new communities and collectives into
being but so too does water scarcity in terms of its impacts. Collecting
water from standpipes and tankers socially connects neighbours
through WhatsApp who may never have spoken to one another
before, and flood–drought continuum impacts reveal the social injustices of precarious or absent water management for neighbourhoods
and regions most at risk. We continue to need a more connective way
of thinking about water across mediated histories of its abundance
and lack, pollution and power. Histories of floods and histories of
drought need to be brought together and integrated with media and
cultural histories. One way to do this is to focus upon water scarcity
in a predominantly 'blue' and watery United Kingdom, to recover the
cultural representation of drought on television and radio which are
held in media archives. Unlike floods, water scarcity is hidden, forgotten and very low on the agenda of many UK industries and society
as a whole, even though the UK passed a 'drought bill' in 1976 and
appointed a Minister for Drought at the time (albeit short-lived), a
role collectively laughed away as a deluge of rain put an end to the
drought in the September of 1976, returning the UK to its status quo:
a wet place.[2] While researchers studying floods in other countries
have noted that changes in land use, rapid urbanisation and impacts
of climate change have increasingly affected the responsive capacity of communities (Coelho and Raman, 2013; Douglas et al., 2008),

---

[2] Baroness Birk stated in the House of Lords on the passing of the Drought Bill: 'My
Lords, I beg to move that this Bill be now read a second time. My Lords, in a country
with a traditional wet profile water has always been a limitless resource, inter-
rupted only when the mains have to be repaired, but in principle available at any
time and in any quantity. Indeed, it has been one of our quaint national character-
istics that steady rainfall could be relied upon throughout the year, particularly in
the summer. This is an assumption we can no longer afford to make. The prolonged

the UK seems yet to address a culture of water scarcity. How, then, can we approach drought in the UK context from a more amphibious (wet/dry) perspective?

Amphibious flows

The emergence of a Blue Humanities in academic circles runs far deeper than the screened spectacles of a massive flood or the BBC's *The Blue Planet* (2001) and *Blue Planet II* (2017). We have in this emergence some new (as well as old) political and cultural economy frameworks for analysing the values of water recirculating in contemporary society, asking critical questions about representation. For example, where are the women in water's history (an issue I focus on in this chapter), and where are Black and minoritised communities? It is assumed that the British rural landscape and waterways are the playgrounds for white people (an issue eloquently challenged in Ed Accura's 2020 documentary *Blacks Can't Swim*). Who then gets to be part of an amphibious culture (one in which people have learned the strategies, skills and knowledge needed to live wet/dry lives)? In our earlier research on flooding in England from Early Modern to Modern, we noted that

> the inhabitants of flood-prone places display 'amphibian' characteristics, as M. Kempe (2007) called them. The grand narrative of flooding as catastrophic and destructive is qualified by personal and community memories of an everyday living with flood risk, flooding and landscape change. … [As] some degree of flood risk is unavoidable, discourses and practices of living in occasionally wet landscapes need to be explored. (Krause, Garde-Hansen and Whyte, 2012: 138)

There are new ways of thinking that are both 'wet-and-dry', as in Franz Krause's (2017) 'amphibious anthropology' that considers 'hydrosocial' relations of volatility, creativity and rhythm. They may be epistemologically in 'flux', as in Chen, MacLeod and Neimanis's

---

drought means everyone has to become water conscious in quite a different sense – to think about the use of water in a conservationist context and to avoid what has always been considered natural waste. If we change our habitual thinking we shall be better able to plan both the development of our water resources and the investment needed to be put into water supply. Drought Bill [H.L.] HL Deb, 20 July 1976, vol. 373 cc690–732. Available at: https://api.parliament.uk/historic-hansard/lords/1976/jul/20/drought-bill-hl (accessed 15 January 2022).

edited collection *Thinking with Water* (2013), which cites Bachelard's *Water and Dreams: An Essay on the Imagination of Matter*, as they introduce 'material metaphors' of flux, flow and circulation in how we think and feel:

> In everyday speech, emotions 'flood,' 'bubble up,' and 'surge'; a 'dry' text is one that lacks feeling and passion. We 'freeze up' with stage fright, join or diverge from 'mainstream' populations. Money 'circulates'; commodities 'flood' the market. The past is a 'depth' and time 'evaporates.' Neither is the realm of theory immune to inspiration from the liquid world: aqueous dynamics of 'flux' and 'flow' characterize qualities of indeterminacy and continuous change within many contemporary epistemologies, whole feminist concepts of 'leakiness' and 'seepage' have been mobilized to identify crucial porosities in bodies and theories alike. ... Just as water animated our bodies and economies, so it also permeates the ways we think. (Chen, MacLeod and Neimanis, 2013: 10)

In media studies we have also thought hydro-symbolically of broadcast channels, communication flows, immersive media and 'twitter storms', as well as the journalistic experience of a drought in 'news'. As I have argued in *Media and Water*:

> Water is in 'media' – represented by television, film, radio and print – and water's actions on human habitats (flooding, drought, extreme weather) produce stories, memories and traumas, offline and online, public and personal. Water produces a sense of place, identity and belonging particularly in countries surrounded by water or with an increasingly dry sense of place. (Garde-Hansen, 2021: 14)

Water's representation in media can be researched in ways that reveal insights into media genres (how we have told and tell stories of water, water as a character, stakeholders as characters), gender (who gets to speak, roles for men and women, 'women's watery work') and generation (the emergence of a climate change narrative, the roles of scientific discourse and folk knowledge, intergenerational communication). But we must think more wet-and-dry, as René ten Bos (2009: 74) noted of Peter Sloterdijk's 'amphibious' anthropology in which 'human beings are switching from one element to another. ... As such, it never sticks to just one environment (e.g. earth, the mainland) but experiences a profound involvement with other environments as well'. With much of this book concerned with living with, in and around water, it also makes sense to focus on cultural memories of living without it.

The UK drought narrative

Drought is widely recognised as a complex phenomenon due to the multiple aspects that concern its onset and, in the science community, the many 'types' of drought recognised (meteorological, hydrological, agricultural and civic). In the Drought Risk and You (DRY) project[3] we explored the many barriers and challenges to communicating drought in the UK, which is defined by its watery sense of place. In the Scottish 'Eden' catchment, the team noted:

> When the idea of drought in Scotland was discussed as a local community issue, many participants tended in the rehearsal of memory to associate drought with warm, sunny weather illustrating their memories of summer droughts. ... Community members generally had nostalgic positive memories of the 1976 drought. (McEwen et al., 2021)

While it might seem odd that media, communication and cultural studies should turn its attention to studying drought when much of the knowledge surrounding it pertains to the harder sciences of engineering, hydrology and ecology, it is clear that drought is not only a natural hazard. It is also a hazard for cultural memory if a lack of water is effaced by popular memory and nostalgia. For if a hazard is not remembered and inherited by a community how, then, can it be prepared for and learned from? Weitkamp, McEwen and Ramirez (2020: 843) make this point in their research on UK drought:

> The '1976 drought' may have become a 'weather memory' (Endfield 2011), but it is only available to older members of society; our interviews suggest a dearth of weather memories relating to more recent drought experiences. This suggests communicators may struggle to tap into experience (Wachinger et al. 2013), which may lead to a

---

[3] The DRY project (http://dryproject.co.uk/ (accessed 27 February 2022)) began in 2014 and the author was one co-investigator representing media and memory research. This £3.2m initiative was aimed at providing new evidence for managing future droughts based on science and experience, with expertise in hydrology, geography, meteorology, agriculture, ecology, culture, media and communications from eight universities and research institutions. The project incorporated voices that would not usually be part of decision making. Using a science-narrative integrative approach, which interweaves science communication with the collection of diverse drought narratives from a range of stakeholders, it aimed to democratise discourses and forms of knowledge related to drought.

normalcy bias (Omer and Alon 1994), with many people in maritime climates underestimating drought risks.

In maritime climates such as the UK's the default is always wateriness, rain and a wet land as key to national and regional identities and the imagined community. Drought happens elsewhere, far away and to others. Yet, drought emerges (often slowly and incrementally) from a complex interplay between the climate (imagined as a system to be predicted) and human activities (imagined as nudge-able). Such a position, which may miss the complex messiness of unpredictable climates and the creativity of human behaviours, requires a better understanding of the 'agency' that human actors may or may not have in a context of 'drought in the Anthropocene' (van Loon et al., 2016).

Drought research is now appreciating the need for improved incorporation of wider societal impacts (Bachmair et al., 2016) into risk, and the necessity for a creative approach to 'drought and community storytelling' (Liguori et al., 2021) and 'anticipatory adaptation' (DeSilvey, 2012) that draws as much on cultural memory as on future scenario-ing. Moreover, there is a recognition that while most studies focus on natural processes or socio-economic causes there is equally a place for the arts and humanities, artists and creatives, and in particular media researchers, to explore the wider human relationship with water stories, or lack thereof, that influence preparedness, lay knowledge and diverse articulations of human connectedness with water and drought. Having a critical awareness of hot weather media templates is key and Gilligan's research makes the point that heatwaves produce media-specific templates in which representations of women stand in for expressing the extremity of British weather and connote the rarity of seeing so much of the female body in an everyday British context:

> The wildfire is the most media friendly of the extreme hot weather subset, and the one with which British audiences are most familiar through television. Print media are more invested in reporting heat wave stories, and appear to be fond of 'blazing headlines' on the subject: the high temperatures of a heat wave lend themselves to illustration with bikini-clad models and are particularly popular with the UK tabloids. Drought is not a specific subject that attracts much attention in the UK media outside of scientific circles. (Gilligan, 2015: 100)

The DRY project explored (in part) how drought narratives might incorporate strong themes of blame, shame, deviance, punishment, control and anxiety, and it explored the overt and sometimes hidden and subtle politics in representations of UK drought and water scarcity from a wide range of stakeholders and communities: water companies, farmers, water users for leisure, heritage organisations, domestic consumers and environmental agencies. This project revealed that narratives of drought, or rather, the daylighting of stories and anecdotes of drought alongside scientific modelling, offered an integration of science and narrative into an effective way of thinking back through drought histories and forwards into drought scenarios for communicating water scarcity. It unearthed everyday experiences and memories of drought from the precise recollections of popular music during hot summers to the discomforting feelings of pregnant mothers unable to keep cool, from the shock of desertification of parks and grassland to the dry-ness of favourite reservoirs and riverbeds alongside the excitement of long evenings of late-night drinking, socialising and a sense of community. The diversity of experiences of everyday stories of drought coalesced around more popular narratives that shape the past, and in particular the summer of 1976, as a mythologisation that needs to be grappled with and incorporated into the much-needed new environmental behaviours and inherited relationships with water.

Drought media

One intervention into drought as a process that produces cultural, social and creative outputs, as much as scientific and governmental responses, is to consider the role of media in historically specific ways in a given national and cultural context. Such an intervention allows for a multi-modal and multi-perspectival approach that considers drought as a nonhuman 'actor' as well as acted-upon by humans, and we can unpack drought representation and experience along certain axioms: urban–rural, public–private, young–old, men–women, weather–war and ability–disability, for example. These would not normally be within the purview of scientific approaches to drought history or to an iconic drought event, such as the period 1975–1976 in the United Kingdom. While the Historic Droughts project[4] created a repository of data from river flows to oral history testimonies (covering hydrometeorological, environmental, agricultural, regulatory,

---

[4] See https://historicdroughts.ceh.ac.uk/ 2014–2018 (accessed 27 February 2022).

social and cultural materials) and integrated this data with a focus on media, it was necessarily socially scientific, using Corpus Linguistics to analyse UK newspaper archives. Weather data and geographical and historical incidences were used to target the social materiality of drought memory, but cultures of living without water in the UK were much less explored.

Therefore, rather than create new narratives of drought from contemporary memory work or confine cultural memories of drought to one media form, it can be equally insightful to bring media archives together: images, adverts, documentaries, film clips, radio reports, radio and television drama, television news items to inform journalistic accounts. A focus on popular culture and popular media offers access to hitherto neglected drought representations. For example, the representation of women in drought stories has been largely considered immaterial and yet to consider them offers wider insights into women's position in society and as human bodies in relation to the natural environment. In 1970s Britain not only did women become particularly visible and vocal but the summer of 1976 has continued to be mediated as a display of women's bodies as much as dry riverbeds. A typical example is the 26 July 2018 edition of the *Express* newspaper, which remediates the now iconic Press Agency photograph of the blonde, slim white woman in a small bikini smiling and sunbathing on an extremely desiccated landscape (Kirkham, 2018). In what follows I introduce the two key media templates of the 1976 drought as a textual, visual and audio-visual representation of women as the 'bearers of water' (domestic work) or as a 'barer of flesh' (sexual work). It is worth noting that the one key but underrated autobiographical book on the experience of drought was written by the journalist Evelyn Cox in which she said: 'I soon realized that piped mains water is the most underrated convenience of the twentieth century. It must have contributed far more to the liberation of women than all the laws of Parliament have put on the statute books in the past few years' (1978: 30).

Living without water: remembering women's bodies

The UK 1976 summer produced a benchmark drought, with days without rain ranging from 45–66 days depending on location, and is more likely to be popularly remembered as the greatest 'heatwave' in living memory if you were an urbanite; or, the worst and most traumatic experience for farming, if you lived in a rural location. There is a 'heat' to city living and urban culture as expressed by Thrift (2004: 57) 'as broiling maelstroms of affect' that is assumed not to apply to rural life. Within the urban memory of 1976 women emerge as visible stereotypes of passive sexuality wallpapering the collective memory of popular culture. This attention to young women's bodies and blazing headlines was established at the time and has been remediated and remembered ever since.[5] The 3 July 1976 article 'Heat wave is making the English act funny' in *The New York Times* reported:

> The heat wave has thus been greeted with uninhibited enthusiasm. On Wednesday three models jumped into the fountains at Trafalgar Square and removed the tops of their bikinis. Admiral Nelson, atop his stone column, did not blink an eye, but the police did. Graciously and slowly – they moved in, told the women that there was an ancient law prohibiting bathing in Trafalgar Square and carted them off to Cannon Street Station, where they were fined $10. (Semple Jr, 1976)

'Heatwave' has been represented as temporary insanity for the national imaginary, it comes on fast and furious, and then is washed away by a deluge of stereotypical rain: the mediated memory template frames the lack of water in the UK setting as a rare but welcome aberration for urbanites and ignores the stories of rural communities. The deadliness of drought (slow, creeping, paralysing) slides out of view from the public imagination.[6]

Recently, as hotter summers have become the norm for Northern Europe and living without water looms as a real prospect, the BBC has re-curated 1976 as a time to reminisce not a time to prepare for drought or learn from drought impacts. The BBC *Breakfast News* Twitter account posted a Tweet at 1.37pm GMT on 24 June 2018, and within it curated oft-repeated archival excerpts from past BBC news

---

[5] A number of blogs and news editorials have proliferated as contemporary heatwaves provide opportunities to recirculate media archive material and reproduce popular memory of 1976. Bradford's *Telegraph and Argus* online article (Ayres, 2020) 'Who remembers the summer of 1976?' uses photographs of three pubescent girls and their wet t-shirts, a boy cooling off with a hose and two women collecting water from a standpipe.

[6] It is worth noting recent calls for heatwaves (described as 'silent killers') to be mediated alongside extreme weather events such as storms through a naming process. 'If it has a name, a hashtag, media coverage, then people pay attention', Baughman McLeod explains in the article in *Euronews* (Frost, 2021).

items into a 'Remember 1976' news video of sixty-two seconds. With the posting stating '☀Incredible weather outside today ... ☀ But does anyone remember this incredible #summer from 1976? #heatwave', there followed the image of young women bathing in 1970s-style bikinis in public, eliciting from the audience many opportunities for reminiscence and nostalgia. While this may have had over 47,800 views at the time of researching the 2018 heatwave (no doubt due to the opening image of women in bikinis), the many retweets and comments served to collectively remember 1976 as one of outstanding weather, youthful love, pop music and socialising. The target audience of BBC *Breakfast*'s Twitter feed were just the right age in 2018 to recall those teenage experiences of hot weather not within a trauma narrative frame such as Evelyn Cox's largely forgotten account of the drought (noted above) but as a way of reminiscing about young women's bodies.[7]

Pathé News's 2014 re-release on YouTube of a 10 minute archival video of silent film rushes of women in London in 1976 is equally confusing in its focus on women's bodies during a heatwave. Erroneously titled 'Heat wave in London: women's summer fashion (1976)',[8] it is clear that 'fashion' is not the focus at all. Over ten minutes and forty seconds of filming, without sound, the viewer's gaze (presumably a 'male gaze') is held within the frame through several long camera takes that focus on female breasts and buttocks, sometimes headless. Not unlike the classic news footage of members of the public's bodies (always headless) used in stock news items of stories from obesity to pandemic, from travel to urban living, the footage has been unearthed and placed on YouTube to demonstrate Pathé News's archival holdings pertaining to this historic hot summer. At the time of writing, it had gathered a surprising number of views (over 465,000). However, it is noteworthy that in 2018, when I first presented this archival footage at conferences, the comments were switched on and I pointed out just how many were of a sexist and predatory nature, with frequent references to 'those were the days' when women were supposedly loose and bra-less and sexually accessible. The comments have now

---

[7] Considering the current scripting of the 'popular memory' of 1976 as a period of hot summers, passions and new styles of music, it is unsurprising, then, to see these tropes re-emerge in recent popular literature for the general reader.

[8] British Pathé (1976) 'Heat wave in London: women's summer fashion (1976)', 13 April 2014. Available at: www.youtube.com/watch?v=vP6hCx5_pYs (accessed 1 December 2021).

been switched off, no doubt due to many of the comments deviating from the archive's intentions. Though it is not clear at all what Pathé News's intentions are with uploading this footage. Nevertheless, this is a framing of the female body during a heatwave as passive material for drought narrative building that does not push that narrative of living without water forward, but places drought and heatwave in a glorious and legendary British weather past. While this heatwave video created the opportunity for viewing women as sexual objects, it also invited (when the comments were switched on) a new currency of 'memory' and urban nostalgia to reproduce a narrative around the video among the YouTube posters, wherein they revealed the 'imagined community' of 1976 as one that has now been lost to political correctness and women's rights. Thus, drought memory says as much about contemporary politics of gender as it does about environmental history.

Living without water: remembering women's labour

A second key example concerns a different but equally iconic representation of older women or housewives (likely to be mothers) passively queuing at standpipes in 1976, or carrying buckets to standpipes, in various television news items, which are then remediated in newspapers and online. A Google image search of 'UK drought 1976' brings to the surface many newspaper images and repeated television news footage of middle-aged housewives standing in queues waiting for water, appearing to chat but mostly patiently waiting. Some of this iconicity pre-dates 1976, as we can find in the Pathé News archive published news footage from 1952 'Rain and drought: water on the ration' in Sussex, wherein much of the footage shows women (dressed in housewife attire) walking to the town pump with their containers; and, from 1959, 'News in flashes', containing film footage showing an older woman at the standpipe during a drought in Edinburgh.[9] In these early examples, film news footage (for cinema release) can be seen to be working hard to make a spectacle of drought, and they do so through two iconic images that have become short-hand for drought and water shortage ever since: the dried and cracked reservoir bed

---

[9] British Pathé (1952) 'Rain and drought: water on the ration', 13 April 2014. www.youtube.com/watch?v=C7m1FUBOiGE; and (1959) 'News in flashes', 13 April 2014, www.youtube.com/watch?v=MBFf5SD6Kek (accessed 1 December 2021).

and the woman at the watering place. Thus, we have footage of a dried out Gladhouse Reservoir in the 1959 footage, followed by some kind of externalised domestic scene, with the woman and the children, ordinarily 'in the kitchen', finding themselves out in the street at the standpipe. Again, they are framed as waiting happily, patiently and politely by news broadcasters. The 'keep calm and carry on' aspiration of British women recurs in 1976 through iconic imagery of women doing what many women around the world still do and will have done in the not too distant past: waited and chatted at the community watering place before carrying home the water.

What we have, then, if we currently search online for media pertaining to the 'UK Drought 1976' is a visual representation of women that is either reminiscent of the misogyny around the 'heatwave' culture of the late 1970s or positions older women (often mothers) as passive actors in water scarcity – waiting for the men to deliver the water, to turn on supplies or to fix the problem. In either case, women are (literally) thrown back in time to a time before liberation and emancipatory social movements of the 1970s. Consequently, women's unpaid domestic 'labour' and relationship building that ensure a resilient community slide out of view as emphasis is placed on getting back to the status quo (which for these women was a return indoors). The 1976 television news footage from the *Channel 4 News* website, uploaded to YouTube in 2012, shows an interview with a woman at the standpipe who states:

> We've all been rather upset to see that half the constituency are, sort of, on and we're off, and I think that, like the war, we don't mind if everybody else is the same as we are but you rather object to carrying buckets and buckets of water every day when you find that someone around the corner has got theirs turned on. (ITN source)[10]

The final interview in the archival clip is with a man in the street who signs off with him laughing to the reporter that he will send the bill for his wife's damaged leg – a reference to the huge amount of water women were expected to carry back and forth that summer.

In this second iconic representation of women in the 1976 drought brought to us by Channel 4's YouTube site, we have user comments switched on and much of the debate pertains to lamenting the loss

---

[10] This ITN footage is available at Channel 4 News, 'Drought 1976: archive pictures of the driest summer', www.youtube.com/watch?v=unJoZHD0AM8.

of 1976. This is a typical comment with the most 'likes': 'The best summer I have ever experienced. England was a much better place then, in EVERY way. Disagree? Go back to 1976 and then you'd see. Every decade has had its problems, but the 1970s were so much better than what we're living in today.' Followed by a retort from a female commenter: 'Sexism and prejudice were a lot more acceptable then. Pictures of naked or near-naked women hung on the walls of almost every garage and discrimination and dirty jokes existed in almost every workplace.'

Living without water: remembering the woman journalist of the summer of 1976

Look beyond the current mainstream social mediation of 1976 and we can find that the popularity of the memories of 'heatwave' or the drudgery of expected women's work at the standpipes and tankers can be countered by significant and extensive shared memories of traumatic drought, particularly in the agricultural sector and rural communities. Evelyn Cox's *The Great Drought* (1978) details in depth and records with close attention to water usage the unusually dry winter which was followed by a dry spring and summer that included sixteen consecutive days of temperatures over 30 degrees Celsius. This resulted in many reservoirs drying up and significant water rationing on her farm, with a water deficit that continued for several months. Paying close attention to drought storytelling is a methodological issue: it requires patience, slow memory and a long durée approach to understanding human relationships with water. It details the daily and time-consuming mitigation practices and the sacrifices neces- sary to ensure the very basics of provision. Living with drought in the UK is neither expected nor remembered well; rather, drought has been reduced to media spectacle, and what is more spectacular than queuing women or desiccated reservoirs, or even both together, as noted above? The reality of UK drought in journalist-turned-farmer Cox's account is representable through slow remembrance, delibera- tively conveyed in writing, and documented as a diarisation of envi- ronmental and mundane domestic experience.

Heatwave media culture (fast, blazing, repetitive and sizzling in its content) only obfuscates the slow memories of living without water and the invisible and slow onset of the drying of the land. Cox's book presents the active and adaptable emergence of a powerful and entrepreneurial female subjectivity but she does this through a dry form of storytelling: documenting, evidencing and detailing each change in circumstance. Such a method of storytelling does not fit with the popular and nostalgic collective memory of the summer of 1976. While it should not be forgotten that the Women's Movement was particularly active throughout the 1970s (we had the 1970 Equal Pay Act and *Spare Rib* magazine in 1972), the patriarchal determination for remediating the summer of 1976 as a peculiarly English heatwave (de-centred from other drought narratives that happen in faraway Global South countries) continues to shape the psycho-geography of a masculine-maritime culture wherein real stories of water scarcity and women's labour therein have been silenced and made invisible. As I noted in *Media and Water* (2021: 110): 'If we continue within the current template of popular narratives of heat-waves, where drought is for scientists and heatwaves are for the tab-loids, we will indeed be taken by surprise every time.' We need a way of representing and remembering water and its lack that acknowl-edges slowness and slow-onset invisible eventhood because water scarcity is very likely to creep up, disable, cripple and paralyse com-munities, and many groups who are silenced or forgotten (especially women and ethnic minorities) will continue to be disproportionately impacted.

Conclusion

In *Disaster Writing: The Cultural Politics of Catastrophe in Latin America* by Mark Anderson (2011), we have an important arts and humanities approach to drought risk and resilience, one that has informed my own media and memory research of drought stories in the UK and Brazil. Water scarcity is not simply a matter of policy (scientific, economic, public engagement); it is also a matter of cultural policy, cultural values and, by extension, cultural narratives (which are nationally specific but also globally shared), and these play a significant part in perception, reception and behaviour. Anderson's chapter on 'Drought and the literary construction of risk' pertains to Brazil and the late nineteenth and early part of the twentieth centuries, and makes the case that as scientific data was absent at the time, then literary data, folk culture and imaginative constructions served as evidence of drought and its impacts. Before science could make drought visible, art and culture served as the early warning systems. Drought, then, requires a persistence of vision across culture and media discourses, forms and practices: drought stories are memorable and sustainable but require multi-modal and interdisciplinary attention. Anderson mentions several types of drought narratives at work in Brazilian literary cultures that construct and ultimately institutionalise drought in the Brazilian national imaginary (there was the Great Drought of 1877–1879 and the drought of 1915 as key events):

> These texts reformulated the vague notion of drought as a purely natural phenomenon of incalculable destructive force into a refined system governed by the interaction of classifiable variables, including social and political factors not formerly considered. More than impartial ethnographies, these novels' meticulous descriptions of local economic contexts, cultural customs, and political and social orders correspond to the calculated objectivity of risk assessment, with its aim of assigning contingent values to unknown quantities. (Anderson, 2011: 66)

In a geographical and socio-political UK context dominated by maritime histories, island mentality and a watery sense of place, drought narratives work against the cultural norms of media templates, cultural memories and gender conformity. There is, however, the short novel *The Drought* (1965) by J. G. Ballard, that is worth remembering in pandemic times. In the story the tipping point has been reached and water is the new currency as humans struggle for survival. In John Harrison's 2014 introduction to *The Drought* he states:

> The drought at the heart of *The Drought* is cultural. Culture is withering. In the guise of rainfall, old social and political meanings run down to the sea and are decreasingly renewed. Where the land seemed fertile, its inhabitants can now admit that it is exhausted. (Ballard, [1965] 2014: x)

In reading *living without water* through media, memory and gender, I have sought to daylight the cultural representations of UK water scarcity in opposition to the dominant narratives of a watery sense of place. The role of women has been fundamental to the mediated spectacle of UK drought as the undressed, tabloid-framed body and in terms of hidden physical (domestic, farming) and cultural (journalism, storytelling) labour. Yet, as Ballard writes: 'Catherine gazed out at the exposed lake-bed. "It's almost dry. Don't you feel, doctor, that everything is being drained away, all the memories and stale sentiments?"' (Ballard, [1965] 2014: 16).

References

Accura, E. (2020) *Blacks Can't Swim*. Available at: https://blackscantswim. com/ (accessed 20 March 2022).

Anderson, M. (2011) *Disaster Writing: The Cultural Politics of Catastrophe in Latin America*. Charlottesville: University of Virginia Press.

Ayres, O. (2020) This month in the past: who remembers the summer of 1976? *Telegraph and Argus*, 28 August 2020. Available at: www. thetelegraphandargus.co.uk/news/18681083.month-past-remembers-summer-1976/ (accessed 20 July 2021).

Bachmair, S., Svensson, C., Hannaford, J., Barker, L. J. and Stahl, K. (2016) A quantitative analysis to objectively appraise drought indicators and model drought impacts. *Hydrology and Earth System Sciences*, 20, 2589–2609.

Ballard, J. G. [1965] (2014) *The Drought*. London: Fourth Estate.

BBC1 (2001–2002) *The Blue Planet* (TV Series).

BBC1 (2017–2018) *Blue Planet II* (TV Series).

Bos, R. ten (2009) Towards an amphibious anthropology: water and Peter Sloterdijk. *Environment and Planning D: Society and Space*, 27, 73–86.

Cabinet Office (2008) The Pitt review: lessons learned from the 2007 floods. The National Archives. Available at: https://webarchive.nationalarchives. gov.uk/ukgwa/20100807034701/http:/archive.cabinetoffice.gov.uk/ pittreview/_/media/assets/www.cabinetoffice.gov.uk/flooding_review/ pitt_review_full%20pdf.pdf (accessed 4 January 2022).

Chen, C., J. McLeod and A. Neimanis (eds) (2013) *Thinking with Water*. Montreal: McGill, Queen's University Press.

Coelho, K. and Raman, N. V. (2013) From the frying pan to the floodplain: negotiating land, water, and fire in Chennai's development. In Anne Rademacher and K. Sivaramakrishnan (eds) *Ecologies of Urbanism in India: Metropolitan Civility and Sustainability*. Hong Kong: Hong Kong University Press, pp. 144–168.

Cox, E. (1978) *The Great Drought of 1976*. London: Abe Books.

Desilvey, C. (2012) Making sense of transience: an anticipatory history. *Cultural Geography*, 19(1), 31–54.

Douglas, I., Alam, K., Maghenda, M., Mcdonnell, Y., Mclean, L. and Campbell, J. (2008) Unjust waters: climate change, flooding and the urban poor in Africa. *Environment and Urbanization* 20(1), 187–205.

Frost, R. (2021) 'A silent killer': why naming extreme heatwaves could help prevent deaths. *Euronews*, 23 August. Available at: www.euronews.com/ green/2021/08/23/a-silent-killer-why-naming-extreme-heatwaves-could-help-prevent-deaths (accessed 23 August 2021).

Garde-Hansen, J. (2021) *Media and Water: Communication, Culture and Perception*. London: I. B. Tauris.

Gilligan, P. (2015) 'Blowtorch Britain': labor, heat and neo-Victorian values in contemporary UK media. In J. Leyda and D. Negra (eds) *Extreme Weather and Global Media*. London: Routledge, pp. 100–126.

Hall, A. (2018) Remembering in God's name: the role of the Church and community institutions in the aftermath and commemoration of floods. In G. H. Endfield and L. Veale (eds) *Cultural Histories, Memories and Extreme Weather: A Historical Geography*. London: Routledge, pp. 112–132.

Kirkham, M. (2018) UK heatwave 1976 in pictures: the scorching summer of 1976 in Britain. *Express*, 26 July. Available at: www.express.co.uk/news/uk/994560/UK-heatwave-weather-pictures-1976-heatwave-pictures (accessed 20 July 21).

Krause, F. (2017) Towards an amphibious anthropology of delta life. *Human Ecology*, 45(3), 403–408.

Krause, F., Garde-Hansen, J. and Whyte, N. (2012) Flood memories – media, narratives and remembrance of wet landscapes in England. *Journal of Arts and Communities*, 4, 128–142.

Liguori, A., McEwen, L., Blake, J. and Wilson, M. (2021) Towards 'creative participatory science': exploring future scenarios through specialist drought science and community storytelling. *Frontiers in Environmental Science*, 8. Available at: www.frontiersin.org/articles/10.3389/fenvs.2020.589856/full (accessed 12 January 2022).

McEwen, L., Bryan, K., Black, A., Blake, J. and Afzal, M. (2021) Science-narrative explorations of 'drought thresholds' in the maritime Eden catchment, Scotland: implications for local drought risk management. *Frontiers in Environmental Science*, 9. Available at: www.frontiersin.org/articles/10.3389/fenvs.2021.589980/full (accessed 12 January 2022).

Morgan, R. (2018) On the Home Front: Australians and the 1914 drought. In G. H. Endfield and L. Veale (eds) *Cultural Histories, Memories and Extreme Weather: A Historical Geography*. London: Routledge, pp. 34–54.

Sarmiento, E., Landström, C. and Whatmore, S. (2019) Biopolitics, discipline, and hydro-citizenship: drought management and water governance in England. *Transactions of the Institute of British Geographers*, 44(2), 361–375.

Semple Jr, R. B. (1976) Heat wave is making the English act funny. *The New York Times*, 3 July. Available at: www.nytimes.com/1976/07/03/archives/heat-wave-is-making-the-english-act-funny.html (accessed 20 August 2021).

Thrift, N. (2004) Intensities of feeling: towards a spatial politics of affect. *Geografiska Annaler* 86B(1), 57–78.

Van Loon, A., Gleeson, T., Clark, J., van Dijk, A., Stahl, K., Hannaford, J., Di Baldassarre, G., Teuling, A., Tallaksen, L. M., Uijlenhoet, R., Hannah, D., Sheffield, J., Svoboda, M., Verbeiren, B., Wagener, T., Rangecroft,

S., Wanders, N. and Van Lanen, H. (2016) Drought in the Anthropocene. *Nature Geoscience* 9(2), 89–91.

Weitkamp, E., McEwen, L. and Ramirez, P. (2020) Communicating the hidden: toward a framework for drought risk communication in maritime climates. *Climatic Change*, 163, 831–850.

Flow

Water circulates and flows in different volumes and at different scales,
and *Flow moves us from the personal lives of boaters and bathers to urban
infrastructures and the more-than-human Anthropocene. Traversing cities,
continents, oceans and time, we see how water spurts, surges and hisses
through and out of pipes and drains, falls from the sky as 'cats and dogs',
ebbs and floods with the tides, and slowly wanders as erratic glaciers. These
watery flows – leaks, raindrops, lagoons, tides, runoffs, rivers of ice – are
no less intimate and everyday, but they illuminate different questions, pressures and problems. Showing how water is managed, measured, diverted
and controlled, the contributors to* Flow *challenge the idea that water can
be taken for granted, or that it belongs to us. Affective ecologies and ecological unravellings of conservation and stewardship reveal a meshwork of lives
at stake and entangled with our own relationships with water. Horseshoe
crabs and sandpipers, lobsters and coral reefs, reveal deep troubles of caring
and environmental crisis below the surface. In* Flow*, water washes over
Western worldviews and borders, and is both our downfall and our hope.*

~

HOW DEEP IS YOUR LOVE?

LI	CAST IRON
CON	CONCRETE
DI	DUCTILE IRON
ECI	EPOXY COATED IRON
GRAN INS OR G	GRANLITE INSULATED
PCI	POLY WRAPPED CAST IRON
PDI	POLY WRAPPED DUCTILE IRON
PE	POLYETHYLENE
PE INS	POLYETHYLENE INSERT
PE BURST	POLYETHYLENE BURST
PVC	POLYVINYL CHLORIDE
FPVC	FIBREGLASS IN PVINYL CHLORIDE
STEEL	STEEL
TWD	TAPE WRAPPED DUCTILE IRON
TUDI	TAPE WRAPPED URETHANE DUCTILE IRON
TR	TRANSITE
YDI	YELLOW JACKET DUCTILE IRON
YUDI	YELLOW JACKET URETHANE DI
AUM	ABANDONED UTILITY-MANHOLE
PRIVATE IRR	PRIVATE IRRIGATION
	PRIVATELY OWNED MAIN
AV	AIR VALVE
B.VLV	BYPASS VALVE
CH	CHAMBER
CV	CHECK VALVE
FON	FLANGED OUTLET
FL.A	FLUSHING ASSEMBLY
LH	LEFT HAND VALVE
M.V	MAIN VALVE
MV VLV	MAIN VALVE IN MANHOLE
MC	METER CHAMBER
PERF	PERF SERVICE
PRV.VLV	PRESSURE REDUCING VALVE
	PRIVATE STANDARD HYDRANT
PH	PRIVATE PUMPER HYDRANT

BASIC HEATH
GEOPHONES CUT-AWAY

COPPER PICKUP PLATES · SOUND PICKUP SPOUT

COPPER RESONANCE PLATES

BOTTOM SOUND CAVITY PLATE

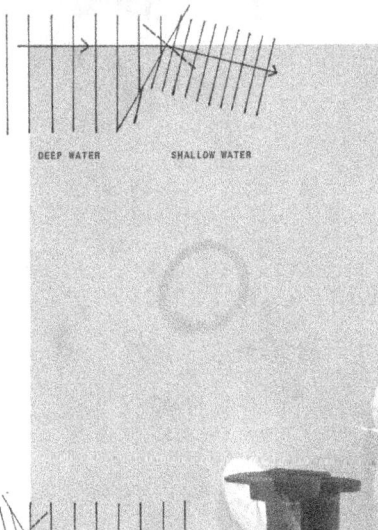

DEEP WATER   SHALLOW WATER

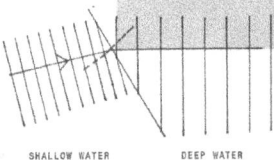

SHALLOW WATER   DEEP WATER

16-24-01-5 DOWNTOWN
Calvin Harris and the Disciples,
How Deep is your Love?

26-24-02-5 MONTGOMERY
Neneh Cherry, Buffalo Stance

15-24-01-5 EAST VILLAGE
Neil Young, Harvest Moon

11-24-01-5 AYLITH
ACDC, Highway to Hell

11-24-02-5 SIENNA PARK/SIGNAL RIDGE
Jeff Beck, Plynth

15 25-01-5 HUNTINGTON HILLS
Gene Kelly, Singin' in the Rain

17-25-01-5 MACEWAN
Whales, Whale Music

22-25-01-5 COUNTRY HILLS
Hayden Desser, No Happy Birthday

11-24-01-5 ALYTH
Nine Inch Nails, Closer

32-25-01-5 EVANSTON
Boston, More Than a Feeling

33-23-01-5 WINDSOR PARK
Led Zeppelin, Rain Music

29-22-29-4 MCKENZIE
Ji Pyeyong Keon, Sad Romance

32-22-01-5 EVERGREEN
Cantor Latine/Beethoven, 5th Symphony

11-24-01-6 ALYTH
K D Lang, Miss Chatelain

2-23-29-4 NEW BRIGHTON
Justin Timberlake, Cry me a River

22-24-01-5 BRIDGELAND
Pink Floyd, Wish you were Here

21-24-01-5 SUNNYSIDE
Renee Desplat, Eliza and Zelda
from 'The Shape of Water'

THIS PROJECT WAS PRODUCED
AS PART OF THE DYNAMIC
ENVIRONMENT LAB, WATERSHED+
www.calgary.ca/CSPS/Recreation/Pages/
Public-Art/WATERSHED+-Dynamic-
Environment-Lab.aspx

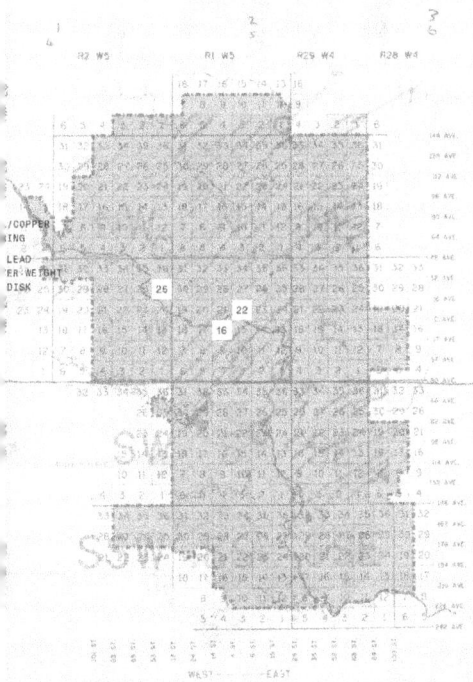

R2 W5   R1 W5   R29 W4   R28 W4

WEST ———— EAST

BECKY SHAW
BECKYSHAW.NET

How Deep is your Love? explores Calgarian's emotional
attachment to their manmade and industrial water infrastructure.
This project focuses on the work of leak location and the leak –
a site of material, geological, social and political pressure.
City Leak locators use extraordinary analogue instruments to listen
for leaks, translating the vibration of the enormous infrastructure
three metres below the ground as it passes through the small
contact surface of the instrument and their attuned ears.
This tour provides a context to listen with geophones, as a way
to experience the vast and the small, the individual and city, and
the above and below, and our strangely distant and intimate
relationship to our manmade and natural environment.

9

How Deep is Your Love? Spurting, surging, leaking and hissing in Calgary's pressurised drinking water infrastructure

Becky Shaw

In 2016–2019 I worked as a commissioned artist exploring Calgarians' emotional attachment to their water system.[1] I (with other artists) was taken to many of the key sites of water management, including for drinking water, sewage and stormwater, and spent time with engineers and managers. Everywhere we went we saw electronic imaging systems monitoring the network of flows and volumes being moved up and down gradients and to the outer edges of Calgary's rapidly expanding 825.3 km² footprint (bigger than New York, just over half the size of London, over seven times the size of Paris).

Calgary, Alberta, has a dynamic and unstable climate – it can snow in almost any month but is also semi-arid. Calgary is notorious for its chinook. This is a sudden hot wind that can raise the temperature by up to 20 degrees in an hour and can make snow sublimate. Calgary's water source begins as rainwater in the Canadian Rockies and Bow glacier. It is transported downhill into the city via the huge Bow River. The Bow and the Elbow River meet in Calgary, and then continue an 800km journey across from West to East, into the Hudson Bay. The Bow and Elbow are a significant part of Calgarian identity, being

---

[1] The period of exploration and resulting work, *How Deep is Your Love?* was commissioned by the City of Calgary Utilities and Environmental Protection, as part of the Dynamic Environment Lab, led by Watershed +, with Sans façon as lead artists. See www.watershedplus.com/news/how-deep-is-your-love-by-becky-shaw-dynamic-environment-exhibition/ (accessed 27 July 2022).

profoundly important to First Nation and Indigenous communities and a site of water sports and 'hanging out' for urbane neighbourhoods. The river was also the site of a devastating flood surge in 2013, and is the source of Calgary's pristine drinking water. In a city Water Services office an old, hand-drawn poster documents the pressure differentials needed to ensure a good supply for all in the city. Beneath the poster is a 'cut-through' model water valve, to train staff. The slice-through reveals the space where water pushes with enormous pressure against the valve top. Not surprisingly, drinking water is produced under the strictest of sanitary conditions, where the social pressure to maintain a healthy supply interlocks with the pressure to maintain the natural environment and the physical pressure to move water to neighbourhoods. The intertwining of social and technical pressure never lets up: at Christmas, Thanksgiving and Stampede (Calgary's world-famous Rodeo) the supply water pressure must be elevated to cope with increased demand.

As part of my research, I spent time in the meter-shed, where staff show me rows of water meters brought in for testing. Water meters belong to the City of Calgary, even when installed in homes and businesses. A political and media storm has recently surged and abated, as customers complained that faulty meters were inflating water bills. The engineer shows me the cavity where the pressurised water forces through the meters and explains that faulty meters under-estimate rather than over-calculate. However, political pressure, Calgary's responsibility as public body and their need to maintain public trust, means they must respect the complaints and run checks. The meters, then, are a single emblematic part of a system of conflicting pressures. The physical and social infrastructure negotiates supply and demand, and balances competing demands of individual household and collective system. The water and its infrastructure is both public service and a product. This is a resource that flows past doors, into every living cell, but also has a cost and produces a 'customer' at the same time as a citizen. It seems that drinking water is a substance where the very nature of publicness is being constructed and contested.

I spent several weeks with Kelly Pyke, a leak locator. The leak location service is a small team of men who travel around the city following reported surface water, loss of service and unexpected meter readings, and routinely inspect ageing services where leaks are common. Kelly is quiet and professional, and initially shy. While the locators sometimes work in teams, leak location is often a solitary job.

Kelly tells me the job suits thoughtful people who enjoy the quiet and sense of freedom while driving miles around the entire city. The city van is comfortable and fit for purpose, and as we travel we see many other city vehicles on the road, with their distinctive civic livery.

We gradually become comfortable with each other, talking about family, health, renovation, history and our two cultures. I was given permission to travel with Kelly on five leak location trips. We picked up his jobs from a central office at the city Water Centre at 5am. We travelled to glassy, wealthy crescents with wide roads, manicured lawns and no evident people; uniform developments right at the city limit, often occupied by 'new Canadians'; and industrial parks. More often, we attended leaks closer to the city; in suburbs mosaiced with Calgary's oldest 'century houses', served by the oldest of water infrastructure. The patched road surfaces in these areas attest to the frequency of mends.

The leak locators aren't always a welcome sight. While residents assume the garden marks the beginning of their property, some City of Calgary water infrastructure sits underneath, with the join between individual and state falling under lovingly maintained grass. Leaks can also turn out to be the responsibility of residents and not the city. The locators need good communication skills to manage difficult conversations and negotiate the interests of residents and the state.

The services in Calgary are buried 3 metres beneath the depth of the frost-line, to avoid freezing and damage. The leak locators use a variety of instruments to diagnose or pinpoint a leak. The instruments all use sound. They seek a change in sonic frequency due to the pressurised spurt of water, or the agitated clicks of pebbles being swirled round in turbulent flow. On site, Kelly starts off with instruments called 'correlators' and a digital aquascope. These digital instruments generate a digital trace and a numerical reading and identify the 'ballpark' area where more detailed locating should then happen.

Kelly then moves on to use the analogue geophone. This is an extraordinary steam-punk-looking instrument with two heavy brass disks that are positioned on the ground around the possible leak site. The disks transmit the pressure of sound waves through the earth, through two delicate vibrating brass and copper plates, and then amplifies it through stethoscopes into the ears of the leak locator. The listener must, then, perform an extraordinary act of translation. The leak locator must bring their understanding of soil types, the wider landscape, the age and material of services, atmospheric noise, household noise, hydraulic forces and pressure to bear on their interpretation of the sound from the two 'touch points' on the ground. The act of translation compresses all this understanding, but also has to perform a fascinating act of spatial translation, from the space between the two 'touch points' on the ground, into a mental conception of this space underground, then back to the surface where they diagnose the site of a leak.

Kelly tries to train me to listen – he describes the need to 'sink under' ambient noise to 'reach' any leak noise. A leak noise is hard to recognise for an untrained ear although Kelly (and other leak locators) make a range of verbal hissing noises to try to describe it. The analogue system means there is no sharable record, only trust in the crew's listening skills. From this diagnosis the repair road crews are authorised, with mistakes leading to potentially thousands of dollars of cost for the taxpayer and occasionally for householders. This gentle act of listening, then, is also high pressure for the locators.

Leak location has its own lore – there are places in Calgary where rogue 'leak' sounds are heard but with no source: these are common places to bring trainee locators – and Kelly also takes me there. There are also stories of leaks flowing backwards, uphill and of householders' pet birds making leak-like noises that confused all locators. Listening with the geophones is an extraordinary experience: part meditation, part spy-movie and part time-traveller. Listening feels intimate and subjective, and generates a peculiar oscillation between feeling alone with the earth and being wired into the vast social infrastructure. It seems to me that the most important thing I could do with my artwork, would be to give other people this experience.

A leak is 'matter out of place' (Douglas, 1984: 36) – a spurting, expensive, specific, disobedient, lively opposition to the orderly, industrial, extensive social infrastructure. I am fascinated by it and decide to make it the 'site' of my public artwork, revelling in the possibility of making a small and intimate work in a giant system. I start by asking the City of Calgary fabricators if they can copy a geophone. This is a unit of engineers within the city who seek to make savings for the public by self-building equipment. I ask them if they can make a smaller geophone, thinking that a reduction in size might amplify the intimacy of listening and reverse our expectation that public art is 'bigger'. Lengthy inspection by a group of engineers indicates that the central 'spine' of the geophone, that holds the oscillating plates at a perfect distance from each other, would be extremely difficult to manufacture. Brent L'Heureux, a skilled engineer, takes the original geophone apart and painstakingly mills a geophone suitable for the hand size of my eight-year-old son, out of the adult one. The fabricators and the leak locators try out the 'mini-geo': it can't reach sound so deep as the 'adult' one and its pitch, like a child's voice, is higher. This is a strange new tool that makes the listener work harder and bend lower to the ground to listen.

At the same time, I fantasise about being able to pass sound through the sterile drinking water system. What if a leak in our own neighbourhood spurts with our 'emotional outburst' – those favourite pieces of music that we listen to, to 'let go' or 'keep going'? How would these individual choices conflict with the need to provide a civic 'public' service? How would the City of Calgary manage the conflict between those who wanted explicit rap, mass-produced elegiac dance music or relaxing whale music, all 'dirtying up' the sterile social drinking water system? While attempts to literally pass sound through connecting valves fail, I start asking staff I meet what music they would want to burst through a leak in their neighbourhood. Kelly imagines k.d. lang's 'Miss Chatelain' and Neneh Cherry's 'Buffalo Stance'. Another leak locator, Chris Steffen, imagines hearing AC/DC or Nine Inch Nails. Denise, a manager who lives in the desirable Signal Ridge neighbourhood, wants Jeff Beck's gritty, screeching furious guitar.

These elements were pulled together into a final, multiform artwork. An exhibition was held in Calgary's extraordinary futuristic-meets-brutalist ex planetarium.[2] A redundant paper City of Calgary repair manual (used in all city vans until a full digital version was developed) was pieced back together into a 12m × 8m floor map, making the vast city scale present alongside the intimate encounter with a full-size and mini-geophone (positioned so the visitor could listen to the heating and water system in the building). Then, for two days this site was the convening point for a guided tour, where we collected the participants, geophones, hi-vis vests and a set of publications that functioned as scripts, tour guides, artworks and souvenirs. Participants were taken onto a City of Calgary-liveried mini-bus and led on a guided listening tour, supported by Chris Steffen. We visited

---

[2] www.contemporarycalgary.com/whats-on/2019/9/26/dynamic-environment (accessed 27 July 2022).

two roadsides in neighbourhoods where staff lived (and had added to the map) and we also visited the place with the 'rogue' leak sound. On the way to the neighbourhoods we played the leak music selected for this neighbourhood, connecting the place above ground with the space of the infrastructure imagined below.

On each site we used both standard and mini-geophone to listen for leaks. The tour group made new friendships as they passed instruments back and forth and suggested new spots to listen. The day of the tour coincided with Calgary's first autumn snow. As we listened, we could hear a strange, gentle, repetitive, drumming noise – the feathers of snow landing on the sensitive geophones.

How Deep is Your Love? sought to give the public the experience of listening for leaks, and through this to melt definitions of what might be considered a negative phenomenon. Nikhil Anand (2020) describes material failure as an ordinary and inevitable part of the assemblages and decompositions of everyday life. Indeed, he writes that failure can generate the conditions from which newly visible infrastructures emerge through the work of maintenance and repair. The leak here generated the possibility for a public artwork that could animate the construction of public and private, dissolve assumed differences between manufactured and natural, and make large-scale institutional structures intimate, tangible and lively.

References

Anand, N. (2020) 'After breakdown: invisibility and the labour of infrastructure maintenance', *Economic and Political Weekly*, 55(51), 26 December. Available at: www.epw.in/journal/2020/51/review-urban-affairs/after-breakdown.html (accessed 27 July 2022).

Douglas, M. (1984) *Purity and Danger: An Analysis of the Concepts of Pollution and Taboo*. London: Kegan Paul.

It's raining cats and dogs

It's raining pocketknives

It's a rain to wet fools

Earth and sand are falling

It's raining like a torrent of pestles

It's raining shoemakers' apprentices

It's raining priests

Tractors are falling

It's raining old women with clubs

It's even raining husbands

10

Rain

Sans façon

It was recently explained to us that all water on earth is alien, that is, it arrived on earth four and a half billion years ago via asteroids, meteorites and comets, or/and (it is not yet known exactly) out of the building blocks of the solar system, which created this planet (Greenfieldboyce, 2020). Fantastical as this sounds to someone who has never contemplated where water came from (we embarrassingly admit we hadn't), perhaps more astounding still is that the water on the planet which arrived at this time is the same water we have today, having over time existed in many states, in the capillaries of plants, as groundwater, in our own bodies, and (with a juvenile glee) the water molecules that we consume as our drinking water are those once expressed by dinosaurs (as pee) (Jha, 2019). Cyclically throughout time, water exists in different states: in 'reservoirs' for varying lengths of time, in rivers and streams for up to a few weeks, lakes potentially a number of years, the ocean up to four thousand years, in the atmosphere (at most) for eleven days, as rain, mere moments (Open University, 2021). How is it, then, that this briefest of states is so emotionally consuming, the avoidance of, the praying for, it hasn't stopped, we haven't had.

Living in the UK we understood that weather, and more specifically rain, was part of our national identity. In the 1990s we both moved to the wettest city in the UK (Smith, 2021), Glasgow (for architecture and art school, not the weather). The weather in Glasgow is credited by some with strongly influencing the city's evident cultural vibrancy, and in part as the reason for the tenacity of its people, the humour,

the creative output, after all when it's raining ... Only later in travelling for our work did we discover that the people of this island are not
alone in their obsession with weather; people in many different places
believe that the weather is part of their identity. When it comes to rain
especially, Glaswegians have competition in their intrinsic relationship to the substance, in Seattleites.

In Seattle rain is credited with contribution in small or large part
to many things: coffee culture, Microsoft and Grunge, the 90s music
scene which brought us Sound Garden, Pearl Jam, Mudhoney and
Nirvana. In the 1996 documentary 'Hype!' Seattle record producer
Jack Endino explained 'when the weather's crappy you don't feel
like going outside, you go into a basement and make a lot of noise
to take out your frustration'.[1] This mid-1990s perspective of a place
on the edge of a continent, the end of the road (before the tech boom
and the modern Seattle of today) was, it seems, compounded by the
weather, or more specifically moisture in the atmosphere.

It is true the North Pacific brings the city a similar number of annual
rainy days as the Atlantic does for Glasgow; however, for this region
weather is especially geographically specific. Forks, which sits on the
west side of the Olympic mountain range west of Seattle, receives
on average over 120 inches of rain annually; 90 miles east, Sequim
(just 50 miles north west of Seattle), sitting within the 'Olympic rain
shadow', receives just 18 inches of rain in an average year (Sistek,
2006). In fact in Seattle the summers especially can be extremely dry
(in rain volume both Miami and Houston have more annual precipitation). That said, as a seemingly proud badge of gritty realness, the old
adage sticks, 'It always rains in Seattle' – even if it doesn't.

Seattle's rain is indirectly what brought us to work in the city.
In 2016 we were asked to work with King County, Washington,
Water Treatment Division (a jurisdiction which includes the city
of Seattle), to develop a plan for the commissioning of artists in
response to their 'combined sewer overflow system' – as unglamor-
ous as this may sound, to the water thinker it is fascinating. As we
all know but rarely contemplate, below the surface of all cities are
the underpinnings of the services we require to function as urban

---

[1] Directed by Doug Pray and produced by Steven Helvey, *Hype!* is a documentary on
the explosion of grunge music that took place in the Pacific Northwest during the
early 1990s. See www.youtube.com/watch?v=uif6ZceSlB4 (accessed 1 September
2022).

centres with millions of people: miles of electrical cabling, internet, gas mains, and thousands of miles of pipes bringing clean water to our taps and sewage to our treatment plants. As part of this system, a network of pipes and infrastructure directly deals with rain that lands on our streets and buildings; 'stormwater' pipes lead either directly to the waterways or to join the sewer systems. In Seattle, as in many cities with older infrastructure, the sewer and stormwater pipes are paired, and, until the recent modernisation, during high-volume rain events (up to thirty times a year) the system would back up, allowing combined sewage and rainwater to run directly into Seattle's Duwamish River, Puget Sound or Lake Washington. The County's actions to mitigate this were citywide, diverse and a huge investment in infrastructure, largely invisible to the public, including rainwater catchments, vast underground basins, and so on. One such project is the Georgetown Wet Weather Treatment Station, a $275 million dollar piece of infrastructure to intersect, clean, store and gradually release rainwater from a significant portion of central Seattle.

The monument to rain

In 1831 the ship *The Beagle* set sail to survey the seas to the Galapagos and South America (1831–1836). Among the twenty-two chronometers (many of which had their own room) were the numerous weather instruments of Admiral Fitzroy, the commander of the ship (this voyage is more famously remembered as that on which Charles Darwin carried out his research, developed the theory of evolution and subsequently wrote *On the Origin of Species*). In addition to charting the seas Admiral Fitzroy made great efforts to understand and study meteorology and climatology (Anderson, 1999); he employed barometers of all kinds, including the so-called 'Storm Glass', a concoction of chemicals held in a glass vessel which, through the careful study of its changing state and appearance, was said to 'correctly indicate the coming rain, high winds, storm or tempest' (Tomlinson, 1863: 95). The accuracy, or indeed value, of the 'Fitzroy Storm Glass', as it became commonly known, is today much maligned but no less apocryphally tantalising. A footnote to this journey: upon his return, Fitzroy established what would later become the British Meteorological office and in 1863 he published *The Weather Book* – in its time a definitive study of the weather.

Today, with billions of dollars invested across the planet in studying, observing, monitoring and planning for precipitation (and conversely its absence), it can be anticipated with a greater certainty and accuracy than ever before, and yet this predictability has had little effect on our human obsession; perhaps it's even fair to propound that the implications of changing climate patterns and the ability to monitor weather from our personal devices at any moment have increased our appetite and this obsession to know what is happening, or about to happen, above our heads. Contemplating the creation of art for the Georgetown Wet Weather Treatment Station, it felt unavoidable that what should and inevitably would take centre stage would be the rain itself, or perhaps more accurately our enduring relationship with precipitation.

The significance of the weather is not lost in the architecture of the station; designed by Seattle-based Signal Architects, the building makes its instrumentality apparent. Rather than camouflaging the infrastructure, they have elegantly made its functionality legible, and in large part publicly accessible, a classroom and community event space being a core component of the building, bringing us closer to the implications of our dynamic environment. In dialogue with the often-invisible instigators of activation at the station above and below ground, the *Monument to Rain* is a large, clear cylindrical column, not unlike a huge museum display cabinet (or 10m tall Fitzroy Storm Glass). On rainy days the column, which is central to the public square at the front of the Georgetown Wet Weather Treatment Station, stands lit but empty, creating a glow to the theatre of the falling rain. Conversely, on dry days it rains within the column at the intensity of the most recent rainfall. The monument holds this perpetual state of raining until the next precipitation occurs, and the cycle continues indefinitely. Rather than pre-empting or reflecting current events as the Fitzroy Storm Glass purports to do, the *Monument to Rain* records and reflects events past, at times just moments ago, while in dry spells it could be weeks or even months.

If you run your hand along the surface of the column you will find imbedded a line of braille running the circumference, a collection of colloquial expressions for 'types' of rainfall collected from communities around the world: 'It's raining stair rods' (UK); 'It's a frog strangler' (Australia); 'It's raining shoemakers' apprentices' (Denmark); 'It's raining pocketknives' (Portugal); 'Tractors are falling' (Slovakia); 'It's even raining husbands' (Spain); 'It's a rain to wet fools' (Colombia);

'It's raining like a tilted pot pouring water' (China), and so on. From a gentle mist to the downpour held in these idiosyncratic phrases read through touch, is a connection of place, people and weather.

To make a monument of any kind is a peculiarity of human-kind; to monumentalise something banal and so commonplace may, by some, be seen as redundant, or irrelevant; after all, we all know rain. Perhaps, however, in the holding of rain in its fleeting state from sky to earth, we have the opportunity to contemplate, as with all monuments, our own relationships, our place in a system, our influence on the dynamics of our environment and perhaps in its ephemerality a certain beauty. For the people of Georgetown, Seattle, at least the moment of rain will be ever present and it will now finally be true to say that it does indeed always rain in Seattle (even if it doesn't).

Acknowledgements

The *Monument to Rain* was realised by Sans façon with frequent collaborators Eldorado Architects, for King County Water Treatment Division, commissioned by 4Culture.

References

Anderson, K. (1999) The weather prophets: science and reputation in Victorian meteorology. *History of Science*, 37, 179–216. Available at: https://articles.adsabs.harvard.edu//full/1999HisSc..37..179A/0000179.000.html (accessed 22 August 2022).

FitzRoy, Rear Admiral R., F. R. S. (1863) *The Weather Book: A Manual of Practical Meteorology*. London: Longman, Green, Longman, Roberts, & Green.

Greenfieldboyce, N. (2020) Where did Earth's water come from? *All Things Considered, NPR News*, 27 August. Available at: www.npr.org/2020/08/27/906791690/where-did-earths-water-come-from (accessed 25 August 2022).

Jha, A. (2019) Why water is so incredibly weird. *BBC Ideas*. Available at: www.youtube.com/watch?v=mPpKhxtFf1Q (accessed 25 August 2022).

Open University (2021) Storage of water in the hydrosphere. Available at: https://www.open.edu/openlearn/nature-environment/environmental-studies/water-use-and-the-water-cycle/content-section-2.1 (accessed 25 August 2022).

Sistek, S. (2006) What is the Olympic rain shadow? *KOMO News*, 4 October. Available at: https://komonews.com/weather/faq/what-is-the-olympic-rain-shadow.

Smith, K. (2021) Four of the rainiest UK cities revealed to be in Scotland. *Scottish Field*, 1 May.

Tomlinson, C. (1863) An experimental examination of the so-called Storm-glass. *Philosophical Magazine & Journal of Science*, XXVl (fourth series; July–December). Available at: https://archive.org/details/s4philosophicalm26lond/page/95/mode/1up?view=theater (accessed 31 August 2022).

11

More than a body of water: disentangling the affective meshwork of the Belize Barrier Reef

Phillip Vannini and April Vannini

We approached Laughing Bird Caye right as the few scattered clouds in the sky began to coalesce into a tenebrous blob of dark grey. The captain of our small skiff had mastered the waves wrought by darker skies before, but as he detected the shifting winds he showed a hint of apprehension. 'Let's keep an eye on the weather guys, the swells are going to start growing soon', he said somberly. We promised him we'd do our work as quickly as we could. Though the island was miniscule – less than two acres – it was alive with people to talk to and things to learn about.

We proceeded to anchor offshore – no dock was available – and for that to occur we had to fit snugly among four other boats floating mere metres away from the beach. We sputtered along gingerly, doing a bit of what looked like parallel parking, the whole scene feeling impossibly incongruent given the vast ocean of space available. The paradox grew in intensity when, a few minutes later, we leapt into the sea to shoot some underwater footage. With the vastness of the Caribbean Sea around us, we and the other few visitors channelled ourselves around the southern side of the caye in a space so confined that our snorkels and fins kept bumping into each other as we swam in circles. 'Oops, sorry!' 'Lo siento!' 'Pardonnez moi'. 'Entschuldigung'. The fish underneath us must have thought humans have an infinite vocabulary for the same expression, large bodies, and very small brains.

Laughing Bird Caye is 19km off the coast of Placencia, in southern Belize, and it draws a handful of small vessels carrying snorkellers, swimmers and sightseers every clear day of the tourist season. The island and the area nearby used to be an important fishing spot. Today it is a no-take zone. Years ago, the Belizean government refused a significant private offer to sell the island and decreed it should be a park instead. Subsequently, a protection plan was put in place. Today the island not only generates tourist dollars, but thanks to the regeneration of multiple species of fish and coral the fishing in the area has improved significantly. We were told it was a trade-off whose value the Southern Environmental Association of Belize (SEA) had worked hard to sell to the fishermen, but the wager was clearly paying off for conservation, extraction and tourism.

SEA is an NGO responsible for co-managing Laughing Bird Caye as well as other sites. SEA, their staff explained to us, are involved in local environmental protection and fish conservation initiatives. They had also been delegated by the Belizean government to regulate access to the island and monitor what goes on there. There is no accommodation on the caye, but day-trippers spend plenty of money to get there and enjoy the feeling of being cast away amid the swaying palm trees and the sea of clear, azure waters. Many of the men around us who previously drew their income from fishing around the caye now work as conservation leaders and tourist guides, piloting small vessels to the tiny island and leading ecologically responsible diving and snorkelling tours.

Infrastructure on Laughing Bird Caye is limited to a small cabin for the warden and a few picnic tables covered by a thatched roof. The caye had been split into two parts by the time of our visit in 2017. In the early 2000s Hurricane Iris hit so hard that it simply cut the caye into two pieces – though you could still cross from one side to the other by wading the shallow waters separating them. As we walked around with the day's warden, we noticed how the island was still relatively heavily vegetated despite the damage wreaked by Hurricane Iris, and several families of birds outnumbered the two dozen tourists on the beach. Turtles nested there too, he told us, though we couldn't spot any.

The Placencia Producers' Co-op had recently worked out a Memorandum of Understanding with SEA. Fishers working far offshore Laughing Bird Caye knew the rules and followed them. This wasn't necessarily the case for distant others. Jamaican fishers were known to fly by night and operate outside the rules, something that aggravated conservationists and local fishers alike. Frustrated by the situation, a few local fishers had given up their old trade and begun farming seaweed nearby. Luckily for them, international seaweed demand was on the rise. But for the most part people felt that their conservation efforts were beginning to pay off. There was hope in the air that the situation would continue improving.

Laughing Bird Caye was facing a few other threats. SEA had realised that snorkellers would occasionally bump into corals, sometimes even stand on them, and cause damage. As a result, they were educating visitors and leading them away from the shallowest zones. Coral had seen plenty of threats lately, largely due to the bleaching caused by climate change. To ameliorate the situation an NGO named Fragments of Hope had been working in the area to restore coral, and we were told we should speak with them and document what they were doing. But it would have to wait for another day. As the winds began packing more strength, we were warned it was time to go.

Back in Placencia the following day, we decided to follow up on the state of the corals. We had travelled to Belize to do fieldwork as part of a six-year multisite project unfolding at twenty World Natural Heritage sites – ten Canadian and ten International. Our work in the waters of Central America was part of a broader study focused on the complexities of different understandings of wilderness and wildness and how those concepts informed conservation practices (see Vannini and Vannini, 2021). Our research was based on a series of inductive and emic encounters with multiple lifeworlds. Besides conducting over three hundred in-depth, open-ended, semi-structured interviews with diverse groups of local residents of heritage sites and surrounding areas, between 2014 and 2020 we spent as much time as possible 'noticing' places (see Tsing, 2015): exploring the sites themselves and observing the multiple ways in which humans and nonhumans there were entangled with one another. Learning about the Belizean sea and its many inhabitants – especially fishers, corals and fish – was a way for us to understand wildness as an affective meshwork. But more on that later.

Placencia lies at the end of a long peninsula jutting out south from the Belizean mainland onto the Caribbean Sea. The small town stretches out on the thinnest part of the peninsula at its very southern edge. On the eastern side is the open sea. On the western side the water flows into a narrow pair of passages separating the peninsula from a half-dozen small islands, forming a lagoon. We asked a local resident named Franco to take us around the lagoon by kayak. Franco had been heavily involved in protecting the lagoon's mangrove ecosystem and had plans to show us how important the lagoon's health was to the coral reef, and in turn to fish stocks. Franco was also a shutterbug and knowing of our plan to film the day's action from the kayak he had gotten us out of bed early. We left at sunrise. As the low-angled light snuck through the mangroves, creating dreamy lens flares with every turn of our kayaks, flocks of birds woke up and took off from the trees, landing elegantly on the calm water. Amid the idyllic scenery, scattered everywhere around us were a few well-hidden million-dollar properties. Franco told us that we were far from being the first North Americans to discover the serene beauty of the place. Every winter scores of Canadians and Americans flowed to their villas cast amid the mangroves and the channels, causing powerful ripples on real estate prices and the local economy.

Franco and his partner Lisa had gotten into the guided kayak-tour business as a way of raising awareness of the work done by Fragments of Hope. Part of what they were trying to achieve was to educate people about the interconnectedness of mangroves, coral and fish. As we paddled our way through progressively narrower mangrove channels Franco explained the trees' importance to us. Coral reef and seagrass ecosystems have fluid boundaries, he explained. As water flows freely around the coast and islands, every sea creature living in the coral reef around here used the mangrove–seagrass ecosystem at some point in their life cycle.

But whereas coral reef ecosystems are widely recognised as both important and endangered, mangroves aren't as fortunate, Franco lamented. Mangroves provide important shoreline protection and nutrient filtering, but because they are not nearly as pretty as coral reefs and atolls, they are more easily subject to development pressures. As they are underwater, mangrove root meshworks are also out of sight and for most out of mind, and so are the complex flows of life they generate. Plenty of mangroves were being pulled up to make space for more sprawling mansions. This had now become a serious environmental and political problem.

In 2009 UNESCO resolved to add the Belize Barrier Reef Reserve to its list of World Heritage sites 'in danger'. 'Management challenges and threats that impact on the integrity of the property', read the World Heritage warning, included 'overharvesting of marine resources, coastal development, tourism, industrial development and proposed oil and gas exploration and exploitation'. Besides functioning as a warning, the relegation had brought a great degree of shame to the small nation.

The Belize Barrier Reef is the northern hemisphere's largest and the world's second largest barrier reef. It is a roughly 300km-long section of the 900km-long Meso-American barrier reef system which runs parallel to much of the Caribbean side of Central America. In the north of Belize, the reef is as close as 300 metres to the land, whereas in the south it lies farther ashore, as distant as 40km. Stretching the entire coast of the country, the reef includes idyllic offshore atolls, hundreds of picture-perfect low-lying sand cays, and a vast network of mangrove forests, river estuaries and coastal lagoons that are home to marine turtles, manatees and marine crocodiles, among countless other species.

The Belize Barrier Reef was inscribed on the World Heritage list in 1996 and subdivided into seven protected areas: Bacalar Chico National Park and Marine Reserve, Blue Hole Natural Monument, Half Moon Caye Natural Monument, South Water Caye Marine Reserve, Glover's Reef Marine Reserve, Laughing Bird Caye National Park and Sapodilla Cayes Marine Reserve. When it was inscribed, it met three of the criteria for inclusion on the List as a Natural Heritage site:

Criterion (vii): The Belize Barrier Reef Reserve System (BBRRS) is unique in the world for its array of reef types contained in a relatively small area. It provides a classic example of the evolutionary history of reefs and reef systems. The rise and fall of sea level over the millennia, coupled with natural karst topography and clear waters, results in a diverse submarine seascape of patch reefs, fringing reefs, faros, pinnacle reefs, barrier reefs as well as off-shelf atolls, rare deep water coral reefs and other unique geological features such as the Blue Hole and Rocky Point where the barrier reef touches the shore.

Criteria (ix): Illustrating a classic example of reef types, including fringing, barrier and atoll reef types, the BBRRS contains an intact ecosystem gradient ranging from the terrestrial to the deep ocean. Including littoral, wetland, and mangrove ecosystems, to seagrass beds interspersed with lagoonal reefs, to the outer barrier reef platform and oceanic atolls, this ecological gradient provides for a full complement of life-cycle needs, supporting critical spawning, nesting, foraging, and nursery ecosystem functions.

Criteria (x): Home to a diverse array of top predators, on land, sea and in the air, the jaguars of Bacalar Chico, the great hammerheads of the Blue Hole, and the ospreys of Glovers Reef are a testament to the property's importance and its ecological integrity. Numerous endangered species are protected within the boundaries of the BBRRS including, the West Indian manatee, the American crocodile and three species of sea turtle. The property also provides valuable habitat for three species of groupers, and the red-footed booby. The BBRRS is also home to endemic species including several Yucatan birds, island lizards, several fishes, tunicates, and sponges, making it an area with one of the highest levels of marine biodiversity in the Atlantic.

During our research in Belize, we travelled to Bacalar Chico National Park and Marine Reserve, Blue Hole Natural Monument, Half Moon Caye Natural Monument, Glover's Reef Marine Reserve and Laughing Bird Caye National Park, and interviewed two dozen people. In all of those places the coral, we were told, was quite simply an endless source of life. Life – in a countless variety of species including humans – flowed around the corals weaving meshworks of material and symbolic significance that gave rise to Belize as a whole. Fragments of Hope was hard at work to ensure that those forms of life would continue flowing for generations to come.

Since 2013 Lisa – a marine biologist who had migrated from California twenty years before – had been at the helm of Fragments of Hope. We met her for a filmed interview at the Placencia municipal pier. Corals, Lisa explained to us, are animals, and as such they can sexually reproduce, but also asexually reproduce just like some plants. 'We can take a cutting of a certain plant and its roots start all over again.' The maximum length afforded by this chapter is not enough to convey the visual and conceptual complexity of what Fragments of Hope does, how it does it and where it does it, so we have created a short video[1] to show that.

Following Hurricane Iris, Lisa told us, Laughing Bird Caye had emerged as the ideal place to begin coral restoration efforts. Fragments of Hope staff began transplanting naturally broken pieces of coral from one site to another in underwater nurseries. Over time, thanks to World Wildlife Fund (WWF) and Inter-American Development Bank funding, Fragments of Hope had managed to

---

[1] https://vimeo.com/215735445 (accessed 16 August 2022).

scale up their efforts, working at one point on nineteen different nurseries all over southern Belize.

'Why restore the reef?' we asked Lisa.

One of the 'main things that reefs do for us is provide so much protein', Lisa said, 'so much food, because they provide home for so many organisms. And so in the Caribbean and other coastal communities throughout the world people do rely on the reefs for sustenance, for protein.' This was one of the most important flows before us, obviously. A flow is a process of circulation, and here we were witnessing proteins circulating from organism to organism, giving life to all along the way. But that source of life was in jeopardy. 'For years we have been documenting the decline of reef health even prior to the hurricane impact', Lisa noted, 'and that is primarily due to climate change effects. And these are coral bleaching and disease events. The first bleaching event was documented in Belize in 1995. The big event famous all over the world was in 1998 when people first began speaking of this.' Bleaching was serious enough to threaten the continued flow of life on the coast and the rest of the country.

Bleaching, she explained to us in simple words, was due to the decaying health of the algae living inside the coral. It's the algae that are responsible for the lively colours of the coral. The corals 'live symbiotically with them, they get their energy, the algae can photosynthesise like plants and get their energy from the sun. Corals are animals that can also feed, but it turns out they get most of their energy from the byproducts of the algae that photosynthesise.' But when the conditions become adverse, as in conditions associated with climate change, the algae tend to leave, they simply flow away. When they do, the coral turns bright white, 'like a skeleton'.

The death of coral, and subsequently of fish, could only spell the demise of the country. And that demise was clearly a possibility. A week later we met Alyssa Carnegie, Communications Director at Oceana Belize, in the village of San Pedro, on Ambergris Caye. As we sat down together for breakfast, she told us that for nearly the last decade the main focus of Oceana Belize had been the fight against offshore oil exploration. The World Heritage designation of the Barrier Reef, Alyssa told us, is something that Belizeans were very proud of. 'But we're not so proud of the fact that it's been listed in danger.' Yet, there was hope this would soon end.

The hope that Alyssa talked about happened to be a recurring theme in our interviews. Unlike other parts of the world, where natural heritage areas are almost forgotten, in Belize people were deeply proud of the UNESCO World Heritage designation. Interview after interview, from fishing folk to environmental activists, from business owners to tour operators, we learned how the reef stood as a national symbol for the young nation. It wasn't just a geological feature; it was clearly a national monument. But while there was shame in its listing as an endangered site, there was just as much hope the situation would soon improve.

'How close are you to getting it off the endangered list?' we asked.

'We need economic research to be able to show the services we currently receive from the marine resources and the value of that versus what we would lose, what we'd be giving up if we were to go the route of just mainstream development.' The key, Alyssa noted, was to stop offshore oil exploration. And Belizeans had begun to unite on that front.

'Their stance has been a resounding "no" to offshore oil exploration', Alyssa told us. 'About six years ago, Oceana held a People's Referendum here in Belize. We had over 30,000 people participate. That's around 10 per cent of the population. They came out and 96 per cent of those people said no to oil. And they continue to say "No to oil" and that opposition has only increased. But what we wanted to get is not just someone to make a statement. We need policy, we need legislation, we need something that would ensure protection for future generations. It's one of those things we know Belizeans care about. They need this, they want this, and they're willing to fight for it.'

The People's Referendum, though it was neither a scientific poll nor a legally binding tool, had seemed to have given the nation hope. The people had spoken clearly that the reef mattered to them.

Over 190,000 Belizeans, by Oceana's calculations, depend on the Barrier Reef for their income, either through tourism or fishing. Twenty-five per cent of Belize's GDP is derived from tourism (in Canada, for comparison, the rate is 6.5 per cent). An oil spill would cripple the country for decades and the reef forever. Oil flows would ebb and drift from coast to lagoon, they would course and ooze from body to body, from species to species, streaming from the habitat of the most minute form of life to the environment of the nation as a whole. 'And that's something I don't even want to imagine, to be honest', Alyssa admitted. 'The loss would be huge, and it would be devastating. Belize is known for this amazing coastline, and that's why people are here. So is fishing, same thing.' And then there was the issue of coastline protection: 'We live in the hurricane belt. And we in recent years have been hit by several storms. And though there have been significant losses they could have been far worse if we didn't have the reef, if we were exposed. The loss would be tremendous, and it would be incredibly detrimental to our country. I think it would change the face, the shape, the nature, our culture, our identity beyond what we know.'

Of all places in Belize, San Pedro had the most to lose from oil exploration. San Pedro became a town in 1984. Until then it had been a quiet fishing village, not significant enough to constitute a municipality. With tourism, it then grew significantly over the next few decades. In 2017 its permanent resident population reached seventeen thousand. Though the number of tourists caused the local population to double during the high season, San Pedro had not yet started to feel like an apartheid community like some resort destinations north of its border, in Mexico. The place had been experiencing some growing pains, but most of the San Pedranos we met seemed genuinely in love with their community and willing to put everything on the line to defend the town and the water around it. And no one seemed more determined to do so than a diminutive twelve-year-old girl named Madison Edwards – Maddy for short.

Like many kids in Belize and around the world's oceans Maddy loved the sea, she told us as we sat down with her and her parents. She loved playing in the water, swimming with her friends and snorkelling. But, unlike many kids around the world who only experience the water while on vacation, Maddy lived close to the reef. Given that proximity and relevance, Maddy had worked up the courage and the confidence to stand in the way of those threatening the waters she called home. Distressed by the prospect of oil exploration, the middle-school girl had decided to raise awareness about the issue by swimming the length of the Barrier Reef (with her parents carefully watching and assisting from a safety vessel). Along the way, she blogged and posted pictures and videos on social media to show everyone the beauty of the place. And while she was at it, she thought she'd pick up litter along the way.

'I snorkelled the Barrier Reef because I just wanted to spread a lot of awareness', she told us, 'because a few months ago there were ships coming to do seismic testing and I wasn't proud of the town Councillor and the Belize government's decision on that. We did walks, we did polls, we did videos, and they just weren't getting the memo, so I wanted to do a swim and I think it's been working.' Maddy spoke confidently, but without an ounce of precociousness. Though self-assured, she seemed shy underneath. 'A lot of people are watching the videos and getting the memo of what I did. I think it's boosting their confidence to not be afraid and to speak out and say we don't want oil drilling in Belize.'

Maddy's trip lasted six days. It was not her intention to swim every inch of the impossibly long journey. To make her point she didn't need to chase records. And she didn't want to miss too much school either, she explained with a smile. Her favourite memory of the journey, she revealed, was seeing dolphins in the wild for the first time. 'One time when we were sailing one came right up to the boat and jumped, I could touch it if I reached my hand out. It was so cool.' Strong in her words was a feeling of hope that change would come soon.

Thanks to the countless efforts of people like Maddy, NGOs and citizen groups, in June of 2018 the Belize Barrier Reef was removed from the list of World Heritage Sites in Danger. Previously, in December 2017, the Belize government had agreed to put an end to oil exploration and had begun to draft legislation aimed at protecting the reef, its resident species and the humans who depend on it.

'Belizeans stood up to protect their reef, with hundreds of thousands more globally joining the campaign to save our shared heritage', commented Marco Lambertini, Director General of WWF International. 'In taking swift collaborative action, Belize has shown that it is possible to reverse nature loss and create a sustainable future.' More recently Belize also adopted regulations to protect the country's mangroves and declared that it would begin to phase out single-use plastics that threaten water-based species and their ecosystems.

The Barrier Reef as meshwork

When we initially learned about the complex web of life and its multiple flows from water to land and back in the Barrier Reef we turned to the concept of the assemblage. Assemblages are defined as 'wholes characterised by relations of exteriority' (DeLanda, 2006: 10), a notion drawn from the work of philosophers Deleuze and Guattari (1987). Writing in their native French, Deleuze and Guattari never quite wrote about 'assemblages' but rather about *agencement* (Phillips, 2006), a process that refers to complex interaction systems. Just like an ecosystem, the 'component parts of a whole cannot be reduced to their function within that whole, and indeed they can be parts of multiple wholes at any given moment' (Dittmer, 2014: 387).

As DeLanda (2006) explains, a particular assemblage is delineated from neighbouring assemblages through dynamics of territorialisation and de-territorialisation. Territorialisation is a movement towards internal organisation and coherence, whereas de-territorialisation refers to forces which rupture and unsettle the whole. There were clear ways, we thought, in which the inclusion of the Barrier Reef on the list of World Heritage Sites in Danger had functioned as a clear de-territorialising process by introducing instability and insecurity. At the same time, we had noticed how the numerous efforts to combat development and oil exploration could constitute dynamics of re-territorialisation.

Another advantage in using the idea of assemblage in our case was its usefulness in describing more-than-human entanglements. Assemblages combine human and nonhuman actors, organic and inorganic materials, discourses and technics. Assemblages knot together 'politics, machines, organisms, law, standards and grades, taste and aesthetics, even the production of sovereign territory and the politics of scale' (Braun, 2006: 647). Assemblages therefore move beyond the 'notion of Nature as singular and universal', as Braun (2006: 644) has noted, and this was an important feature for us. The Barrier Reef waters are home to fish, birds, mammals, plants, fishers, tour operators, and countless people who live by the water or who visit the coast and its many atolls, and this entanglement was knotted together by shifting laws and economic processes which we thought we would dissect in order to study how wildness came together as a social product. These were just our premature observations, finding space in our field journals next to observations and early insights.

However, the more time we spent in and around the water in Belize, the more the notion of assemblage seemed to fall short of the ideal conceptual tool we needed. To begin with, the notion 'territorialisation', with its etymological root grounded in *terra firma*, felt insufficiently aqueous for our concerns with water. Moreover, there was something overly mechanical about the core image of an assemblage. We felt the need for a sensitising concept that was more organic, and soon we turned to the work of Ingold, whose ideas on the subject we found particularly original. Rather than an assemblage, Ingold proposed the notion of a meshwork. Dictionaries define a meshwork as an open fabric made of either string or rope that is woven or tangled together at regular intervals. The material, however, does not really matter, and patterns need not be so regular or symmetrical. Therefore, a meshwork is essentially a tangled web. To us, this was not unlike the roots of mangroves reaching for soil underwater, giving shelter to countless species who spawn and radiate life outward. And while root systems have always been everyone's preferred example to explain meshworks, the shape of corals to us seemed equally adequate, if not superior, to exemplify a meshwork unfolding. Even the tangled web of a net used to catch fish, and therefore to feed people, felt like a particularly fitting, exemplifying image.

A meshwork is not quite an assemblage, nor a network. As Ingold (2010) explains, the meshwork is made and constantly remade by tangled lines of growth and movement, just like mangroves and the fish, or the corals branching out and regrowing underwater. The concept of the network refers to something quite different. That key difference, Ingold (2010, 2015) argues, lies in the openness of the meshwork. Network-based metaphors divide the world into points of contact among connected nodes, whereby something is either inside or outside the network. The meshwork metaphor, in contrast, describes a world in constant formation. This is an open world of becoming that is constantly unfolding along paths of movement, just like the underwater world flourishing alongside coral webs.

The more we thought about the meshwork, the more we found it useful. But there was something else, something quite aqueous as it happened, that really drew us towards Ingold's idea of the meshwork. According to Ingold, Western worldviews are characterised by the logic of inversion, a logic that is so deeply entrenched in our ways of thinking and acting that it is actually quite difficult to become sensitised to it. 'Through this logic', Ingold (2010: 68) explains:

> the field of involvement in the world, of a thing or person, is converted into an interior schema of which its manifest appearance and behaviour are but outward expressions. Thus the organism, moving and growing along lines that bind it into the web of life, is reconfigured as the outward expression of an inner design. Likewise the person, acting and perceiving within a nexus of intertwined relationships, is presumed to behave according to the directions of cultural models or cognitive schemata installed inside his or her head. By way of inversion,

beings originally open to the world are closed in upon themselves, sealed by an outer boundary or shell that protects their inner constitution from the traffic of interactions with their surroundings.

In exemplifying how the logic of inversion works, Ingold (2011) used the example of how we typically draw a fish. When asked to draw a fish most of us would normally draw a roughly oval shape, add a triangle-like tail, then a fin above and below the body, and finally a couple of beady eyes and a mouth. Normally, that's what a fish looks like in our minds. By doing so, however, we reveal the logic of inversion at work. A thing, in this case a fish, is converted into a schema that reduces its 'being' to its appearance and physiological boundaries with the outside. Inside the drawn shape we thus find fishness. Outside of it we may find water, air, the kitchen table or something else; something other than fish and its fishness. In this way, a being that is originally fully immersed in the water world becomes closed in upon itself, sealed by the edges drawn by our pencil and our cognition, and fully dissected from the currents of its entanglement with the world.

But why, Ingold asks, represent (and think, and imagine, and know ...) a being in virtue of its boundaries, rather than in virtue of its entanglements, its movements and its becoming? Why not draw, for example, a zigzag to denote the fish's swimming and a few wavy lines on top and below to denote the flow of the currents it swims in (Ingold, 2011)? Why not draw lines knotting the fish with the mangrove root systems where it is given life? Why not extend lines to the coral reefs where it dwells? Why not capture its flows into fishers' nets and eventually into the belly of a human? It was that kind of thinking and imagination of the coral reef as a web of lines and a tangle of intersecting flows that the metaphor of the meshwork invited us to engage in.

Meshworks force us to confront life as becoming, as movement, as something entangled in multiple currents of formation. Meshworks invite us to treat life as lived in the open, even if underwater, in a fluid world that is not pre-constituted or occupied by things existing independent of other things. The meshwork is not so much a metaphor, but rather an essence of sorts, or a core image that pushes us to understand how more-than-human life is experienced and practised as a kind of flow. Flow, movement, circulation, is the quintessential way in which more-than-human existence manifests itself. Flow generates relations and weaves the knots that bind humans and nonhumans together. And that flow, according to Ingold (2010, 2015), cannot be understood outside of the traces – or the 'trails' – that it takes place in and that it creates. 'Neither beginning here and ending there, nor vice versa', he explains (Ingold, 2010: 71):

> the trail winds through or amidst like the rot of a plant or a stream between its banks. Each such trail is but one strand in a tissue of trails that together comprise the texture of the lifeworld. This texture is what I mean when I speak of organisms being constituted within a relational field. It is a field not of interconnected points but of interwoven lines; not a network but a meshwork.

What we call 'the environment' or an 'ecosystem', or more precisely in our case a Barrier Reef System, might then be better envisaged as a domain of entanglement. It is within such a tangle of interlaced trails, currents, flows, lifelines continually ravelling here and unravelling there, that beings like fish, corals and human beings grow or 'issue forth' along the lines of their relationships. This tangle is the texture of the world. In this ontology, beings do not simply occupy the world, they *inhabit* it, and in so doing – in threading their own paths through the meshwork – they flow together into its ever-evolving weave (Ingold, 2010: 71).

Towards an affective meshwork

The idea of the meshwork served our purposes beautifully, yet there was something else in the air and in the water in Belize, we felt. Something that the meshwork metaphor did not fully capture. It was something present in every one of our interviews and in the words and the actions of everyone who had mobilised to fight unsustainable development. It was something that seemed to push, to drive, to urge people. We had noticed it in speaking with Lisa and Franco, when we realised how much they cared about a Barrier Reef inhabited by healthy coral. It was in the fishers' vision of a better and more sustainable future. We had picked it up when we heard from Alyssa about the love that Belizeans had for their country's waters. We had detected it even as we sat down with twelve-year-old Maddy, whose vision for the future had galvanised countless Belizeans to act to defend their reef. That something was quite simple and yet very powerful: hope.

There is little space for affect in discussions of meshworks (or assemblages, for that matter), but affect matters deeply. Affect animates, enlivens beings to 'issue forth', to thread new relationships, to enact new flows, to fuel and direct new movements. It was clear to us that this is what hope was doing in Belize; it was driving the re-territorialisation of an ecosystem, indeed an entire nation, destabilised by the realisation that their watery lifeworld was in jeopardy (also see Todd, 2017). And it was that mobilising affect, that hope, which ultimately led to the removal of the Barrier Reef from the list of endangered sites. Hope worked, to borrow from Les Back's (2021) reflection on how hope circulates. Hope engendered a heightened kind of awareness to the world, it enlivened flows of 'emergent alternatives, directions, or possibilities' (Back, 2021: 4).

In Belize, but clearly elsewhere too, people and water-dwelling species can be understood as 'beings with simultaneously parallel and entangled biographies' (Kirksey and Hemreich, 2010: 552). In light of this understanding, coral and mangroves are not just key to the functioning of an ecosystem, but a bona fide cultural keystone species that is key to the functioning of an entire society (Haggerty et al., 2018; also see Garibaldi and Turner, 2004). To borrow a concept from Anna Tsing (2015), coral, mangroves, fish and people can be seen as 'mutually flourishing' companions. Affect is central to this vision of ecology, to this kind of *affective ecology*.

Affective ecologies are entanglements that help us think about the kinship connecting humans and nonhumans as alive, open to change, mutually interdependent and based on the equality of all constituent members (Singh, 2018). As Singh (2018: 3, emphasis added) writes, 'thinking in terms of affective ecologies inspires and enables an ecopolitics rooted in *care* for the material world not as "impersonal nature at a distance" but from a lived-in or kin-centric ecological perspective'. This is not a patronising care, observes Hinchcliffe (2008: 95), but a 'care for others ... in the sense of being open to others, or being curious about others', as a type of kinship that is 'produced with and as others'.

It is all too easy to treat hope as a human affect, as something only our species is capable of (Todd, 2017). We do not have the 'hard data' to prove that fish, corals or mangroves can experience and practise hope, but maybe those data are unnecessary anyway. Within an affective ecology, and an affective meshwork, lifelines are continuously in movement and so is the affective energy that vitalises them.

'Hope floats', the old expression goes, and perhaps as it flows from being to being, it energises as much as it connects, binding humans and nonhumans together (Todd, 2017). Western worldviews find it challenging to envision nonhumans as spiritual and emotional beings, but Indigenous ontologies help us in moving beyond dualist perspectives. As Lakota/Dakota scholar Kim TallBear (2011) argues, there are dangers in splitting humans apart from animals and other organisms. Disconnection implies and provokes separation. Disconnection is the origin of domination and the possible genesis of colonial subjectification and environmental violence (also see Rose, 2015; Watts, 2013). By moving beyond disconnection, we realise that 'human nature [in all its myriad forms] is an interspecies relation' (Tsing, 2012: 141), where everything – including care – is related (also see Deloria, 2001).

Hope, we want to simply argue with this short writing, is central to the formation of kinship. It is central to the functioning of meshworks. Hope, as a type of care, flows and binds species together. Hope can heal too (see Haggerty et al., 2018). As Métis/Otipemisiw scholar Zoe Todd (2017) writes, if we humans thought of ourselves as co-constituted with the lifeworlds that we share with nonhumans – as opposed to different and removed from them – we would learn to view ourselves as part of a kinship with all beings. 'Tending to the reciprocal relationality' inherent in such kinship, Todd (2017: 107) writes, 'is integral to supporting the narrow conditions of existence in this place', our shared planet. This is what is known as a kin-centric ecology. In kin-centric ecology everything is relative and interconnected and there is no need for categories of thought, such as affect, that separate wildlife from humanity (Salmón, 2017).

No longer stranger to each other, no longer mere dots in a network, no longer just agents in an assemblage, we left Belize viewing humans, corals, mangroves and fish as bound together by the waters they call home, and the affects flowing within. And with that our notion of wild had changed. Wild was no longer feeling something foreign, removed, untouched by human hand. Wildness – just like the corals restored by the NGOs who cared, just like the fish conserved by the fishers who hoped to see them grow, just like the waters defended by united Belizeans – was more something like reciprocity and kinship between very different, but connected, species (for more see Vannini and Vannini, 2022).

References

Back, L. (2021) Hope's work. *Antipode*, 53, 3–20.

Braun, B. (2006) Environmental issues: global natures in the space of assemblage. *Progress in Human Geography*, 30, 644–654.

DeLanda, M. (2006) *A New Philosophy of Society: Assemblage Theory and Social Complexity*. New York: Continuum.

Deleuze, G. and Guattari, F. (1987) *A Thousand Plateaus: Capitalism and Schizophrenia*. Minneapolis: University of Minnesota Press.

Deloria, V. Jr (2001) American Indian metaphysics. In V. Deloria Jr and W. Wildcat (eds) *Power and Place: Indian Education in America*. Golden: Fulcrum Publishing, pp. 1–6.

Dittmer, J. (2014) Geopolitical assemblages and complexity. *Progress in Human Geography*, 38, 385–401.

Garibaldi, A. and Turner, N. (2004) Cultural keystone species: implications for ecological conservation and restoration. *Ecology and Society*, 9(3), 1.

Haggerty, J., Rink, E., McNally, R. and Bird, E. (2018) Restoration and the affective ecologies of healing: buffalo and the Fort Peck Tribes. *Conservation and Society*, 16, 21–29.

Hinchliffe, S. (2008) Reconstituting nature conservation: towards a careful political ecology. *Geoforum*, 39, 88–97.

Ingold, T. (2010) *Being Alive*. London: Routledge.

Ingold, T. (2011) Introduction. In T. Ingold (ed.) *Redrawing Anthropology: Materials, Movements, Lines*. Farnham: Ashgate, pp. 1–19.

Ingold, T. (2015) *The Life of Lines*. London: Routledge.

Kirksey, E. and Helmreich, S. (2010) The emergence of multispecies ethnography. *Cultural Anthropology*, 25, 545–576.

Phillips, J. (2006) Agencement/assemblage. *Theory, Culture & Society*, 23, 108–110.

Rose, D. (2015) *Wild Dog Dreaming: Love and Extinction*. Charlottesville: University of Virginia Press.

Salmón, E. (2017) No word. In G. Van Horn and J. Hausdoerffer (eds) *Wildness: Relations of People and Place*. Chicago: University of Chicago Press, pp. 24–32.

Singh, N. (2018) Introduction: affective ecologies and conservation. *Conservation and Society*, 16, 1–7.

TallBear, K. (2011) Why interspecies thinking needs Indigenous standpoints: theorizing the contemporary. *Cultural Anthropology*, 24 April. Available at: https://culanth.org/fieldsights/260-why-interspecies-thinking-needs-indigenous-standpoints (accessed 16 August 2022).

Todd, Z. (2017) Fish, kin and hope: tending to water violations in Amiskwaciwâskahikan and Treaty Six Territory. *Afterall*, 4, 102–107.

Tsing, A. (2012) Unruly edges: mushrooms as companion species. *Environmental Humanities*, 1, 141–154.

Tsing, A. (2015) *The Mushroom at the End of the World*. Princeton: Princeton University Press.

UNESCO (2009) Belize Barrier Reef Reserve System: integrity. Available at: https://whc.unesco.org/en/list/764/ (accessed 25 August 2022).

Vannini, P. and Vannini, A. (2021) *Inhabited: Wildness and the Vitality of the Land*. Montreal: McGill-Queen's University Press.

Vannini, P. and Vannini, A. (with Vannini, A.) (2022) *In the Name of Wild*. Vancouver: On Point Press/UBC Press.

Watts, V. (2013) Indigenous place-thought and agency amongst humans and non-humans (First Woman and Sky Woman go on a European world tour!). *Decolonization: Indigeneity, Education & Society*, 2, 20–34.

12

Shifting tides: Anthropocene entanglements and unravellings in the Bay of Fundy

Aurora Fredriksen

The highest tides in the world flow in and out of the northern end of the Atlantic's Gulf of Maine, in the Bay of Fundy. At their highest point, in the Minas Basin (an inlet of the larger bay), a spring tide[1] can rise 16 metres vertically and spread 5 kilometres horizontally. At low tide boats at dock sit on sand, and water can only be seen far in the distance. Visiting a dock at low tide brings to mind images of boats in the desert where the Aral Sea once was. But the impression is fleeting, as the tides bring the sea back each day, twice a day, and the flood tide is fast, faster than you can walk in some places. We – myself and a film-maker friend – almost lost two Go-Pros to the flood tide on the day we set four of these little waterproof cameras out on the sandy shore to film the tide flowing in to submerge them in real time. The flow was too fast though and inrushing seawater submerged them quickly, washing them off the sandy bottom. We eventually found them swishing in some rocky shallows several feet from where they had been set. We grabbed them and headed back to the truck at a jog, wet almost to our waists with seawater. This wasn't the first or last time in the fieldwork that the extraordinary flow of the Bay of Fundy's tides changed our plans, spoiled our 'data', soaked our legs.

---

[1] A 'spring' tide does not refer to the season but the high tides that come with the full and new moon, which are the highest in the lunar tidal cycle, getting steadily lower as the moon waxes and wanes towards a 'neap' tide at the half moon.

I was in the Bay of Fundy in the summers of 2017 and 2018 to research the controversy surrounding tidal energy development, and particularly the tensions between tidal energy proponents and independent and Indigenous fishers. In both years a friend came up from New York to film as I researched, to make a visual record of movement, more-than-verbal encounters, flows. Throughout the research and after, the Bay of Fundy – its waves and tides and all the things and relations it involves – was more than the setting or container of the controversy over tidal energy; it was a central thread running through the entangled stories of living with continuity and change in a time of disorienting environmental shifts. In spending time there, talking to people, going out in trucks and boats, watching birds and getting alternately soaked and left high and dry by its tides, I came to appreciate the Bay of Fundy not as a body of water in the North Atlantic, but as a flowing meshwork of unfolding, entangled, more-than-human lifeways (Ingold, 2010). And, indeed, perhaps too as something exceeding meshwork, stretching beyond its material entanglements to 'permeate senses and imaginations, emoting the "marine" and the "maritime"' (Peters and Steinberg, 2019: 294), drawing bodies and imaginaries into relations that unfold and flow within a wider affective ecology.

In the liminal zones of seacoasts, the Anthropocene comes 'down to earth' (cf. Latour, 2018), making global environmental changes legible in the intensifying forms of coastal erosion and flooding caused by rising seas, in redrawing the edges of things at sometimes alarming rates. In stratigraphic terms the Anthropocene proposes a new geological epoch marked by human impacts on earth systems, readable in the rocky strata of the deep future. Colloquially, the Anthropocene is increasingly becoming shorthand for this planetary moment of disorienting environmental shifts, ecological unravellings and cascading elemental catastrophes brought about by (certain) humans and their excesses. Sea-level rise, as Elizabeth Doherty argues, is particularly generative of imaginaries of planetary change through the rising of an interconnected world ocean (DeLoughrey, 2017: 34). But while imaginaries of the Anthropocene often come into focus through global forces – sea-level rise, global warming – or disaster – super storms, floods, wildfires, extinctions; as Stengers (2021) points out, global disaster is also a difficult lens to think with or through.

The everyday, or the ordinary, by contrast, offers itself more readily to the task of reflecting on and making sense of the many

small and large ecological dislocations of a given place. The 'ordinary Anthropocene' (Fredriksen, 2021) shifts the lens away from the
global future and on to the ongoing, everyday and less-than-planetary
moments where epochal environmental shifts flicker into view, where
they are sensed or lived through, or where they come together in the
flow of ordinary practices and ways of knowing and relating (Stewart,
2007). In this chapter I explore such ordinary moments of planetary
trouble through a series of small stories shaped around the diurnal ebb
and flood of tides as they flow through the unravelling and reweaving
of meshy, affective ecologies in the Bay of Fundy.

Flood

Approximately 14 billion tonnes of seawater flow through the
5km-wide passage to the Minas Basin on an average flood tide,
with tidal currents around 10 knots or 5 metres/second. The speed
of the water at flood tide and the precision at which the timing of
flows can be known has long interested energy developers. The size
of the 'tidal resource' in the Minas Passage is estimated at 7,000
megawatts, making it an attractive prospect for energy companies
looking to diversify their portfolios, venture capitalists seeking investment opportunities and the government of Nova Scotia as it looks to
reduce its dependence on coal. To this end, in 2009 the Fundy Ocean
Research Centre for Energy (FORCE) was set up as a government–
private industry partnership in the Minas Passage as a testing site for
in-stream tidal energy devices.

FORCE promotes its test berths to tidal energy companies with the
lure of testing their technology against the 'Fundy Standard': the idea
that if a tidal turbine can be shown to function and produce energy
in the Bay of Fundy's Minas Passage, with the strongest tidal current
in the world, equivalent to a class 4 hurricane, then it can be confi-
dent of functioning anywhere in the world. To date none of the tidal
turbines tested at FORCE has met the Fundy Standard, though several
have had their enormous blades bent or even ripped off in the attempt.

As well as the location of the FORCE test berths, the Minas Passage
is one of the Mi'kmaq creator Kluskap's homes (the other being
Cape Duaphin on the east coast of Cape Breton Island). It is where
he created the world and its people, animals and other living things.
The immense flow of water in and out of the Minas Basin with the
tides is integral to the living ecologies around not only the Minas

Basin, but also the wider Bay of Fundy and its surrounds. The area Mi'kmaq Nations were not consulted about the siting of FORCE in Kluskap's home, an oversight that has not only been 'heart wrenching', as one Indigenous leader described it to me in an interview, but also one that speaks to the ongoing dispossession of the Mi'kmaq from land/water by the settler-state's governing of land/water as property or resource (see Pictou, 2020; cf. Simpson, 2017).

The area Mi'kmaq Nations were not consulted about the siting of FORCE because the parameters drawn around the testing site do not overlap with those drawn around the nearshore waters of the Bay's First Nation land reserves. Concerns raised by some area First Nations about the potential ecological impacts of the tidal turbines have been side-stepped for the same reason. In line with the legal requirements of federal and provincial law, legal responsibility for, and authority over, knowledge about how the turbines deployed at FORCE may affect environmental processes and marine ecologies is spatially restricted within the 1.0 × 1.6km area of seabed leased by FORCE from the British Crown Estate – which is the legal owner of Nova Scotia's nearshore seabed – and the water column above it (FORCE, 2016: iii). Private companies deploying turbines at the FORCE site are responsible for monitoring the 'nearfield' environmental effects of their turbine, defined as those occurring within a 100m radius of their device, while FORCE is responsible for monitoring the 'midfield' environmental effects of turbines, defined as the remaining area within the boundaries of the 'Crown Lease Deployment Area' (the area of seabed leased by FORCE and the water column above it). Any potential environmental effects of turbines outside the Crown Lease Deployment Area are not monitored (FORCE, 2016).

The Euclidean imaginary of bordering state authority and private property through line drawing is so ingrained in Western terrestrial practices that it is now being transposed onto the sea despite the apparent difficulties with demarcating fluid oceanic space in this way (e.g. Bear, 2013; Kerr et al., 2015; Peters, 2020). While recognising the shortfalls of simply drawing a square around the turbines on a map to study lively marine waters, for many of the marine scientists involved in environmental monitoring who I spoke with, it was the most practical way of delimiting their study area.

Troubling this 'common sense' approach, one Mi'kmaw activist I spoke with explained, the infringement of the test site area on Kluskap's home was not merely a matter of cultural insensitivity; the imaginary of bounded ocean spaces in which to measure environmental effects was also in contradiction to the ethic of socio-ecological responsibility taught by the Kluskap creation story:

> When I talk about the Kluskap and this attachment, people kind of think well that's in the past. But those creation stories really ... they speak to this responsibility, this reciprocal relationship to the land and to the waters that we use. (Interview, 10 August 2017)

As a collective of Mi'kmaq and allied scholars (*M's-it No'kmaq* et al., 2021) explain, the circular process of (re)telling and listening to stories is a central way of deepening knowledge and care for land/water in *L'nuwey* (the Mi'kmaw way of seeing/being in the world); in each new telling/listening new lessons, nuances, understandings may emerge (*M's-it No'kmaq* et al., 2021). Looking at the effects of turbines only within a nearfield geometric parameter drawn on a map around the berths does not meet the requirements of responsibility and reciprocity with the larger Bay taught by the story of Kluskap's act of creation. The bordering of knowledge/authority over discreet parcels of seabed and the water columns above them – with First Nations only involved in decisions over the water immediately offshore from their settler-state-designated territories – is incapable of knowing in the context of the perpetual flow of this creation, of the affective ecologies and entangled lifeways that take shape in these tidal waters.

By most accounts the few tidal turbines located at the FORCE test site are unlikely to have any significant impacts on the vast tidal ecologies of the wider Bay of Fundy. Yet the precedent they set for extending land-based property rights (and their Euclidean imaginaries) into lively tidal waters speaks to the ongoingness of colonisation. On the surface, the fact that the seabed on which the berths are located and cables trailed are legally the private property of the British Crown Estate, to be leased out at that organisation's discretion, speaks plainly to this point. A concern raised by Indigenous and white fishermen alike in my research was the extension of property rights more widely across the seabed in the Bay of Fundy; after the testing phase, would successful technologies be scaled up? While there is no official plan for any such scaling up, rumours of investor meetings where companies pitched a vision of thousands of turbines spread up and down the Bay of Fundy loomed large. There is, however, a more fundamental issue at stake here: it is not just that the seabed in the Bay of Fundy is owned by the British Crown Estate, but that the seabed is *owned* at all. The former speaks to a history of colonisation, the latter to the ongoing condition of colonisation, in which entangled, reciprocal relations with land/water are governed through a Western legal framework that necessarily positions land/water as property or commodity (Pictou, 2018, 2020; *M's-it No'kmaq* et al., 2021).

Ebb

Growing up in the landlocked US state of Vermont, my first memory of the sea is from a day trip to Fire Island when I was seven, the day after an uncle's wedding on Long Island. I remember very little of the detail from that trip, only that the sunlight was dimmed by a thick summer haze and that the air was full of the smell of salty rot from the horseshoe crabs stranded onshore by the ebbing tide after mass spawning at the height of the spring tide overnight. Horseshoe crabs, those strange emissaries from deep time[2] more closely related to spiders than actual crabs, have survived as a taxonomic group through the earth's first five mass extinction events, only to encounter serious peril in what many ecologists now believe is a sixth mass extinction, victims of the great 'Anthropocene defaunation' (Dirzo et al., 2014). Along with the loss of suitable coastal places for spawning due to the construction of 'hard engineering' sea defences and seafront properties, horseshoe crabs are harvested by the hundreds of thousands for use as fishing bait. When horseshoe crabs decline, so do shorebirds like red knots and other sandpipers that consume their eggs, fuelling up in critical stop-offs timed precisely with horseshoe crab spawnings before non-stop flights across thousands of miles of open ocean on their way from their breeding grounds in arctic Canada to their wintering grounds in South America (Mizrahi and Peters, 2009).

These little birds and their entanglement within complex ecologies involving ancient sea creatures, modern commercial fishing and vast expanses of the north and south Atlantic seacoast were on my mind on the day I first arrived on Nova Scotia's Bay of Fundy in 2017. I walked out onto the expansive mudflats exposed in the afternoon's low tide at Evangeline Beach on the southern shore of the Minas Basin

---

[2] The taxonomic group to which horseshoe crabs belong, Xiphosura, has been found in fossils from the Ordovician Period, 450 million years ago, while the species we encounter today are nearly unchanged since the Jurassic Period (Funch, 2017; Van Roy et al., 2010).

looking, in particular, for semipalmated sandpipers. These diminutive wading birds are one of the wonders of the Bay of Fundy summer,
beloved for their habit of flocking by the thousands in shifting areal
shapes over the shore in the evenings. This afternoon they were down
by the edge of the receding water, skittering back and forth on the wet
sand eating the tiny mud shrimp that were everywhere exposed by
the ebb tide. I was cautious not to get too close, knowing that startled
birds will take flight, using up valuable energy they should be preserving for the journey ahead.

In the Minas Basin's tidal mudflats the semipalmated sandpipers
that seemed so numerous to me on that day have been in 'moderately
rapid decline' over the past two decades (Birdlife International, 2016).
Like their kin who depend on horseshoe crab eggs further down the
Atlantic coast, their decline seems to be due to the combined effects
of decreases in key food sources (here the tiny mud shrimp on the
Minas Basin mudflats), the destruction or disturbance of coastal
habitats, and increases in extreme weather and sea-level rise (which
induces them to use up valuable energy flying over high water) (Mann
et al., 2017). The loss of wildlife in the Anthropocene is not only a
story of individual species decline, but is one of mass unravelling of
ecologies, the undoing of long-standing Holocene relations as losses
cascade through interconnected lifeways (Rose, 2013; van Dooren,
2014; cf. Dirzo et al., 2014 for a scientific interpretation of the same).

The unravelling of ecologies in the Anthropocene – the unpick-
ing of intricate meshworks – was a constant presence in my research
on tidal energy and fishing on the Bay of Fundy. Sometimes threats
to particular wildlife or wider ecologies were explicit, as when fishermen brought up threats to whales and harbour porpoises seen in
the area of the turbines, or pointed to larger possibilities for ecological havoc caused by removing energy from the flow of tidal currents.
Other times, it was more of a shadow, the memories (sometimes personal, sometimes passed down from the previous generation) of the
past collapse of Atlantic Canada's cod fishery in the early 1990s and
the resulting losses of tens of thousands of local livelihoods.[3] At yet
other times it was the looming shadow of a future collapse in the
lobster fishery, foretold by the pattern of boom and bust slowly pressing northward through the Gulf of Maine. In southern New England

---

[3] As well as fishermen who suffered job losses from the collapse of the cod fishery,
many thousands of associated jobs in fish-processing plants were also lost.

lobster fisheries crashed a decade ago after years of rising landings, and the same pattern is now creeping northward from Massachusetts to Maine; the first signs of decline are just starting to show in the statistics on lobster landings in the Gulf of Maine's northern edge in the Bay of Fundy (Albeck-Ripka, 2018; Luck, 2021). Decades of warming waters in the Gulf of Maine have brought more lobsters, but when the water gets too warm the population crashes (Le Bris et al., 2018).

The need to care for the larger ecologies of the Bay to ensure the health of lobster populations was a central point of discussion on the day we went out on a lobster boat with the captain and his four-person crew. We filmed the lobster traps being laid on the seabed in the bright morning sun. Strung together by the score, they were pulled off the deck and down into the water by the force of a sinking anchor at one end and the movement of the boat out from under them at the other, marked by a GPS-tagged buoy. The captain was keen to show us how the practices and technologies used by independent fishermen in the Bay of Fundy were adapting to meet the ecological challenges of the present. The crew tossed female lobsters laden with eggs back into the sea with the bycatch. The metal cage traps came fitted with small windows through which smaller lobsters and other bycatch could escape and were held together with biodegradable bindings so that traps lost at sea (as happens when lines attaching them to buoys break or are cut) would not continue to 'ghost fish' indefinitely on the sea floor. The captain linked these conservation measures to a larger vision of stewardship over the Bay of Fundy's diverse ecologies and to the connection he felt personally to these ecologies having spent much of his life out on this water. More pragmatically, he said it was also a business decision – no lobster fisherman wants to see a decline in lobsters.

I almost never made it to that discussion on the boat that day. We had left Halifax at 3am to make it in good time to our meeting at the wharf at 5:30am that morning but around 5am we ran out of gas, barely making it to a gas station off the highway about a 15 minute drive from the wharf. The station was closed, there was no off-hours pay at the pump, opening time was at 6am, but the Tim Horton's attached to it was open an hour before the pumps (only in Canada, I thought). I called the boat's captain using the wi-fi from the Tim Horton's. The captain was graciously understanding, but the boat couldn't wait for the gas station to open at six. The tide was going out and they had to disembark by 5:30, 5:45 at the latest, before the water sank too low for the boat to safely navigate to open water, well before it would be sitting on the sandy bottom at dock. So we missed the boat, literally left high and dry.

Fortunately for us, the tides in the Bay of Fundy are diurnal, flowing in and out twice daily, such that the time between high and low tide is just under six and a half hours. At 6am we filled up the tank and killed time until, approaching midday, we drove out to the wharf where the boat came in to collect us at the rising tide. We had to clamber down a ladder to the deck, which was about six feet below the dock. We had missed filming with the rising sun, but at least we had made it on board.

In the intervening hours between missing the boat that morning and our reprieve from the consequences of poor planning, I was left to reflect on the ways the tides continue to evade human mastery. They don't wait for petrol stations to open or pause for you to find your Go-Pro. They don't flow nicely past in-stream tidal devices to turn their blades without ripping them loose in the process. In the Anthropocene tides are the vanguards of rising seas, pushing against the edges of land faster than hard engineering solutions can adapt to hold them back. Countries with significant coastal areas are now looking to develop 'coastal realignment' plans, accepting that 'holding the line' against the pressing tides will shortly become financially, and soon thereafter technologically, unsustainable (see, for example, Haasnoot, Lawrence and Magnan, 2021). This realignment of policy marks a startling change from the long dream of mastery that has led up to, *has caused*, the great environmental dislocations of the present. The hierarchical imaginary of human stewardship over tidal ecologies is exposed as unintelligible in the flowing present of ecological feedback loops and planetary tipping points.

Flood

The rhythmic pattern of repetition and change in tidal zones is what Owain Jones (2011) describes as the rhythmpatterning of place, a flowing movement that lends tidal zones the distinction of enacting a constantly shifting timespace in which elements are mixed, separated and remixed at a timescale fully accessible to human senses and temporalities (unlike, say, the movement of Massey's mountains (2005)). For many human observers the rhythms of tidal shores are part of their appeal, the meditative atmosphere of flow and interchange, the ways that edges are created and washed away by the crashing wash of waves and steady ebb and flood of tides. Captivating though it may be, however, the ways that tides shift the shoreline, raise and lower sea levels at dock, and mix salt- and fresh water into unwieldy brackish estuaries is not so amenable to the demands of global capital. Accordingly, one of the great aims of the Modern era has been what Jones (2011) calls the 'smoothing' of tidal rthythmpatterns: the building of breakwaters, seawalls and causeways, impounding bays to create perpetual high water for ports, and dredging, draining and damming estuaries in the name of 'land reclamation'.

The Bay of Fundy has been no exception to this destructive global effort, with the draining of estuarine and salt marsh habitats for agriculture dating back to the Acadian dyke systems of the seventeenth century and the more recent hubris of the twentieth century's hard engineering disrupting estuaries up and down the Bay. One such artefact of hard engineering can be found in Annapolis Royal, about midway up the eastern edge of the Bay of Fundy, at the Annapolis Tidal Generating Station, a newly defunct tidal barrage stretching across the Annapolis estuary.

Essentially marine dams, tidal barrages impound the flood tide behind a wall for later release through turbines embedded in the wall to generate electricity. In the 1970s, with successive oil crises destabilising energy supplies across North America, plans were drawn up to build a massive tidal barrage across the Minas Passage. The amount of energy generated from such an endeavour would have been considerable, but so might the consequences for coastal communities down the coast. A marine scientist long involved in tidal energy research recalled that,

> I had by that time become seriously concerned about any idea of building a barrage in these tidal waters because, for example, one of the designs that they have, if they had built it, would probably have flooded Boston, and that is not a very good solution. You can get an awful lot of energy out of it but Boston and a lot of the communities along the Gulf of Maine coast are right at the high water mark. So, if you raise the tides down there then you have serious implications. (Interview, 4 August 2017)

Despite misgivings like these, plans for a tidal barrage in the Minas Passage were promoted widely around Nova Scotia. Fortunately for Boston, the idea was abandoned when oil prices dropped in the opening years of the 1980s.

A smaller tidal barrage was built, however, as a test site, in Annapolis Royal, where the Annapolis River flows into the Bay of Fundy. The Annapolis Royal Generating Station came online in 1984, generating 30 million kilowatt hours of electricity per year until 2019, when it was permanently shut following the failure of a crucial generator component and a subsequent order from the Department of Fisheries and Oceans (DFO) following a review by the Canadian Scientific Advisory Secretariat (CSAS) on fish mortality associated with the site (Gibson, Fulton and Harper, 2019). Evidence of dead fish around Annapolis Royal was not new; indeed, the CSAS report highlighted the absence of recent data, basing its review largely on studies from the 1990s. Along with calls for more updated research, CSAS suggested that the province of Nova Scotia had failed in its duty to adequately monitor or report fish mortality at the site (Pope, 2019).

Regardless of where the failure in environmental monitoring/reporting occurred, the evidence, both scientific and anecdotal, points to significant ecological damage of the Annapolis estuary behind the Annapolis Royal Tidal Barrage. As quickly became apparent during my research in the Bay of Fundy, memories of disputes over the construction and operation of the tidal barrage at Annapolis Royal and its ongoing ruination of the estuary behind it (thirty-five years of socio-ecological damage cannot easily be undone) have haunted the dispute over the development and testing of a different tidal energy technology, in-stream tidal, in the Minas Passage.

Almost all of the fishers I talk to point to Annapolis as a reference point for what they fear about in-stream tidal energy development in the Minas Passage. Reflecting on the impact of the Annapolis Royal Tidal Barrage, one area lobster fisherman set it in terms of its impacts on the Annapolis River recreational fishery, saying:

> I grew up fishing for striped bass in the river, and the world record striped bass was caught right here in Annapolis Royal and they've been extirpated from the river, they are not there anymore, and the shad are being severely depleted. Sturgeon, which are a listed species, are routinely chopped to bits and washed ashore around the turbine. (Interview, 3 August 2017)

In-stream tidal turbines are a completely different technology from tidal barrages, of course. They don't impound tides like a dam, they sit on the sea floor turning in the tidal stream like underwater wind turbines letting the tidal waters flow around them.

Yet, as the former chief of an area Mi'kmaw Nation explained to me, the Annapolis Royal Tidal Station doesn't loom large in the current debate because people confuse the two technologies; it does so because it stands as a living memory of the dispossession of the Annapolis First Nation from its living estuarine ecology in the name of energy experimentation in the Bay.

> Those turbines [at FORCE] are experimental, and the big distrust is because we have the Annapolis Royal Tidal Station ... that was just an experimentation and here we're stuck with this permanent feature. ... My grandmother, who was chief at the time, was writing letters to the newspapers of great concern and here we are all these years later and of course we're looking at these environmental effects. (Interview, 10 August 2017)

Proponents of tidal energy defend FORCE with the need to 'just get these things in the water to test them' (Interview, 27 July 2017) and the adamant claim that 'theclimate emergency is real' (Interview, 9 August 2017). The latter is rhetorically powerful, but the reality of climate change was not in dispute. The fishers I met with and those publicly opposing FORCE were acutely aware of warming seas and their impacts on the current health and future prospects of the fisheries they rely on for their livelihoods. They are not only witness to the ecological damage climate change is bringing to the Bay of Fundy, but also deeply entangled within the affective ecologies being undone there.

As for the need to 'just get these things in the water' to test their effects, the former chief quoted above went on to raise the question of who bears the greatest risk from testing new technologies. There's a history in Canada, as elsewhere, of experimentation going hand in hand with ongoing colonial violence, of the promise of economic development overriding consideration of First Nation treaty rights (see, for example, Pictou, 2018, 2020). Testing these technologies in the Minas Passage – a sacred site in Mi'kmaw cosmology – without buy-in from or benefit to the Mi'kmaq First Nations along the Bay is, like the bordering of knowledge and authority discussed earlier, a testament to ongoing colonisation structured by Western relations of property and capital (Pictou, 2020).

The significance of Annapolis Royal as a precedent for destructive 'testing' was also a key concern of the non-Indigenous fishermen opposing FORCE, though they don't speak in terms of colonisation and dispossession, a largely unfamiliar and uncomfortable topic for white fishermen. Instead, as the lobster fisherman explained to me, the significance of the Annapolis Royal Tidal Barrage is what it says to fishermen about the order of priorities:

> The precedent set on tidal energy here in Canada by that turbine [at Annapolis Royal] is that you can be proven to have a serious effect on species, you can extirpate a unique genetic strain of striped bass from the river and not be shut down. The tidal turbine in the Annapolis River is still operating on a test permit after thirty-two years, thirty-three years now in operation, and the purpose of the test was to assess a tidal turbine's effects on the ecosystem. (Interview, 31 July 2017)

With the DFO order finally ending the long ecological experiment of the Annapolis Royal Generating Station, it is unclear what the future holds. Fish will no longer get chopped to pieces passing through the turbine, yet the wall in which the turbine was embedded is not coming down. Indeed, among the findings of the CSAS report was that much of the ecological damage to the estuarine habitat behind the tidal barrage pre-dated the turbine there by decades, when the original causeway which was later developed into the tidal barrage was built to 'reclaim' land from estuarine salt marsh for arable agriculture. As the report notes, the construction of the causeway in the early 1960s

> transformed the estuary upriver of the causeway from a well-mixed estuary with about a 10m tidal range (similar to many around the Bay of Fundy) to a highly stratified salt wedge estuary with a tidal range around 0.5m. The Annapolis TiGS [Tidal Generating Station] was constructed at the causeway and has been in operation since 1985 ... its operation increased the tidal range upriver of the causeway to about 1–1.5m. (Gibson, Fulton and Harper, 2019: 5)

The tidal barrage, destructive as it was, had at least allowed some tidal water to re-enter the estuary, not much and not enough, but some. The barrage wasn't the original destroyer of the Annapolis estuary, the causeway came first. Yet the tidal barrage was part of the same pattern of undoing relations, the same attempt to master, or smooth, the tides for economic gain, irrespective of any socio-ecological wreckage it may cause. The fear expressed to me in different ways by different respondents was that in-stream tidal devices, though apparently less damaging than tidal barrages, were also part of these patterns of undoing.

Ebb

Not long after my last trip to the Bay of Fundy in 2018 the controversy over tidal energy began to subside. The only tidal energy turbine then deployed at FORCE, and the subject of most of the dispute, had stopped working for the second time. The turbine was a joint venture of OpenHydro and Emera, and when the former declared bankruptcy in 2018 the latter pulled out. For some time thereafter various parties argued over who would be responsible for removing the turbine as it continued to sit, 'damaged beyond repair', by the tides (Quon, 2018).

Though tidal energy development had stalled, the anxious atmospheres of my fieldwork remained, sustained by a downturn in lobster landings. Then, in September 2020, the Sipekne'katik Nation launched a self- (rather than DFO-) regulated 'moderate livelihood' fishery out of Saulnierville, near St Mary's Bay at the southern edge of the Bay of Fundy. Issuing their own licences and starting before the DFO-authorised commercial lobster-fishing season, the Sipekne'katik Nation took this action as an assertion of their Mi'kmaw treaty right to earn a 'moderate livelihood' from fishing, affirmed (though poorly defined) by the Supreme Court of Canada's 1999 Marshall Decision.

Perceiving a threat to their livelihoods, despite no evidence thereof, members of Nova Scotia's non-Indigenous fishing community showed up on land and on boats in the water in protest. These protests quickly escalated into racist acts of intimidation, violence and vandalism against Sipekne'katik people and property. Over the ensuing weeks acts of intimidation and violence on land and sea continued; Indigenous fishers and leaders were assaulted, flares were fired at Indigenous fishing boats, their lines were cut and 350 of their traps were pulled one night and dumped in front of a DFO building (see Bilefsky, 2020 for a summary account of events). In early October a Sipekne'katik lobster pound (a type of outbuilding for housing live lobster before sale) was burned to the ground overnight (Cooke and Chisholme, 2020). The RCMP (Canada's federal police force) failed to contain the violence and, according to Sipekne'katik accounts, DFO officers only contributed to the atmosphere of harassment by pulling their traps and 'taunting' Indigenous fishers out on the water (quoted in Withers, 2021).

Fisheries experts in Nova Scotia noted that the number of traps licensed by the Sipekne'katik Nation were negligible in the context of the hundreds of thousands of commercial traps licensed in the Bay of Fundy by the DFO (Smith, 2020). Indeed, the 10 boats with a combined total of 500 traps licensed by the Sipekne'katik Nation to fish in Lobster Fishery Area (LFA) 34 in 2020 were dwarfed by the 965 boats licensed to fish with up to 400 traps each in that same area (DFO, 2020). And while LFA 34 is seeing a decline in lobster landings, linking this to the Sipekne'katik fishery is dubious at best. Declining landings in LFA 34 mirror declines being seen across the wider Bay of Fundy, and they pre-date the launch of the Sipekne'katik moderate livelihood fishery (DFO, 2020; Luck, 2021).

Following all of this from the confines of what was beginning to feel like a perpetual Covid-19 lockdown in the UK that autumn cast new light on my earlier conversations with commercial fishermen. The captain that had convinced me of his commitment to ecological conservation two summers ago on the day we went filming out on his boat, was quoted by the CBC, this time using the discourse of ecological stewardship to justify his opposition to the Sipekne'katik fishery. I wondered how many other folks I had spoken to and spent time with over those summers might now be engaging in acts of racist violence (discursive or physical) against Indigenous fishers. It was a sinking feeling.

At the height of the controversy over tidal energy testing in the Minas Passage, the Bay of Fundy Inshore Fishermen's Association and Fundy United (a loose coalition of fishermen and other 'concerned citizens') were pushing hard on the potential negative ecological impacts of the tidal turbines. The former had even sought (unsuccessfully) to gain an injunction in court against the impending deployment of a turbine in 2016 based on their assertion that the environmental impact assessment was inadequate. At the time there seemed to be a promising, if uneasy, allyship emerging between commercial and Indigenous fishers based on their mutual entanglement in and care for the marine environment.

Four years later, however, the former head of the Inshore Fisherman's Association, who had spearheaded the failed court case against FORCE, was giving interviews opposing the Sipekne'katik Nation's moderate livelihood fishery using the discourse of ecological conservation. Ignoring the evidence to the contrary, and disputing the DFO position that lobster landings were down in LFA 34 due in part to a corresponding drop in the number of boats on the water and days spent fishing (combined under the DFO statistic 'units of effort'), the former Association blamed 'Shubie' – shorthand for the Sipekne'katik First Nation – for the decline:

> There's no lobster there to fish for, so they [white fishermen] had to leave. Normally they'd fish every day there for the first three weeks [of the season]. Now the [lobsters] are gone in four or five days because they were already caught by Shubie. (Quoted in Withers, 2020)

In the case of the in-stream tidal turbines at FORCE, there was similarly little evidence to suggest a few turbines would have any significant impact on fish, lobsters or the wider ecology of the Bay of Fundy. Enrolling a discourse of ecological care and responsibility in that case, however, was a way of opposing the logic of ocean privatisation, of reaching out to understand and ally with Indigenous ways of thinking about interconnectedness. Or was it? The new turn gave me doubts. The use of the same discourse to oppose Indigenous groups from exercising their treaty rights seemed only disingenuous, covering up less noble motives.

The circular process of (re)telling and (re)listening to stories lends new meanings and insights (*M's-it No'kmaq* et al., 2021). In its retelling, the story of a white fisherman's concern for the environment revealed a more reactionary, less collaborative tone. In its undertones it reflected a mode of thought rooted in the unthought white supremacy of settler colonialism that lurks within many of today's seemingly benign environmental discourses (Gandy, 2021). This is a mode of thought structured by settler-colonial imaginaries of nature without humans, of environment-as-resource/property and of the linking of stewardship with economic self-interest. This is a mode of thought that does not see its own entanglement within the meshworks of more-than-human affective ecologies.

~

In drawing global environmental shifts into the everyday, the ordinary Anthropocene can be disorienting, forcing realisations that old ways of knowing and being within complex, affective ecologies are no longer feasible. In the Bay of Fundy, as with the rest of the wider Gulf of Maine, lobster landings are down, storms are getting worse, waters are acidifying, undoing enmeshed lifeways as thread after thread is pulled or changed beyond recognition. In Europe and North America tidal energy development is generally positioned as a good news story – a hopeful narrative in which humans might gain redemption through the casting off of fossil fuel dependence. This narrative is difficult to reconcile with my research in the Bay of Fundy, where tidal energy was extending terrestrial property relations and modes of authority into the sea, displacing other relations in its wake. At the same time, resistance to this displacement opened up a space, a fragile and fleeting one as it turns out, for allyship between commercial and Indigenous fishers. The passing of this moment, the re-emergence of deep fractures between these groups, makes for a depressing ending to this chapter. But it is not the end of the story. Some non-Indigenous fishers from my fieldwork and beyond spoke out in support of the Sipekne'katik fishery and hundreds of non-Indigenous Canadians marched through the streets of Halifax in solidarity with Indigenous groups to protest the violence against the Sipekne'katik Nation. This story and the others that make up this chapter are all still unfolding, flowing with and through the deep troubles of caring within meshworks that are rapidly losing threads, fraying at the edges, as well as the uncertain work of weaving new ecological relationships in a time of environmental crisis (Haraway, 2016; Tsing et al., 2017).

References

Albeck-Ripka, L. (2018) Climate change brought a lobster boom. Now it could cause a bust. *The New York Times*, 21 June. Available at: www.nytimes.com/2018/06/21/climate/maine-lobsters.html (accessed 20 September 2021).

Bear, C. (2013) Assembling the sea: materiality, movement and regulatory practices in the Cardigan Bay scallop fishery. *cultural geographies*, 20, 21–41.

Bilefsky, D. (2020) In 'Lobster War,' Indigenous Canadians face attacks by fishermen. *The New York Times*, 10 October. Available at: www.nytimes.com/2020/10/20/world/canada/nova-scotia-lobster-war.html (accessed 20 September 2021).

BirdLife International (2016) *Calidris pusilla. The IUCN Red List of Threatened Species*, 2016: e.T22693373A93400702. Available at: https://dx.doi.org/10.2305/IUCN.UK.2016-3.RLTS.T22693373A93400702.en (accessed 5 November 2021).

Cooke, A. and Chisholm, C. (2020) Large fire destroys lobster facility in southwest Nova Scotia amid escalating fishery tensions. *CBC News*, 17 October. Available at: www.cbc.ca/news/canada/nova-scotia/lobster-facility-nova-scotia-fire-1.5765665 (accessed 20 September 2021).

Gibson, A. J. F., Fulton, S. J. and Harper, D. (2019) Fish mortality and its population-level impacts at the Annapolis Tidal Hydroelectric Generating Station, Annapolis Royal, Nova Scotia: a review of existing scientific literature. *Technical Report of Fisheries and Aquatic Sciences 3305*. Dartmouth, Nova Scotia: Center for Science Advice (CSA), Maritimes Region, Fisheries and Oceans Canada.

DeLoughrey, E. (2017) Submarine futures of the Anthropocene. *Comparative Literature*, 69(1), 32–44.

DeLoughrey, E. M. (2019) *Allegories of the Anthropocene*. Durham: Duke University Press.

DFO (2020) DFO Maritimes Region, LFA 34 & St. Mary's Bay lobster landings by season – 2002–2020. Data released to CBC. Available at: https://docs.google.com/spreadsheets/d/1f8i7ZandwJNp5PSq2d4yfwotEoTVDs4v/edit#gid=1011334929 (accessed 20 September 2021).

Dirzo, R., Young, H. S., Galetti, M., Ceballos, G., Isaac, N. J. B. and Collen, B. (2014) Defaunation in the Anthropocene. *Science*, 345, 401–406.

FORCE (2016) *Environmental Effects Monitoring Programs*. Halifax: Fundy Ocean Research Center for Energy.

Fredriksen, A. (2021) Haunting, ruination and encounter in the ordinary Anthropocene: storying the return of Florida's wild flamingos. *cultural geographies*, 28(3), 531–545.

Funch, P. (2017) Synchronies at risk: the intertwined lives of horseshoe crabs and red knot birds. In A. L. Tsing, N. Bubandt, E. Gan and H. A. Swanson (eds) *Arts of Living on a Damaged Planet: Ghosts and Monsters of the Anthropocene*. Minneapolis: University of Minnesota Press, pp. 141–154.

Gandy, M. (2021) An Arkansas parable for the Anthropocene. *Annals of the American Association of Geographers*, 112(2), 368–386.

Haasnoot, M., Lawrence, J. and Magnan, A. K. (2021) Pathways to coastal retreat. *Science*, 372, 1287–1290.

Haraway, D. J. (2016) *Staying with the Trouble: Making Kin in the Chthulucene*. Durham: Duke University Press.

Ingold, T. (2010) *Being Alive*. London: Routledge.

Jones, O. (2011) Lunar–solar rhythmpatterns: towards the material cultures of tides. *Environment and Planning A*, 43(10), 2285–2303.

Kerr, S., Colton, J., Johnson, K. and Wright, G. (2015) Rights and ownership in sea country: implications of marine renewable energy for indigenous and local communities. *Marine Policy*, 52, 108–115.

Latour, B. (2018) *Down to Earth: Politics in the New Climatic Regime*. Cambridge: Polity.

Le Bris, A., Mills, K. E., Wahle, R. A., Chen, Y., Alexander, M. A., Allyn, A. J., Schuetz, J. G., Scott, J. D. and Pershing, A. J. (2018) Climate vulnerability and resilience in the most valuable North American fishery.

Proceedings of the National Academy of Sciences of the United States of America, 115, 1831–1836.

Luck, S. (2021) Lobster landings data released by DFO show complex picture. *CBC News*, 8 March. Available at: www.cbc.ca/news/canada/nova-scotia/lobster-landings-data-released-by-dfo-show-complex-picture-1.5935393 (accessed 17 September 2021).

Mann, H. A. R., Hamilton, D. J., Paquet, J. M., Gratto-Trevor, C. L. and Neima, S. G. (2017) Effects of extreme tidal events on Semipalmated Sandpiper (Calidris pusilla) migratory stopover in the Bay of Fundy, Canada. *Waterbirds*, 40(1), 41–49.

Massey, D. (2005) *For Space*. London: Sage.

Mizrahi, D. S. and Peters, K. A. (2009) Relationships between sandpipers and horseshoe crab in Delaware Bay: a synthesis. In J. T. Tanacredi, M. L. Botton and D. Smith (eds) *Biology and Conservation of Horseshoe Crabs*. Boston: Springer US, pp. 65–87.

M'sit No'kmaq, Marshall, A., Beazley, K. F., Hum, J., joudry, shalan, Papadopoulos, A., Pictou, S., Rabesca, J., Young, L. and Zurba, M. (2021) 'Awakening the sleeping giant': re-Indigenization principles for transforming biodiversity conservation in Canada and beyond. *FACETS*, 6(1), 839–869.

Peters, K. (2020) The territories of governance: unpacking the ontologies and geophilosophies of fixed to flexible ocean management, and beyond. *Philosophical Transactions of the Royal Society* B, 375: 20190458.

Peters, K. and Steinberg, P. (2019) The ocean in excess: towards a more-than-wet ontology. *Dialogues in Human Geography*, 9(3), 293–307.

Pictou, S. (2018) The origins and politics, campaigns and demands by the international fisher peoples' movement: an Indigenous perspective. *Third World Quarterly*, 39(7), 1411–1420.

Pictou, S. (2020) Decolonizing decolonization: an Indigenous feminist perspective on the recognition and rights framework. *South Atlantic Quarterly*, 119, 371–391.

Pope, A. (2019) Testing the future of tidal energy in Nova Scotia. Canadian Geographic, 29 August. Available at: www.canadiangeographic.ca/article/testing-future-tidal-energy-nova-scotia (accessed 3 September 2021).

Quon, A. (2018) Cape Sharp Tidal turbine was 'damaged beyond repair' in September. *Global News Canada*, 13 November. Available at: https://globalnews.ca/news/4644316/cape-sharp-tidal-turbine-damaged/ (accessed 20 September 2021).

Rose, D. (2013) What if the angel of history were a dog? *Cultural Studies Review*, 12(1), 67–78.

Simpson, L. (2017) *As We Have Always Done: Indigenous Freedom through Radical Resistance*. Minneapolis: University of Minnesota Press.

Smith, E. (2020) 'Scale of Sipekne'katik fishery won't harm lobster stocks, says prof. *CBC News*, 22 September. Available at: www.cbc.ca/news/canada/nova-scotia/mi-kmaw-fishery-moderate-livelihood-megan-bailey-conservation-dalhousie-university-1.5734030 (accessed 17 September 2021).

Stengers, I. (2021) Putting problematization to the test of our present. *Theory, Culture & Society*, 38, 71–92.

Stewart, K. (2007) *Ordinary Affects*. Durham: Duke University Press.

Tsing, A., Swanson, H., Gan, E. and Bubandt, N. (eds) (2017) *Arts of Living on a Damaged Planet*. Minneapolis: University of Minnesota Press.

Van Dooren, T. (2014) *Flight Ways: Life and Loss at the Edge of Extinction*. New York: Columbia University Press.

Van Roy, P., Orr, P. J., Botting, J. P., Muir, L. A., Vinther, J., Lefebvre, B., El Hariri, K. and Briggs, D. E. (2010) Ordovician faunas of Burgess Shale type. *Nature*, 465(7295), 215–218.

Withers, P. (2020) The lobster catch in St. Marys Bay is down, but there's little consensus on why. *CBC News*, 6 October. Available at: www.cbc.ca/news/canada/nova-scotia/lobster-st-marys-bay-mikmaw-fishery-1.5751040 (accessed 17 September 2021).

Withers, P. (2021) An appeal for calm as tensions rise again over N.S. Mi'kmaw lobster fishery. *CBC News*, 11 August. Available at: www.cbc.ca/news/canada/nova-scotia/appeal-for-calm-as-tensions-rise-mikmaw-lobster-fishery-1.6136858 (accessed 20 September 2021).

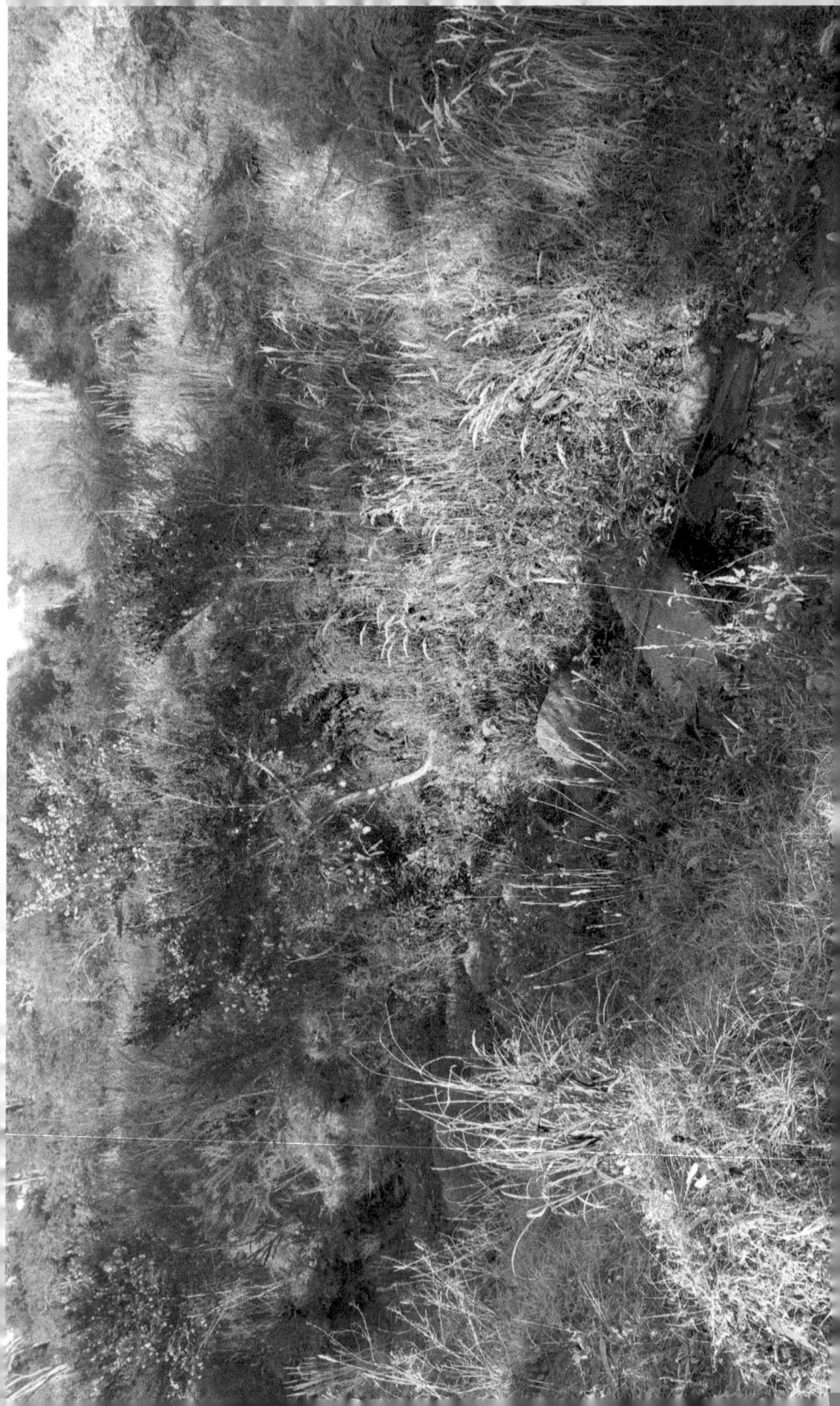

13

Follow the water

Perdita Phillips

I have been travelling intermittently from Whadjuk Noongar country to Menang country in the southwest of Western Australia. My visits to Albany/Kinjarling were prompted by the *Follow the water* project, which experimented with different strategies of experientially knowing water and drains.

One meaning of 'Kinjarling' is 'place of rain'. The city is dominated by two granodiorite hills whose bald rock surfaces shed water that runs either southwest, through the older town and its stone drains, down to Princess Harbour, or southeast along Yakamia Creek, through more recent suburbs, industrial areas, drained swamps and the peri-urban fringe, into Oyster Harbour. Albany began as a British military outpost in 1826. The recent dual naming of Albany means that the hills now have more nuanced identifiers. Mt Melville is Kardarup and Mt Clarence recedes as the *genus loci* of Corndarup regrows.

The steep slopes above and through the old town have always been prone to flash-flooding. Originally wooden and then open stone drains were built to handle the flow; to transport water as quickly as possible, to *get rid of the problem*. The construction of drains in the late eighteenth and early nineteenth century represented a considerable civic investment as well as a history of extraction. Rock was quarried from the nearby mounts and interceptor drains were built into each hill in an attempt to control the flow of water. There was care in the crafted construction of these drains, with each stone skilfully placed. But water is elusive and always finding its way. Even on into summer, water still exudes from underground in small seeps, across footpaths, onto roads, slowly making its way through the urban fabric, downhill.

On the other side of the two hills, settler colonialism turned what was once a large area of swampy ground covered in Wattie (*Taxandria juniperina*) into cow paddocks, rubbish tips and then sports grounds. Along its course Yakamia Creek repeatedly turns from drain to creek to drain again. But water remembers. It returns to flood low-lying areas. The amount of phosphorus, BOD (Biological Oxygen Demand, a measure of organic pollution potential in water) and *E. coli* are carefully measured for their collective impact on Oyster Harbour/Miaritch. At the mouth of Yakamia, slow sea-level rises are reclaiming swampy ground that, in geological terms, had only recently been a shelly inlet.

I originally came to Albany/Kinjarling to listen to places. In the first half of the project I created opportunities for others to *follow the water* from their house or workplace, down to the nearest waterbody. At the end of each walk we listened to the soundscape and made an on-the-spot cyanotype recording of what we had experienced and collected.

Later, working with local historian Malcolm Traill and civil engineer Fred Wallefeld, we created a public walk, *Dealing with the runoff*, that went downwards, from the drinking water tanks in the bushland on Mt Melville to the oldest stone drains near the heart of the city. Following an acknowledgement to country, people listened to historic newspaper reports on municipal budgets, stories of cholera, sewage, flooding and engineering philosophy as they descended through bushland and streets.

~

The white-tipped tail of a nocturnal Ngwayir/Western ringtail possum is made for climbing. It curls lifeless, on the side of the road, where its body, just smaller than a cat, has crawled after being hit by a vehicle. The sight of the inanimate body was, and remains, paralysing. So much loss and extinction in the reckoning. Like much that faces us in contemporary life, nothing substantial can be done in this immediate moment, other than being 'with' (Boscacci, 2018). And yet water remains in an animate reflection. It is a matter of working out how to act in impure and difficult circumstances – and how to act at different scales at different times (Phillips, 2022).

This conundrum of how to act in entangled circumstances was present in many forms in *Follow the water*. It was present in the environmental weeds that lined the waterways of Albany. The designation of weeds – as plants out of place – depends upon complex cultural values bound up in settler cultures with belonging and unbelonging (Trigger et al., 2008; Trigger and Mulcock, 2005). Weeds displace and overwhelm other species, but they are taking advantage of water in a Mediterranean climate – and the often forgotten spaces of drains dug through the landscape. It is a good example of what Lauren Berlant (2016) refers to as the *awkwardness* of the commons. Where is the agency of the weed? Where is the agency of the *other* plants that are overwhelmed? What happens when there is a *flood* of weeds? Do we need to hold onto opposing ideas – weeds and non-weeds – at the same time? I take three environmental scientists on a walk to rediscover the quiet paths of Yakamia Creek. 'Yuckymia has turned back into Yakamia', one of them says. They see the weeds, but also the need to hold in their thoughts, the flourishing of impure places.

In common with those of many cities, the drains of Albany were originally built as hard, impervious surfaces to convey a problem away, out of sight, to a receiving water body, as quickly as possible. More recently, I witnessed the building of the Centennial Park Biofiltration Wetland on Yakamia Creek as an example of newer conceptions of sustainable urban stormwater design. The function of stormwater management has expanded outwards from preserving infrastructure or public health and safety to 'protect and restore the health of waterways, estuaries, wetlands and oceans ... [and to] improve the liveability of urban communities' (Department of Water and Environmental Regulation, n. d.). By diverting peak water flow *out* of Yakamia Creek, nitrogen and phosphorus can be absorbed by reeds and plants living in and around the overflow basins. At the same time, the weedy overgrown channel had been engineered into a trapezoidal drain profile lined with geotextiles to smother weeds and encourage the growth of selected 'native' species. But returning to Albany a year later I saw how the water was quick to wash away the precisely modelled spillway and otherwise modify the human-designed facility. The weeds were returning.

How can places be made that restore and flourish without purity? How can settler culture give up some of its notions of engineering and control? How can we be 'both' and 'and' at the same time? Building upon the works of Berenice Fisher and Joan Tronto (1990), and María Puig de la Bellacasa (2017), I use the term 'porous repair' to map a process which takes the more difficult course of looking forward instead of restoring back to a past state. Porous repair can be small; working across, in and through boundaries. It can be open ended and speculative. Porous repair is wrapped up in failure at the same time as it is hopeful and preparing for future worlds (Phillips, 2022).

This sequence of photographs brings together some of the contradictory states of porous repair. Each pair welds the uncertain state of both/and together in visual form. 'There is risk; but there is also a sharing' (Pollock, 2010: 831) implied in these works: no matter how impoverished or uneven, life carries on, all the way down to tiny globules of algae, taking advantage of any available water seepage, to grow and flourish.

Acknowledgements

As a visitor to Kinjarling/Albany, I pay my respects to elders past, present and emerging of the Menang Noongar people. Parts of this project were supported by the City of Albany through the Vancouver Arts Centre and the State Government of Western Australia through DLGSCI-funded SymbioticA Residencies for Western Australian artists and researchers.

References

Berlant, L. (2016) The commons: infrastructures for troubling times. *Environment and Planning D: Society and Space*, 34(3), 393–419. https://doi.org/10.1177/0263775816645989.

Boscacci, L. (2018) Wit(h)nessing. *Environmental Humanities*, 10(1), 343–347. https://doi.org/https://doi.org/10.1215/22011919-4385617.

Department of Water and Environmental Regulation (n. d.) *Stormwater*. State Government of Western Australia. Available at: www.water.wa.gov.au/urban-water/urban-development/stormwater (accessed 18 July 2021).

Fisher, B. and Tronto, J. (1990) Toward a feminist theory of caring. In E. K. Abel and M. K. Nelson (ds) *Circles of Care: Work and Identity in Women's Lives*. Albany: State University of New York Press, pp. 35–62.

Phillips, P. (2022) Seeping, maintaining, flooding and repairing: how to act in a both/and world. *Swamphen: A Journal of Cultural Ecology*, 8, 1–25.

Puig de la Bellacasa, M. (2017) *Matters of Care: Speculative Ethics in More than Human Worlds*. Minneapolis: University of Minnesota Press.

Pollock, G. (2010) Aesthetic wit(h)nessing in the era of trauma. *EurAmerica*, 40, 829–886.

Trigger, D. S. and Mulcock, J. (2005) Native vs exotic: cultural discourse about flora, fauna and belonging in Australia. In A. G. Kungolos, C. A. Breddia and E. Beriatos (eds) *Sustainable Development and Planning II*, vol. 2. Southampton: WIT Press, pp. 1301–1309.

Trigger, D., Mulcock, J., Gaynor, A. and Toussaint, Y. (2008) Ecological restoration, cultural preferences and the negotiation of 'nativeness' in Australia. *Geoforum*, 39(3), 1273–1283. https://doi.org/10.1016/j.geoforum.2007.05.010.

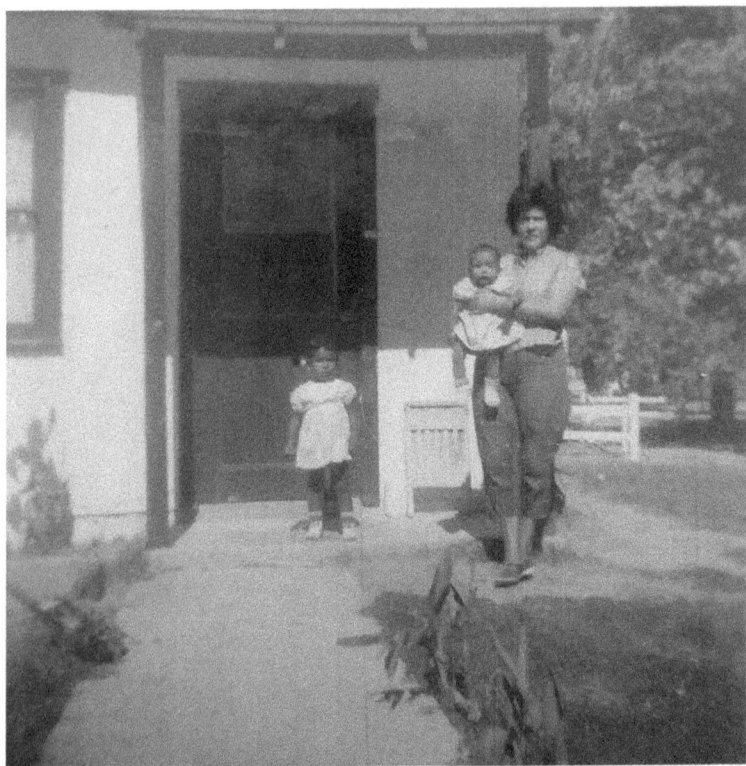

14

Glacial erratic

Stephanie Krzywonos

Lake

Mount Pisgah, a sand dune, watches Lake Michigan, a wide freshwater sea. I ascend the dune's crest through a forest of beeches, maples and oaks on a zig-zagging wooden staircase. Near the top, trees yield to wispy shrubs, pastel grasses and a dayblue sky. An observation deck tops the summit; hands and wind have smoothed its wooden railings. I try to glimpse the other shore. I can't.

On the foredune, near the level beach below, spiky marram grass grows in patches; its underground rhizomatic web buffers the mountain of sand from water. Below the railing, the dune is a bare basin, a 'blowout'. Naked sand, the colour of light brown sugar, slides towards the water. Too much traffic has killed the vegetation and now wind eats this dune. A neighbouring beach designates dunes for human play; hills of finely ground quartz cushion running feet and tumbling bodies perfectly. But Mount Pisgah is off-limits to people. Instead, sand reed grass moves into the basin like platelets towards a wound. It was here, as a girl, that I learned from a sun-bleached placard how glaciers formed the lake.

~

The pictures on the placard only show the pale back of the glacier, its face burrowed into the ground, gouging the earth. I know the lake is deep, but I don't know what glaciers are. My dad explains the ice age, that all this was frozen, that glaciers are just ice. I stare at the shimmering water and try to fathom a heavy sky-sized mountain of ice, something blue and white and cold, but all I can imagine are sledding hills and remnants of ploughed snow in parking lots that last long into Michigan's spring. I ask if the glaciers are all gone and dad tells me glaciers live on mountains and congregate at the top and bottom of the earth. That this lake and these dunes are a massive footprint the glacier left on the land as it headed north.

~

Glaciers, by definition, are always moving. In their abandoned homes, glacial ghosts are everywhere. During their wanderings north and south, they scratch rocks. Their graffiti – long striations. They mould hills, scatter ponds and lakes, carve fjords and valleys as they seek suitable habitats. Glaciers are migrants and great collectors of things, picking up earth, even slabs of bedrock, as they rove elsewhere. Their piles of debris – sand, gravel, boulders – are called moraines. Long Island, in New York, is a moraine.

Glaciers also leave subtle traces. A pebble, rock or large boulder whose colour, shape and substance don't resemble its surroundings – a non-native – is likely a glacial erratic. Erratics take their name from the Latin word *errare*, which means to wander, roam, ramble. *Errare* also means to make a mistake. Through erratics, glaciers speak. They say: You are entwined with us. They ask: Who is a glacier? And what or who is an erratic?

~

Flora Yolanda, my mother, is from California. She met my father, Stephen, a Pennsylvanian, at a pub in England, where they were stationed with the US Air Force. I was raised in Michigan because my mother's brother Ed married Perla, who lived in the same makeshift neighbourhood for migrant farmworkers. One evening, in the fertile valley between California's coast and mountains, my Tia Perla's sister Gloria visited a new bar with her girlfriends and met Grimaldo, who was visiting from Michigan, a lush peninsula. They married and pulled Ed and Perla along to Michigan with them. After a scouting trip, as my family drove back to Pennsylvania to pack our things and move to a part of Michigan colonised by the Dutch, I kept scratching my neck – chickenpox. Moving, I thought, was an error.

~

I leave my classroom to use the bathroom and pause in an empty hallway to inspect my class's artwork. I'm seven. We were each given an outline of a face and instructed to 'colour ourselves in'. I am one of three kids who scribbled dark hair and dark eyes. We are brown, surrounded by blues, hazels and blondes. I sense difference, and the difference makes my stomach hurt.

My mom volunteers to translate English to Spanish for my school-mates' parents; she helps their relatives fill out paperwork and find jobs besides farm labour. Hearing Spanish spoken embarrasses me.

Sometimes, when I leave the house for school in the mornings, I find the gift of a five-gallon bucket of whatever is ripe sitting on our doorstep. My favourites are buckets of blueberries, each little fruit a dusty dark blue. Once, I plunged my whole arm in. It came out sticky and coated in red juice.

~

Another teenager asks me if my family came here legally. The question baffles me. My grandparents, Josefina and Eduardo, came to the United States because the US Government recruited Mexicans to work on American farms in the 1950s, offering green cards and sending buses to bring them. They migrated to the United States with their two young sons in a pick-up truck, which they lived in for a week, parked under an old and wide tree. My grandfather drove to work every day, leaving my grandmother and young uncles in the tree's care. When the truck broke, he walked, departing before sunrise and returning after sunset. Eventually, they moved into a sod house in a settlement called Medio Camino – 'Half Way' – by its residents.

~

I'm twenty. After a crushing meeting with a psychiatrist – who assures me I'm not demon-possessed, but pills will help – I drive to the lake, as usual, for solace. The beach is empty except for a driftwood stump, smooth and naked of bark, upright and planted on the border between water and shore, its roots reaching into the sand. I stand on the stump, staring at the soothing horizon, where the lake mingles with the sky.

The glacier is gone, but it has marked me. I don't know this yet, but in eight years I will follow glaciers geographically and they will carry me deep into the past.

Glacial till

We live during earth's fifth major ice age, the Quaternary System, which began 2.6 million years ago, the same time the Pleistocene began. An 'ice age' means glaciers exist somewhere on earth. Epochs without glaciers – when earth's poles and tops of mountains are ice free – are called greenhouse periods.

Ice ages experience pulses of warmer and cooler weather. During cold pulses, 'glacial periods', glaciers bloom. The last glacial period began about 115,000 years ago and was one of about twenty glacial periods that occurred during the Pleistocene. We live in a warm pulse, when glaciers wilt, an 'interglacial period' called the Holocene, which began almost 12,000 years ago at the end of the Pleistocene. Graphs of glacial–interglacial cycles depicting temperature, carbon dioxide and methane shifts look like a heartbeat.

~

During the Pleistocene, glaciers perched in Arizona's mountains; runoff from their vigorous glacial streams created canyons. Alluvial fans of debris that spilled from canyons' mouths are still there, in what is now the desert. Between 14,000 and 12,000 years ago, the glacial period ended and the last of the Arizonan glaciers died. The region dried and the modern Sonoran Desert ecosystem was born.

~

During a visit to Arizona, my mother wept at her mother Josefina's kitchen table because she could not get pregnant after three years of trying. My grandmother's neighbour, a traditional healer, walked by and heard my mother's voice breaking through her tears. The neighbour walked into the Sonoran Desert, among the long-rooted mesquite trees and saguaro cacti, to gather plants for tea. A few weeks after my mother drank it, she became pregnant with me.

When I was three, I remember standing under the cutting board that pulled out from the counter in Granma Josie's kitchen. As she rolled round tortillas above my head, white flour floated to the ground around me like snow.

Granma Josie grew up as the daughter of a single mother, a baker of large chewy tortillas in the border town of Nogales in the Sonoran Desert. She told me when she was born she had blisters on her cheeks from her mother's pregnant belly being too close to a hot stove.

In my oldest family story from Mexico, two ancestors met by the River Sonora. She washed clothes in the river; he passed by on a horse and noticed her. I picture her in a simple dress and her thick black rope of hair tucked under her hat. Love was instant and she married him in his village that evening.

~

In 2008, archaeologist Jason De Leon began documenting debris the estimated half a million Latin American migrants per year leave in the Sonoran Desert on their journeys to the United States. Sun-bleached backpacks, food wrappers, water bottles, toilet paper, ragged t-shirts, empty cortisone cream tubes, packets of refried beans, cigarettes and sun-dried children's shoes dot the sand. Most of what he finds is considered trash. To Jason, the scraps are important, artefacts of a larger story. Sometimes he finds bones and human remains. Jason hopes more people will see this desert as sacred ground and the people who cross it as more than statistics.

Trough

Fourteen thousand years ago, as the planet re-warmed, the glacier that formed Lake Michigan – a lobe of the Laurentide Ice Sheet – began retreating, 'ablating', northwards. The Laurentide covered most of northern North America for tens of thousands of years. For a long time, experts believed the Laurentide's northward retreat opened an ice-free path – and humans arrived in North America. A closer inspection of glacial erratics revealed experts were wrong. The morphological dance of the Laurentide and Cordilleran Ice Sheets caused ice-free corridors to repeatedly open and close, but no easy ice-free path correlates with when we believe humans first arrived in North America from Asia. Either humans came much earlier than originally thought or humans came via the coast or over ice. We don't know. But we know humans and glaciers were migrating in the same place around the same time.

~

On an evening flight from Seattle to Anchorage, on my way to a job I took so I could see glaciers, the sun lowers itself into the Pacific as the plane departs. The further north we travel, the brighter the evening becomes. The plane traces the land's curve along the Gulf of Alaska, the route humans took to enter North America. From the plane's port-side oval window, I see them. I'm shocked by how many there are. The glacier-lined coast resembles cilia. The ice, like veins, bleeds into the sea.

~

My friend Jacob and I walk to the foot of Exit Glacier, a toe of the Harding Ice Field, a remnant of the Pleistocene. We picnic with wine, cheese and bread from a grocery store. Giddily, we eat chunks of ice broken from the glacier. The ice crackles as it dissolves in our mouths; we inhale the released ancient air. Jacob scoops nearby sand and lets it fall through his fingers, over and over.

~

On a mute foggy morning, a few companions and I kayak through an Alaskan fjord to watch Aialik Glacier calve. We paddle through the fjord's nave, leaving mossy trees behind for rock walls, soon inhabited by ice. The air chills. Shrivelled ice floats past. Shy harbour seals stretch their necks and peer at us from icebergs, scanning for threat. Aialik appears, a soft cliff, bone white and faint cerulean blue. I stop paddling and undulate in the water, eating bread and waiting for the crash of ice falling into the sea.

The elders of the Alutiiq people, indigenous to this place, say Aialik means something like 'dangerous, fearful, surprising place to be respected and revered'. One elder says Aialik can mean something akin to: 'OH MY GOD!' Other Alaskan elders say glaciers are wilful, capricious, easily excited by human intemperance, but placated by quick-witted human responses. If people are not deferential in their presence, glaciers are known to swallow people. They also respond to human insolence with deluges of water. Aialik's roar echoes as it self-amputates into the bay. Through my body, through the kayak's thin hull, I feel the bay respond with heavy rolls of water. The walls of the fjord quiet. It seems irreverent to keep eating. Something immense is present here besides the glacier.

~

The lodge I work at in Alaska has a sauna, a hewn log cabin, on the banks of the Kenai, a glacially fed river. Its steaming, fragrant wood stove illuminates our faces in the dark. When we get too hot, we ease into the frigid river, careful to evade the current's grip. The sharp temperature change awakens our skin.

The river's water is a vivid and surprising creamy blue. My coworker says glaciers grind the land and rocks beneath them into a powder so fine the particles suspend in water instead of sinking. 'Rock flour', reflecting sunlight, creates bright blue water. When she tells me it's possible to work in Antarctica, where most of the glaciers live, I know where I'm migrating next.

Desert

At their maximum, Pleistocene glaciers covered one-third of earth's surface. Now, they cover only 10 to 11 per cent. The 'Snowball Earth' theory says glaciers covered the entire planet (or left a band of slush at the equator) during three separate epochs. Glaciers can belong anywhere.

The third Snowball Earth ended 635 million years ago, a time before our oldest animal fossils, and the second Snowball Earth ended about 710 million years ago. Each lasted about 10 million years. But the first time earth glistened as a white ball happened 2.2 billion years ago – half the age of the planet. Scientists link this epoch to the oxygenation of our atmosphere – the creation of the air we breathe. Some believe all three Snowball Earths paved the way for the Cambrian Explosion, the emergence of complex multicellular organisms. Before, the only life forms were protists, organisms that are neither animals nor plants nor fungi.

~

Through a window, on my fifth migration to Antarctica, I watch chunks of glaciers laze their way north through the sea. Then open water disappears. Beyond firm cliffs of ice, snow unfurls as far as I can see, and my world becomes an orb of ice. The only visible land-masses are nunatuks – the tops of 'lonely mountains' – emerging from ice. The sun watches glaciers as they slide around these elderly peaks.

~

It's June, winter in Antarctica. I'm in the dark in the desert with the glaciers. After the sun abandoned us in April, the sky rippled towards complete darkness. When civil twilight disappeared in May, my world – everyone and everything – ended at the edge of the research station's floodlights. Tonight, I'm rummaging through a Mormon-run genealogy website exploring my father's family tree. I trace roots for thousands of years. Born in Hungary, died in New Jersey. Born in France, died in Quebec. Born in first-century Jerusalem, died in Britain. Ancient names read like obscure flora: Cerwyn, Dunvallo, Numa, Withemir, Boudicca, Waldrada. Penardin of the Druids. Vandalar of the Osogoths. Laodice of Syria. Born in China. Born in Norway. Born in Sparta. Accuracy aside, the net of their names, their years and their places cradles me in the dark.

   In a few days, my mom will receive her 23 and Me DNA test results. Blended with our known Yaqui and Portuguese ancestry is Ashkenazi Jew. I have never contemplated Jewish people seeking a new life in Mexico.

Mountain

Five glaciers remain in Mexico. Three of them – Pecho ('chest'), Panza ('belly') and Suroriental – live on Iztaccíhuatl, 'sleeping woman', a dormant volcano and Mexico's third-highest peak. The other two – El Norte and Noroeste – live on Citlaltépetl, 'star mountain', also a volcano, Mexico's tallest mountain and the continent's third-highest peak.

   On air-conditioned buses, I watch Iztaccíhuatl and Citlaltépetl in the distance. Their ice-tipped peaks, the colour of bright white clouds, look stark against the sky. Even though these Mexican gla-ciers are surrounded by recent snowfall, they are starving. The air is too warm for them to sufficiently feed. The surrounding arid land-scape offers no escape route.

Hugo Delgado, a glaciologist who has spent his career studying Mexico's glaciers, estimates all five will be extinct by 2050. Empty volcanic slopes and stones 'scattered like bones' will be all that's left.

~

On this trip to Mexico – my first as an adult – I didn't journey to see glaciers, but to visit different migrants, the eastern monarch butter-flies in their winter home.

Around 20,000 years ago, the Laurentide reached its maximum southern point. As it retreated, the butterflies expanded their migra-tion northwards, as far as Canada. No individual monarch makes the round-trip journey; it takes at least three generations to complete the migration. The butterflies know how to get to a forest in Mexico they haven't been to. How long the butterflies have been migrating is a mystery.

My partner Nathan and I are in Mariposa Monarca Santuario El Rosario, ascending a small mountain forested with Oyamel pines with our guide, an old woman with a chestnut horse named Estrella. My paltry Spanish embarrasses me, but we manage to communi-cate. Dead butterflies and parts of dead butterflies sprinkle the path like petals. As we climb higher, the clusters of rusty scales on conifers grow thicker. Orange wings bloom overhead. The movement of but-terflybodies sounds like soft rain. It feels right to be here.

Not all monarchs migrate, but nearly all these butterflies will dis-perse northward. Their grandchildren or great-grandchildren will be the ones to seek refuge in these trees. Some will be born in Canada, north of Lake Superior, a glacial footprint deeper than Lake Michigan. As they pump their wings, flying thousands of miles to this forest, the migrants will make an erratic turn, navigating around a mountain that no longer exists. Some scientists believe the mountain may have been one of the highest in North America, now gone for millennia. All that's left of the mountain is the butterflies' flight path. Memory, deep in the flesh, can outlast even a stone.

Submerge

The urban Liffey and the rural Churn, the disappearing tarn on kunanyi, the mountain springs in the Cairngorms, the stagnant swimming ponds of the de Moeren estate – each invites us to question what happens if we take the plunge and submerge our own watery bodies in other bodies of water. Exploring questions of ownership, trespass, transgression and transformation, Submerge is a reflection on the boundary-dissolving capacities of water. Dipping our bodies through the silky murk, swimming with the Goddess Cuda, under trees, and in ink, with silt-slicked skin and numb fingers and toes, we move through water, through worlds and through words, ending the collection soaked through.

~

15

17 bridges

Vanessa Daws

There is a sense of empowerment as we stride through the city bare foot in our togs, swim caps and goggles. At that moment we own the Liffey, this is our space, we are indestructible. The cars honk their horns and people stop us in the streets and ask what we are doing. We climb up rather ungainly, helping each other, making sure we don't fall before we jump, we line up on each bridge, an audience gathers, the anticipation of the jump.

At what point do we trespass?

While standing on the railings of a civic structure spanning the city's river?

Or once we have left that bridge and are flying through air, the gap between land and water?

Or once we have broken the river surface with our toes and shot beneath it into the brown depths of the Liffey where we eventually stop going down, our bodies adjust and we start to float back up through the veil of bubbles to catch our breath at the surface.

But can you swim in the Liffey?

Who do you ask?

Who owns water?

16

Churn

JLM Morton

In 2021, I swam, walked and waded along the River Churn in Gloucestershire, UK, just over 23 miles from its source at Seven Springs to its confluence with the Thames at Cricklade. I followed the river slowly but surely, out of any order or sequence and often trespassing, picking out sections to swim-walk when cracks of time opened up in my life as a writer and mother to young children. I usually headed off spontaneously and travelled light with little more than an ordnance survey map, dry bag, phone camera/voice recorder and my lovely, daft dog, Biscuit. The rough field notes from these experiences can be viewed online by scanning the QR code below.

A native of Cirencester, the Churn is my home river. I've known it for over forty years, playing in and around it as a child growing up, watching the water voles dart through the crowsfoot, paddling and fishing for snotty dogs and minnows, shooting along it on tractor inner tubes where the flow ran high at the water meadows. What I had anticipated would be a project about movement, migration and invasion, developed during the journey into a playful poem sequence with found text marginalia that responds to a fascination with home, belonging, motherhood, ritual and a conversation with the genius loci embodied in the iron age 'goddess' of the Cotswold hills and rivers, Cuda.

I: Source

and I have been away but you run through me

your whole life ahead behind around

a whole floodplain of pastness and presence

compressed into oolite blue clay cornbrash

urgent as longing dragging at my body

water's memory is a home I stumble

into a tacky shrine to a source of life

littered with wax and metal white cider

libations poured into headwaters

that run below the A436

and dump in a stagnant pub-side pond

Cuda's place Cuda's wold oh goddess Cuda

summoned and churning ex nihilo

your body's secretions inquire of my need

Stone Inscription
HIC TUUS O TAMESINE
PATER SEPTEMCEMINUS
FONS / 'Here, O Father
Thames, is your sevenfold
spring'.

**Trip Advisor Seven
Springs Pub Review**
*** 'Not the best'
* 'Wouldn't visit again
unfortunately'

Field Note
Attachment to place is a
kind of family.

II: Coberley

I bring bread and apples to your stone relief

spill my blood on your minerals my wound

a request for love the soft plates of my feet

are pestled on the debris of a

tropical sea and its upheavals

a river on its bones I follow

my desire path walking a borderland

where the way follows the water follows

wall between wildness and civility

brimming cow parsley mother die ground ivy

last year's white weeds ossified the buzzards

circle above the agrochemical drift

my body falls in a bed of iris

spears my silt slicked skin an offering

Plant Folklore

Another vernacular name, 'Mother die' or 'Mummy die', was used to frighten children into thinking that if they picked cow parsley, their mother would die. This was intended to deter children from potentially picking deadly hemlock.

III: Rendcomb, South Cerney

I clamber on your winter wreckage

a wildfire looking for the comfort

of water in the valley of nettles

dead trees are snagged with feedbags grey green
sludge

amphibious tails of filth road after road

fence and spike and gate and barb Private Land

Keep to the Path! do not go in search of

flying things: meadow brown wagtail wood pigeon

as ordinary as home is here

reaching for your arterial walls grown

thick with fireweed for the stink and bloom

of elderflowers that grow in easy crevices

I have gone astray searching for my owner

where poplar sings of courage to the wind

Field Note
I divert and head
downriver walking the
shallow riverbed and am
soon met with four strings
of barbed wire fencing
off land and river. I climb
through.

WhatsApp Message
That's Colesbourne
Estate, Marsden Estate
and College land. It's all
private.

Trespass
In England, if you're by
a river, in a river or on
a river, there's a 97%
chance you're not allowed
to be there.

IV: Water Meadows

I follow the cow path cow dung dock down

to the watering place full with water mint

with longing grabbing over the stock fence

and find others who are searching too

hunched and hooded figures looking for what?

are we fools holding fast to a notion

of permanence in this place of childhood

of swim and play the knowing even then

a sacred line was crossed latchkey kid

left lonely to rummage in the river

netting minnows snotty dogs sticklebacks

lifting stones to see what lurked beneath

I see mum in red beads tie-dye sundress

childhood's one bright day and what I'm chasing

Being You

We perceive the world not as it is, but as it is useful to us.

Field Note

I take the breeze block step over the barbed wire fence and into the corner of the water meadow. Head for the stretch of river I know best of all. But there is a strange man there with his dog throwing a stick in the water. He clearly lives here, seems surprised to see someone else, has the air of someone at home.

V: City Bank, Memorial Gardens

I follow you into the tunnel

of dusk and overgrowth where brown trout show

their speckled backs to the bypass verge

to the car park edge slithering over

an earthslide of patio slabs a coat

floating cloak of Genii Cucullati

guardian spirits shape shifters signal

crayfish shoot upriver and take flight

over a passing pizza van

this ritual each step a sacrifice

to roaming in these limestone spaces

this world of stateless yearning things

I lose you heron at the sluice gates

see how home is the shrine I am carrying

'Do Humans Have a Religion Instinct?'

'When you begin to do some kind of practice like ritual, over time that area of the brain seems to shut down ... the boundaries between self and other – another person, another group, God, the universe, whatever it is you feel connected to – the boundaries between those begin to dissipate and you feel one with it'.

Museum Label Votive Relief

Group consisting of three Genii Cuculatti and a seated Mother Goddess found in Watermoor Road, Cirencester.

Twitter

Lots of American signal crayfish in the River Churn by Hereward Rd today; lovely animal, wrong location. #WildCiren

VI: Confluence

I am a foal upright and running

through you my precaution against grief

you're there are you there you are here here

in the dark where I went to put away

my questions submerge my fear make my mouth

an ossuary lips inscribed with gold

let the horses do their work and run

the river's current release the lines

on the map see how water shifts land's shape

by simply being for love is the riverbed

of our lives and Cuda is gift and gain

shrined in a molecule my bones

at watersmeet the open dogrose of my heart

is warming in the sun and asks for nothing

Corinium Museum label
gold staters
The first coins in the Cotswolds date from the 1st century BCE. Inscriptions on coins are the first examples of writing in Britain and evidence of the earliest named people in the Cotswolds ... Dobunnic coins feature a triple tailed horse motif. This symbol could represent the power and status of horses in the Iron Age Cotswolds.

Britain
The river Churne, when it hath left Circester behind him, six miles neare to Dounamveny, an ancient seate of the Hungerfords, joyneth with Isis.

Sources for found text marginalia

I

Information board at the source of the Churn, 'Welcome to Seven Springs. The ultimate source of the River Thames'. Trip Advisor reviews of The Seven Springs pub. Field Note, 24 April 2021.

II

'Cow Parsley'. Woodland Trust. Available at: www.woodlandtrust. org.uk/trees-woods-and-wildlife/plants/wild-flowers/cow-parsley/ (accessed 1 August 2021). Agrichem website. Available at: www.agrigem.co.uk/ (accessed 1 August 2021).

III

Field Note, 24 April 2021. WhatsApp message, discussing access to the river with my brother, 23 August 2021. Hayes, Nick (2020) *The Book of Trespass: Crossing the Lines that Divide Us.* London: Bloomsbury.

IV

Seth, A. (2021) *Being You: A New Science of Consciousness.* London: Faber & Faber. Field Note, 12 July 2021.

V

Neuroscientist Andrew Newberg quoted in 'Do humans have a "religion instinct?"' *BBC Future*. Available at: www.bbc.com/future/ article/20190529-do-humans-have-a-religion-instinct (accessed 1 August 2021). Label, votive relief, Corinium Museum, Cirencester. Twitter @WildCiren, 18 September 2016.

VI

Label, stater board, Corinium Museum, Cirencester.

Camden, W. (1610) *Britain* (trans. Philemon, Holland), London:
George Bishop and John Norton.

17

Submerging bodies in cold waters

Charlotte Bates and Kate Moles

Stories are like water, they pull you in and shift your perspective, they awaken your senses and take you into other social worlds. The stories in this chapter dwell in and focus on the moment of entering the water. The starting point of every swim, this moment is specific, situated and contextual, providing rich accounts of water, swimming practices and the meanings they hold. Each encounter and each body of water – pond, river, sea, lake and ice – magnifies and teaches us something distinct about wild swimming and our relationships with water, offering insights into the liquid boundaries and entanglements between cold water, bodies, wellbeing and risk.

Thresholds

So swimming is a rite of passage, a crossing of boundaries: the line of the shore, the bank of the river, the edge of the pool, the surface itself. When you enter the water, something like metamorphosis happens. Leaving behind the land, you go through the looking-glass surface and enter a new world, in which survival, not ambition or desire, is the dominant aim. (Deakin, 2000: 3)

Thresholds are beginnings, and they are brinks, they mark boundaries, and they are the spaces in between. We can think about embodied thresholds of pain and pleasure, physical and psychological lines we cross that take us to new ways of being and knowing ourselves and our environments. Thresholds are also material, the edge of the land where it meets the water, the point we step in and swim. Social life at the threshold is a space of tensions, contradictions, emergences and provocations. The act of crossing, and the social practices around the edges, bring alive new ways of being, different ways of understanding and alternative modes of interaction. Thresholds bring into relief the assumptions and expectations that form the social worlds that lie on either side of the boundary, the rules that govern our behaviour and the understandings that we hold about how to be. The closer we get to the boundary, the more ambiguity emerges, and the norms and regulations that govern how we act become more slippery. In this chapter, we think about crossing the threshold between land and water through the moment of entering the water to swim. As Roger Deakin described in *Waterlog*, entering the water is a deeply important physical and metaphysical moment, whereby both we and the environment we are part of change and are changed. This chapter takes this moment as a point of entry and departure, as we move deeper and become submerged.

Boundaries have long been attended to as particular sites of meaning making, identity formation, and changes in relations and interactions with other people and the social and physical world around us (Shields, 1991). The boundary itself is a liminal zone, a place of existing between two states, during which one stage is left behind but another has not been fully entered – betwixt and between. As the anthropologist Victor Turner (1967) described, during liminal periods of all kinds, social hierarchies may be reversed or temporarily dissolved, continuity of tradition may become uncertain, and future outcomes once taken for granted may be thrown into doubt. Moving through the boundary, and into the social world on the other side, there is an incorporation, a full submersion into the final destination, and a settling of cultural expectations and reduction in the fluidity and flux of the liminal period.

In the act of entering cold waters, we can see these stages unfold and we can feel the transitions occur. The separation from terrestrial ways of being, the cultural standards of land-based life, are replaced by a different set of expectations and demands – on our norms and values, through our senses, and in and about our bodies. Bodies are exposed to wind, water and each other. As you step in, the shock of the cold touching skin provokes swearing and shrieks from even the most stoic of swimmers. The pain is replaced by a numbness, as the cold water creeps up your legs, biting and stinging as you move deeper in. If you are wearing a wetsuit, the shock is delayed until the water seeps in through the zip and trickles down your back. Understanding these sensations to be pleasurable and desired is one of the suspensions of normal understandings that takes place in wild swimming. The idea that cold water sensations are pleasurable is learned and understood within the context of wild swimming and the cultural norms and values that entails.

As you wade in further, the cold continues to creep, but you are committed to the process and understand that this is something you want to do. The sensations become part of the welcomed transition into being a swimmer, and the framing of bodily sensations shifts as you are embraced by the water, just as you embrace the changes in the way you feel. This is a time of ambiguity and disorientation – understandings of what should be are fluid and malleable. Bodies, values, time and space are all reinterpreted from the perspective of the threshold, and within this moment everything is in flux. Waves crash against your body, sand shifts below your feet, stones trip you up and stub your toes, rocks are slippery, but all these things become insignificant as you push off and start to swim.

In this moment of commitment and submersion you cross the threshold between land and water. A rite of passage, through which you are incorporated into the water, no longer ambiguous in your identity as land or water dweller. Becoming part of the water you swim in, your body moves from vertical to horizontal, it floats and bobs in different ways, the coldness stops biting and wraps itself around you, just as you wrap yourself around it. You move together, up and down in the swell, pulled along by the currents and movement of the water. Your perspective shifts and the points of reference change. Your body finds a rhythm and a way of moving through the water, and on the best days you enter a state of flow that allows your mind to soar free and to be released from the ways of knowing you experience on land. The experience of being in the water is different depending on the water, the season, the kit you are using. It changes depending on how you feel, your stroke and the people you are with. But each swim, every time you enter the water, is marked by the commitment to crossing thresholds and moving from land to water, and this involves new ways of being and becoming together.

Cold

> Entering the water. I step down into deep water. Breathe. Swim a
> few strokes. Face in the water. Cold. Jingling cold. Sometimes as the
> seasons change just grippingly cold. Today it's bracing cold. Embracing
> my entire body. A flush of pleasure. The word 'yes' and a deep sigh. I
> look around for my friends. We smile. And we swim. (Swimmer)

There is something extraordinary and almost unimaginable about
the act of submerging bodies in cold waters. Most people choose to
bathe in hot water and swim in indoor heated swimming pools, only
entering natural waters on holidays in warmer climates. Compared
with indoor swimming pools, which vary in temperature from
around 26 to 31 degrees Celsius, outdoor waters in the UK range from
the mid 20s in peak summer to as low as zero degrees in winter. This
makes them colder, year round, than any indoor pool. Swimmers are
exposed to a much wider range of temperatures when swimming
outside, and come to know and feel cold in many different ways.
As Karen Throsby writes, 'open water immersion produces a much
more detailed delineation of temperatures, where a single degree
makes a tangible difference to the experience of being in the water
in ways that would be unintelligible to those outside of the community' (2013: 14). The Outdoor Swimming Society's temperature guide
(Rew, n. d.) classifies cold water in finely tuned bands, from Baltic to
fresh. To outdoor swimmers, pool temperature is 'arguably unpleasant', and there is something missing from 'lazy-hazy' summer swimming. The exhilaration of cold water only begins below 16 degrees,
when water feels 'fresh'. At the lowest temperatures 'water has bite,
skin smarts and burns'. This is winter swimming – jingling, gripping
and bracing.

Crossing the cold water threshold opens up a new world, in which
cold is experienced through a different range of emotions and sensations. Reluctance, dread, anticipation, excitement and exhilaration
can be experienced at each stage, from the first tingle on stepping into
the water to the shriek as it rises up your body or seeps inside your
wetsuit. These new ways of thinking and feeling about cold water take
time and dedication to accomplish – bodies need to adjust and accli-
matise to cold before they can feel superhuman. To become a hardened
outdoor swimmer, you need to embrace cold and understand its risks,
which include cold water shock, hypothermia, drowning and death.
Sudden immersion in cold water can cause a sharp intake of breath,

a gasp that floods the lungs with water and can lead to drowning. In cold water, your breathing rate and blood pressure increase, blood rushes to vital organs in the core, and blood flow to limbs is reduced. If this reaches extreme levels, it can weaken arms and legs to a point where you can no longer swim. Staying in cold water too long can result in hypothermia, a drop in core body temperature so severe that it can lead to loss of consciousness and heart failure. As the water temperature drops it necessarily changes the way you swim – a guide is to allow one minute in the water for each degree of cold – so in the coldest months, and without a wetsuit, swimming becomes dipping, making the moment of entering the water all the more significant. The feeling of cold lingers and can even worsen back on land – afterdrop is common after swimming in cold water, and can leave swimmers shivering violently, growing faint and feeling unwell. Knowing all this, outdoor swimmers embrace cold water and actively seek it out.

How can an experience that disorientates your senses and takes you close to the edge of survival be good for you? Science understands the dangers of cold water better than the benefits. But there is growing evidence that submerging in cold water boosts your immunity and has an anti-inflammatory effect. Swimmers tell us that they are less susceptible to colds, and even that they feel the cold less – needing fewer layers of clothes in winter and using less heating in their homes. We also think that cold water acclimatisation can help people adapt to other stresses more easily and help them to live with depression. While medical trials are difficult to conduct and science cannot fully explain the active ingredient in cold water swimming, extreme physiology gives us some insight into how cold water affects the body, from the flow of blood to the rush of adrenaline and the release of endorphins. This information helps swimmers to stay safe in the water and warns them against the dangers of swimming for too long, and it can save lives (Tipton, 2021). But, as Samantha Walton writes, 'What will be lost if we focus only on the benefits of the cold water itself, and not the meaning and the sensory richness of the lake, river or sea? What about the ritual of the swim, the sense of freedom and empowerment, and the relationships we form with other swimmers?' (2021: 45). This is where we begin.

Entering the water

The stories in this chapter are based on our immersive and multisensory ethnography of wild swimming in the UK – a year and more of forming friendships, sharing thoughts, notes and images, keeping in touch and sometimes swimming with women through the changing seasons. It is important to recognise that the wild swimming community mainly comprises white, middle-class, middle-aged women. Elsewhere we have written about the lines of exclusion that are drawn in and around the water (Bates and Moles, 2022). In this chapter, we acknowledge that while this community is inclusive and embracing in many ways, the pleasures of belonging – in the community and in the water – are limited, and divisions and exclusions still exist. Through the project and within these limits, we have come to know the ways swimmers feel and experience cold water, how they understand well-being, joy and risk, and the bonds that are created and sustained through these encounters. This chapter gathers together some of the accounts and encounters with water that have been shared with us. These experiences are multiple, emplaced and embodied, sometimes tacit and always rejuvenating, and they show us that wild swimming is much more than a physical response to low temperatures. In writing about these moments, we seek to share what wild swimming feels like and what it brings to our lives. Each story takes the reader to a different body of water to explore the pivotal moment in which bodies cross the threshold and become submerged. These bodies of water are grey and murky, brown and frothy, black, green, clear, soft, salty and frozen solid. More than simply 'bluespaces', they show that wild swimming challenges ideas about health and clean waters.

Pond

We were supposed to swim at the Blue Lagoon, a former slate quarry now flooded by the sea. The name alone is alluring. Bordered by beautiful beaches and craggy rocks, the lagoon is a popular spot for cliff diving and wild swimming. But a storm had blown over the weekend, and the sea was rough. It would be too dangerous to attempt the steep descent down the cliff face, too difficult to lower our bodies safely into the water or to scramble back out onto the rocks again. Instead, I receive coordinates for a different location. I search the map and find a small blue mark connected to the sea by a blue wiggly line.

Sea foam agitated by wind and waves floats through the cold grey air and lands on the rippling surface of the pond. Thirteen women are gathered at its edge, chatting and stripping and leaving piles of clothes, tins of cake and hot thermos flasks on the soggy grass.

The pond feels exposed and the wind chills the swimmers' bodies, raising goose bumps on their naked arms and legs. We all agree that on this blustery January day the pond is uninviting. Woolly hats and swimming caps are pulled on, and two women stand at the water's edge, offering their hands as a makeshift ladder. Nobody wants to swim. But one by one, the swimmers cross the threshold into the water. Stepping into the brown silt with resolve and a polite 'thank you ladies', shortly followed by a series of loud expletives. Shrieking and swearing fill the pond as the cold water rises up the swimmers' bodies, enveloping all but their heads. I hold back, observing the scene from the other side of the threshold. No normal human would do this. But within a few minutes the swearing has turned to laughter, and the bobbing heads are lit up with bright eyes and smiles. Submerged in cold water, bodies, fears, pain and sadness dissolve like the organic matter that floats in giant bubbles on the pond's surface.

~

Swims change with the weather – not in the vague and erratic sense of the popular saying 'you change with the weather', but in a material and social way weather and water are intertwined, and swimmers learn to read and make judgements about where and when to safely enter the water. Jennifer Mason (2016) writes that weather is ingrained in our lives, shaping what we do and feel, in ways that are best described as 'living the weather'. Swimmers live the weather and learn to know it, because weather changes water and water changes weather. One of the first things a swimmer will do before they leave home is check the forecast. The effects of weather on coastal waters are particularly unpredictable. Waves formed by wind travel for days across oceans, changing in strength and direction over distance and time. Storm surges, big tides and tidal streams all make water dangerous to enter. Wind affects waves and shapes the surface of water, roughing it up and making it unpredictable and difficult to swim. Wind and rain also make it colder, both in and out of the water – in the exposed moments before and after a swim. This is not to say that swimmers always seek calm waters. On the contrary, many revel in the liveliness of the sea and are energised by the sensation of being thrashed about by water. Big waves can be exhilarating, and they can wash us away: as one swimmer wrote, 'feeling utterly relaxed after letting the waves take me'. Water and weather, then, can create different experiences as well as present different risks.

But sometimes, weather can make a swim too difficult and dangerous, and committed swimmers will seek safer waters or be forced to stay on dry land. Days like this can lead swimmers to waters like the pond. Uninviting and unappealing, but accessible and safe. Connected to the sea by a small tributary, the pond has none of the romanticism of the Blue Lagoon. But it does hold a certain magic of its own – hard to see at first, but knowable once you cross the threshold. As the swimmers step through the 'looking-glass surface' (a surface that is not clear or blue, but brown and murky) and enter a new world, the pond fills up – it is full, not only of water, but of bodies, shrieks and laughter, swearing, jokes, solidarity and conviviality. The pond is both exposed and sheltered. Exposed and exposing, it sits in a bleak landscape, a road lies close by from which naked bodies made pink by cold water and whipped by wind can be seen by passers by. Bodies of different shapes and sizes, young and old, watermarked and scarred in other ways. Bodies that are remarkable and courageous – bodies that enter cold water. Emotions are exposed too – hesitation, trepidation and resistance as the swimmers coax and encourage each other into the water (though no judgement is made of any who stay behind on land). Even the most seasoned and stoic swimmers shriek and swear as they meet the cold water. Sheltered from the bad weather and rough sea, and offering shelter – a refuge and retreat from life and land. The simple act of entering cold water binds swimmers together, creating bonds that endure back on dry land, and whatever the weather.

Swimmers' stubborn attachment to water makes small and otherwise insignificant bodies of water like the pond remarkable, and reveals a commitment to immersion that goes beyond scenic or idyllic notions of wild swimming. Water and weather gather swimmers together in an act of 'weathering', which Astrida Neimanis and Jennifer Mae Hamilton describe as a particular kind of relation to the environment and a different kind of sociality, one that 'makes distinctions between the meteorological and the social rather leaky' (2018: 81). Through weathering, we learn to live – with the weather, with each other and with water. As a form of biopolitics that lies somewhere between resilience and vulnerability, weathering and wild swimming go hand in hand. Submerging in cold water simultaneously reveals our strength and our vulnerability, and swimming both exposes us to wildness and shelters us within the natural world.

River

The swimmer treads lightly across the frost-white grass and approaches the river. An early morning mist swirls gently above the water's surface. At the riverbank the ground is brown and muddy, and the swimmer's neoprene socks squelch in the sodden earth. She steps in and reaches down to touch the moving water. Beneath the surface, the undercurrent tugs at her legs, her feet slip and slide, and the river playfully pulls her body in. Faster than anticipated, the swimmer is submerged. She swims.

~

For many swimmers, an early morning dip is the best way to start the day – even when the ground is frozen, the air is cold and the water is even colder. Like the weather, swimming is ingrained in our lives – an essential part of the day or week, an everyday routine that keeps us coming back to the water year round. Missing a swim, especially in winter, can quickly lead to the body becoming un-acclimatised to cold, so that the next swim feels colder, harder. As one swimmer wrote, 'I have missed three swims and worry that the water has dropped its temperature in my absence. I had a cold shower last night to remind me of the sensation.' Trepidation and doubt can creep back in, so it is important to maintain a constant relationship with the water – even if it is mediated by a domestic shower. Missing one too many swims can also leave swimmers feeling frustrated, sad and miserable. For all these reasons, the swimmer wakes early, drags herself out of bed, slips on her swimsuit beneath her warm clothes and walks through winter alone to meet the water. Peeling off layers and changing her boots to neoprene socks, she stands on the muddy threshold. She is swimming 'skins' (just a swimsuit – no wetsuit to insulate her body or offer protection from the cold), but the addition of a woolly hat and neoprene socks helps retain body heat and protect extremities, without restricting movement or hindering the contact between cold water and skin.

There are many different rituals that swimmers use to enter cold water. Some clap their hands, others speak words aloud; as one swimmer wrote, 'When I get into the water I speak encouraging words to myself – delicious, delightful, warm, rejuvenating, refreshing – and sometimes I chant!' Some swimmers stand in the water, splashing their wrists and necks, waiting for their bodies to adjust and accept the cold. Some ease their bodies in slowly, keeping their arms raised, feeling the water inch up their bodies, touching their thighs, wrapping around their waists, approaching their shoulders, resisting immersion until the last second. Others rush towards the water, knowing that they need to get in without hesitation. Whichever approach you take, there is a moment of no return, in which you must commit to taking the plunge. But on this swim, the river claims the swimmer before she is ready. Catching the swimmer off-guard, the water leaves no time for ritual greetings or hesitation. She is submerged, swirling gently with the mist and the water, away from the riverbank and into the swim.

River water behaves differently from other bodies of water, it has its own rules. In the coldest months of the year still bodies of water can freeze over, but rivers mostly continue to flow. Swollen with rain and obstructed with debris, fallen branches and loose rocks, rivers present untold risks and unique experiences. The continual flow of water shapes and changes rivers and their banks, and can make familiar places unfamiliar quickly. Currents need to be judged, depth ascertained and plant life negotiated. Safe entry and exit points need to be searched for and found – and are rarely in the same place, as currents carry swimmers downstream and away from their clothes, which need to be returned to on foot. Rivers can also be harder to access. In Scotland, swimmers have a right to swim as part of their right to roam. But in England and Wales, access to rivers is often disputed. Fishing rights dominate, and private landowners – who own bank and bed, but not the water that flows past and over – can be unwelcoming, and many rivers are fenced off with barbed wire, impossible to reach. In a few places, where people have traditionally swum for a long time, or in hidden, secret spots, it is possible to swim in flowing water and be carried by currents. As the Outdoor Swimming Society warns, should a weed tug at your leg, try changing your stroke to a modified doggy paddle and gently extricate yourself without kicking or thrashing around – breaststroke will only get you more entangled.

Immersion in cold water has long been associated with healing, and the search for the 'nature cure' is still compelling today (Walton, 2021). But healthy bodies and healthy waters are entangled. In the UK, rivers are increasingly polluted with chemicals, sewage discharge and the runoff from agriculture, and swimmers need to know what a healthy river looks and smells like. Unhealthy rivers are rancid, scummy and cloudy, and bodies that enter them can suffer unpleasant effects. This does not necessarily stop swimmers: as Samantha Walton writes, 'Keeping my head dry, I return again, immersing my vulnerable body in the vulnerable water' (2021: 29). This is the bind – a different way in which the fates of bodies and water are bound together.

Sea

The morning is bright and blue, clear and cold. Swimmers dress and undress along the headland path, squeezed between rock and sea, exchanging smiles and quick greetings. At the end of the peninsula, land meets salty water. Man-made steps used by swimmers for over a hundred years to move between worlds are almost submerged by the high tide. Rusted metal handrails plunge downward, and the sea rises up to greet each swimmer, frothing, swirling, pulling. The water is clear, and beneath the surface the steps sink deeper and deeper, out of reach of the swimmer's feet, land dissolving into water. The swimmer does not descend with them; instead, she leaves land and drops instantly into water, floating out to sea. As the sun rises over the horizon, the swimmer begins her day submerged. With each stroke and breath she is pulled further away from land, and life.

~

Stripping down outdoors, exposing bodies to air, wind and sea, is part and parcel of wild swimming – it comes with the territory. Normal expectations about bodies and nudity, along with ideas of comfort, decorum and decency, are temporarily suspended, and instead practicalities take over. Proximity to water, shelter from wind, a place to stash dry clothes become the focus. Nakedness becomes essential and accepted, and the negative emotions we often associate with nudity, from shame to embarrassment (Górnicka, 2016), are washed away. People talk to each other as they undress, swimmers huddle together in groups, using each other's shoulders to balance as they pull off socks and haul on wetsuits. Wild swimming introduces a proximity to nakedness that is not found in many other social and spatial spheres – or at the indoor swimming pool, where nearly naked bodies are regulated, socialised and civilised

(Scott, 2010). This acceptance of exposure and of other bodies contributes to an appreciation of all bodies, a feeling of belonging, and a sense of community.

Entering the sea means putting your body into a huge, moving, living mass of water, salty and sublime. Sea waters vary widely – the colours, the conditions, the points of entry and egress all shift and change with the seasons and on any given day. Tides ebb and flow daily, changing with the position of the sun and moon. Swimming conditions vary according to these rhythms – outgoing tides are best avoided, slack waters and incoming tides offer safety against being pulled out by the sea. Tides also affect places of entry and egress – steps that are hidden at high tide, muddy beaches that cover you up to the knees at low. Sea waters can be turquoise and clear, with light streaming through revealing the sea floor as you swim above it. Or they can be opaque and murky, full of sand and mud and other things it is probably best not to think about. Even the saltiness of the water varies, though the taste of the sea is distinct and universal. The sting of salt on your tongue, or in your throat when you stay in longer, is a reminder of the ways coastal waters do not quite flow seamlessly with your own bodily fluids. The saltiness of the sea also makes swimming in it distinct – salt alters the density of water and gives it buoyancy, so that the sea holds you and helps you to float. All these differences mean that every sea swim is different; as one swimmer wrote, 'Entering the water always gives me a sense of excitement; will it be too rough, too cold, how about that undertow?'

This time, the conditions are good and the sea is calm and welcoming. As the swimmers take their last steps on land and drop into the sea, they cross a threshold with a long history – people have flocked to the coast to bathe in the sea for centuries and this threshold is worn and rusted. But at high tide the steps are superfluous, and the swimmers quickly transition from land-bound verticality to horizontal fluidity. No longer rooted by their feet, they glide through the water and drift out to sea. As arms find their stroke, the swimmer's gaze shifts down – a change in perspective that reveals another world beneath the surface. Our understanding of how to move in water, the embodied, sensual act of swimming, is indivisible from the water it takes place in; we move in and are moved by water. These 'techniques of the body' (Mauss, 1973) are situated, historical and contextual. Entering the sea, we immerse our bodies in cold water and surrender into a way of being and a way of belonging. It is a new social world, having crossed the threshold and become a swimmer.

Sea swimming offers particular joys and challenges in becoming submersed. While many swimmers have saltwater in the blood and love the sense of adventure that comes with sea swimming, others live far from the coast or choose to seek out quieter waters. The sharpness of the entry and the challenge of motivating yourself to do it are particular to the temperatures found off the coasts of the British Isles. There are much colder waters, and much warmer, but the temperature of these waters year round combines the thrill of the cold on entry with the challenge to endure it long enough to swim. It provides a source of wellbeing and relief for swimmers all around the country, marked by a sense of achievement on completion of swims and comradery forged through the accomplishment.

Lake

Three friends quickly undress at the edge of the lake. Pulling on bikinis and swimsuits, caps and goggles, they hurry to the water. The seasons are turning and there is no time to waste. Without hesitating they walk barefoot into the still, clear lake. The water gently ripples around their ankles in reply. A few more steps and they are waist deep. The swimmers pause, laughing and swearing at the cold, holding their arms high out of the water, resisting getting wet for another moment, and then their bodies plunge in.

Gasping and shrieking punctuate short, sharp breaths and strokes. The water, colder than air, takes hold. The swimmers look at each other, checking and reassuring one another, taking strength and resolve from being submerged together. And then they swim.

As these cold water warrior women return to the shallows, two young men edge apprehensively into the lake. Stopping waist deep, they stand in the water for a few minutes before hastily retreating. The women swim again.

~

The communities around the lake change with the seasons. In summer, the lake is busy and men in wetsuits train for triathlons, pounding the water and counting the kilometres, measuring swimming in distance and time. But as the water temperature drops, things become quieter. Small groups of women wearing bikinis and swimsuits return to reclaim the water. These three women are swimming through winter together. They have made a promise to each other, to encourage, support and watch for each other in the water. Swimming in cold water requires a special kind of comradery. The water introduces new vulnerabilities, and you need to trust those you go in with. This group of women watch out for each other, they share the responsibility of care and reciprocate moments of joyful adventure. Their shared enjoyment of the water can be heard in the shrieks and laughter as they enter, and their shared commitment gives them the strength and resolve to keep swimming. Swimming in cold water invites people to be vulnerable and brave, to open themselves up to the elements while wrapping themselves up in their friendships. As one swimmer wrote, 'I have found my tribe, and they will support and join me in my next goal and beyond'.

The communities that exist around the edges of bodies of water are as diverse and multiple as the waters they swim in. The composition of these groups fluctuates, from small pods of close friends to expanded swim-families and big flocks of swimmers, all gathered together by water. Swimming communities of all shapes and sizes have grown and proliferated over the last few years as the benefits, culture and sense of belonging connected with swimming outdoors are increasingly shared and celebrated. They offer a space of support and friendship, welcoming diverse bodies and varying levels of experience and expectation into the fold. The groups offer support far beyond time in the water, with vulnerabilities opened up and emotions laid bare. Spaces of acceptance, inclusion and care, these groups of women are bound together in the waters they swim, and in the huddles around tea and cake that happen afterwards. The swimmers get up early and swim as the sun rises, come together for full-moon swims and evening dips, and meet for regular plunges that punctuate their everyday lives. These are special spaces where women feel they belong and can support each other through the act of entering cold water and all that comes with it.

These bodies of water are also spaces of power, courage and strength. All over the UK, women enter cold waters where and when others do not follow. Rethinking traditional ideas of strength and fitness, these warrior women endure cold, enjoy challenges and display impressive levels of commitment. Connected through the act rather than drawn apart through competition, they find strength in each other and in the water. From swimming through winter to dip-a-day challenges, women are quietly getting in the water and getting on with tearing up the record books, often in contrast to the more bombastic displays that male swimmers undertake. Outdoor swimming is a space where women are not just taking part, but are equal to, and often exceed, their male counterparts in terms of times, distances and feats undertaken, challenging the idea that women's sporting bodies have lesser abilities compared with men's (Throsby, 2013: 103). It opens up potentials and different narratives for women's participation and offers new accounts of what open water can mean for women.

This makes the water a space where new ways of being a woman can exist. Bodies that are 'overlooked or problematised' (Throsby, 2013: 17) can be celebrated because of their diversities, their strengths and their vulnerabilities. The shared shrieks and swears on entering the water bring alive a sense of freedom and release, the kick of the cold and the ability to endure it spark understandings of strength, resilience and courage, and the coming together after the swim, huddled against the cold and getting changed, holding tea and cake with cold fingers, opens up spaces of sharing, warmth and community. Water brings people together in unexpected and intensive practices, and binds them together in enduring and special ways.

Ice

It is deep winter and the loch is frozen. Craving the cold hug of the water, the swimmer wades through the shallows, breaking thin shards of ice and throwing them aside to find a way in. The ice vibrates and the sound travels across the loch, bouncing over the frozen surface, resounding. Keeping close to the shoreline, the swimmer seeks a place to submerge. Lying down, she pushes her body into the icy water, basking like a seal. She has made contact with the cold that she sought.

~

After an exceptionally hard year the swimmer has new-found need and longing to enter the water. The frozen surface does not deter her, and the thrill of breaking the ice to enter becomes part of a new experience of cold water. Water that is frozen takes a different texture and form, and the silky touch of the loch, its brown and green tones, are now hard and white. The threshold is no longer liquid, but still holds the promise of cold immersion underneath. The sensation of breaking through ice and lying in freezing waters offers a chance for this body and mind to reset and re-emerge from the water renewed. Ideas of wellness and wellbeing are prevalent in rationales for embracing cold water, and are particularly connected to narratives of resetting and restoring. Swimmers recognise the power of water to calm and to comfort, and often describe water as their 'happy place', offering an escape from land-bound troubles and hardships, and an affective transformation 'from cranky sea lion to smiling dolphin' (Throsby, 2013: 15). As one swimmer wrote, 'It's always been my cold hug, my confidante and friend'.

Ice swimming is wild swimming at its most extreme, the ultimate cold challenge through which swimmers inhabit the margins of survival, on the edge of enjoyment. The levels of difficulty and risk only add to feelings of commitment and understandings of reward, enlivening the experience and marking these swims apart. Reaching for a hammer and swimming in icy slush can make swimmers feel superhuman, giving them renewed confidence in their bodies and binding them to water even more tightly. Swim groups and events encourage and celebrate these feats. Penguin and Polar Bear Challenges (which have different rules for swimming with or without neoprene) and the International Ice Swimming Association's Ice Mile offer swimmers motivation to swim in deepest winter, edging them closer to their limits and pushing them to rethink what they can achieve. These swims demand high levels of commitment, temporal and mental, and train bodies to endure what lies far beyond normal understandings of what is good for us.

Afterglow

The cold starts to nag a bit more insistently and fingers and toes start to grow cold and turn pink. It is time to get out of the water. Leaving can be disorienting, cold legs struggle to stand, the water that has just been holding you up drags you down as you try to wade out, swimsuits and wetsuits feel heavy and cold. The wind prickles and stings against your skin and your temperature drops. Shivering starts pretty quickly, hands shaking as you try to grab a towel or a changing robe, teeth clatter. Fingers fumble as you try to hold a cup of warm tea, and the tea burns as it sloshes out of the cup. Then, as warmth returns to your body, your skin tingles with aliveness, and a sense of achievement and of relief floods through your body. You look out across the water that you have so recently been in and feel the connection extending through your body. You can still taste the water you swam in, and your hair and skin will hold the smell until you rinse it away. As you relax into warmer clothes a calmness will wash through your body and your mind, and exhilaration will diffuse inwards to your body's centre, bringing deep and enduring energy. The glow of shared smiles and joy, friendship and connection through supporting and encouraging each other will stay with you all day.

Submerging entangles bodies and water, bringing us closer to ourselves, each other and the natural world. Crossing the threshold and entering cold water, we learn, unlearn and relearn how to swim and how to survive, how to be and how to belong. The waters we usually encounter in everyday life – the waters we drink, wash in, or in indoor pools – are sanitised, still and safe. Ponds, rivers, seas, lakes and lochs are natural waters, and on the other side of the threshold, there are new rules, risks and rewards. These bodies of water disorient social worlds and challenge our bodies, but they also hold us. Entering them, we learn to be vulnerable, to understand risk, to know water, and to trust ourselves, each other and the waters we swim in. We make friends with other swimmers and with the water, forming close bonds that endure. We leave the water with renewed strength and hope, and with a longing to return.

References

Bates, C. and Moles, K. (2022) Bobbing in the park: wild swimming, conviviality and belonging. *Leisure Studies*. Online first, 5 June. https://doi.org/10.1080/02614367.2022.2085774 (accessed 1 August 2022).

Deakin, R. (2000) *Waterlog: A Swimmer's Journey through Britain*. London: Vintage.

Górnicka, B. (2016) *Nakedness, Shame, and Embarrassment: A Long-Term Sociological Perspective*. Wiesbaden: Springer.

Mason, J. (ed.) (2016) *Living the Weather: Voices from the Calder Valley*. Manchester: University of Manchester, Morgan Centre for Research into Everyday Lives.

Mauss, M. (1973) Techniques of the body. *Economy and Society*, 2(1), 70–88.

Neimanis, A. and Hamilton, J. M. (2018) Weathering. *Feminist Review*, 118, 80–84.

Rew, K. (n. d.) Cold water: a temperature guide, *The Outdoor Swimming Society*. Available at: www.outdoorswimmingsociety.com/cold-water-feels-temperature-guide/ (accessed 1 August 2022).

Scott, S. (2010) How to Look good (nearly) naked: the performative regulation of the swimmer's body. *Body & Society*, 16(2), 143–168.

Shields, R. (1991) *Places on the Margin: Alternative Geographies of Modernity*. London: Routledge.

Throsby, K. (2013) 'If I go in like a cranky sea lion, I come out like a smiling dolphin': marathon swimming and the unexpected pleasures of being a body in water. *Feminist Review*, 103, 5–22.

Tipton, M. (2021) Mike Tipton on how our bodies respond to extreme conditions. *The Life Scientific*, BBC Radio 4, 25 May. Available at: www.bbc.co.uk/programmes/m000w9t5 (accessed 23 August 2022).

Turner, V. (1967) *The Forest of Symbols: Aspects of Ndembu Ritual*. Ithaca: Cornell University Press.

Walton, S. (2021) *Everybody Needs Beauty: In Search of the Nature Cure*. London: Bloomsbury.

18

How to swim without water: swimming as an ecological sensibility

Rebecca Olive

How was the forest today? How was the sea? Did you hear the bubbles under the trees, see the fish in the leaves, the birds in the corals? Did you listen to their dawn chorus? Did you feel the breeze created by your kicking feet, feel the waves that roll through the trees? Did you marvel at flying so high on the water, did you see the clouds drift by beneath you, did you take a deep breath and float on the grass and soil? Does the air catch at your fingers as you pull yourself forward, drawing against the tension of the sky? Did the currents drift you from the path to a quiet glade, did the waves fill your lungs? Tell me what you learned, tell me what you felt, tell me who you met and what you saw.

Immersion

For bluespace and water researchers the sea can feel like air; an element that land-focused researchers themselves rarely consider the weight of. But for those whose work is immersed in water, we always know it's there. We feel the wetness of it – the ebb and flow and wash and pull and power and immensity – even if we don't admit it. Barbara Humberstone (2011, 2018) has long thought about spiritual aspects of watery play, while Easkey Britton (2018) encourages us to 'be like water'. In Australia, Aotearoa/New Zealand and the UK, lisahunter and Lyndsey Stoodley (lisahunter, 2019; lisahunter and Stoodley, 2021) and Hannah Denton, Charlie Dannreuther and Kay Aranda (2021) talk about being in, with and on the sea, and Clifton Evers

(2006, 2021) has always centralised waves in his feminist and queer readings of becomings-with, with his recent work thinking about bodies in relation to 'polluted leisure' experiences. Kimberley Peters (2019) reflects on what it's like to study oceans when you rarely get wet yourself, while Kanaka Māoli woman, Karin Amimoto Ingersoll (2016), writes about 'seascape epistemologies', highlighting how Native Hawaiian ways of knowing cannot be separated from the seas that surround Hawai'i.

If you're familiar with my work at all, you might have noticed the sea is always there too. Admittedly, mostly as a context; an inevitability. That is what seas and oceans and coasts are for many surfers and swimmers, and is certainly what they have been for me. But some time ago, while reading and thinking and writing about being in oceans, it became clear to me that I'd had a difficult relationship with oceans, which I had not yet accounted for. These uncertainties and questions were raised in different ways at different times. They were raised in Aotearoa/New Zealand, where I lived in a beachside cabin with an expansive view to the west across the Tasman Sea. The almost two-years of living with this coveted view brought me to a point where looking across the ocean felt like looking at a searing desert. I came to feel it as a barren view of relentless light, death and pain, against which I kept the curtains closed through the day. I could only see the impossibility of survival there, both on the surface in the scorching sun, and under the water with no way to breathe. I couldn't see the abundance of the saltwater, I could only imagine its limitations. Other questions came from a time of deep, raw grief, during which surfing brought on upwellings of sadness that made it difficult to paddle out into the waves. The amplification of grief I felt when out in the waves highlighted that I'd never really experienced the ocean as a space of renewal and cleansing. Instead, I found it to be a place where I could not hide from myself (Olive, 2021). There is great value in such reflections, but still, I found I increasingly sought the cool consolation of green, shady, bird-song-filled forests.

To admit this in the company of other water researchers is no small thing. We're supposed to love oceans, to promote their health and wellbeing value, to always find ourselves in them, to be water people (Peters, Moore and Brown, 2018). To admit that I have questions about the capacity of seas and oceans to offer comfort and restoration feels like a betrayal of the very ideas I promote. And so, I've been confused by the challenges in my relationship to seas and oceans. But thinking through my relationships, through my experiences and responses, through the saltwater and waves, I've realised that the solace I'm more recently finding in the depth and volume of forests is also oceanic. Among the trees and green, the warmth and cool of light and shade and wind on my skin, the movement and shapes of clouds flowing so high above me, the flight and song of birds, I am immersed.

This oceanic perspective on green spaces highlights how oceans and other bodies of water offer ways of thinking that are different from the terrestrial ones we're so used to. Like my watery research field itself, in my research I am immersed in an ocean of words and publications and perspectives and knowledges. To help me better navigate the scope of possibilities in the vastness of these bodies of literature, I started thinking of them in terms of volumes and depths, climates and currents (Steinberg and Peters, 2015; see also Olive and Enright, 2021). Thinking in an oceanic framework helps me imagine research as a system of tides and flows and tempests and storms and calm and multispecies and nonhuman interactions – with bodies, animals, plants, minerals, rubbish, things, histories, knowledges, critiques – and to see how I am immersed in ways of knowing that are entangled in diverse human/nonhuman relationships, communities, histories and networks of power.

Over the last few years, I've been extending these ideas to consider swimming as a way of thinking, knowing and being in oceans. Swimming is how I move through water, but it's also a way of learning about and navigating water and my relationships to multispecies worlds. But moving this way is not just relational. It requires a reorientation of my body, my breath, my relationships, and to how I think about myself as part of it all. Swimming is much more than a form of mobility or a mode of movement. Swimming is ecological. As I swim I am in encounter with other people as well as fish, dolphins, rays and sharks, birds, rocks, sand, plastics, pollution, and many other things and beings. I am also in encounter with the possibilities of the conditions I'm immersed in and over which I have no control; the weather, waves, tides and currents.

These are powerful shifts in my thinking, and they follow me out of the water. When I'm on land, under a tree, I notice how the birds dive and swim through the leaves, just as the fish fly and soar through underwater coral and rocks. I notice how the light filters and diffuses, following the patterns of the air, currents, leaves and clouds.

I can't help but stop and swim when I'm under a tree.

What is swimming?

Of course, I'm describing a sensibility. That is, it's a way of thinking about and experiencing myself in relation to multispecies places and communities. I don't swim without water in the sense of how I move my body under a tree, so much as how I experience moving and sensing my body in relation to the ecology that I'm part of. Such a claim is consistent with how we already talk about swimming as a practice of immersion.

Most fundamentally, swimming is a way of moving our bodies through water. While in this discussion I'm focused on swimming for leisure and recreation, swimming is also practised as a competitive, high-performance or endurance sport (e.g. McMahon and Penney, 2013; Throsby, 2016) and as a cultural practice of labour that includes collecting food (e.g. Kato, 2007; Stronach and Adair, 2020). Swimming is undertaken using our own physical power, sometimes with various technologies and mobility aids. Usually attired in swimwear, swimmers might also wear goggles, a silicone cap, snorkel, flippers/fins or hand-paddles. If they're swimming a long distance, swimmers might attach a float to their waist, and in colder waters they might don a wetsuit, booties, gloves or a woollen hat. However, like runners, swimmers are largely moving their body around with limited technological intervention. The key thing for swimming is water, and our bodily immersion in it. It is the water that encompasses us, washes over us, around us, buoys us, weighs us down, creates the resistance we move with and against.

Accounting for all of this, Shane Gould (Gould, 2019; Gould, McLachlan and McDonald, 2021) writes that swimming is more than the common representation of us pulling our horizontal bodies forward through the water with our arms and hands, while at the same time propelling ourselves by kicking our legs and feet. When we lie this way along the surface our face is in the water and we breathe by turning our head to the side in a rhythmic pattern every few strokes. However, Gould argues that many people swim vertically, focused more on immersion and sensory pleasure than swimming as an activity for fitness. Vertical swimmers bob and float in the water with their feet below them or use breaststroke to move forward with their face out of the water. In some swimming places I've visited, the freestyle/Australian crawl stroke that is so connected with swimming in Australia (Osmond and Phillips, 2006) is scowled at as too splashy

(Moggach, 2019). Instead, breaststroke is popular in cold water climates such as the United Kingdom, where swimmers advocate the benefits of cold water immersion and decorate their heads with knitted 'bobble hats' (Roper, 2018).

Swimming, simply put, is a physical activity that describes a way of being immersed in water and/or propelling us through water. Of course, there are politics and hierarchies around participation in all forms of swimming, but in the terms of this discussion, horizontal and vertical forms of swimming have been equally pleasurable, valuable and influential experiences. Like Gould, I have found that

> the experience of immersing in water in a swimming-like way, is interactive, whether vertical, horizontal or suspended or not. Feelings of; bouncy suspension, feeling light, complex interesting pressures and flows, feeling unstable yet safe, and more … sensations from which pleasurable appeal and scary anxiety of swimming derives. (Gould, 2019: 196)

For Gould, swimming is less about being out of our depth than is it about being aware of the water: 'Perception of the water while swimming and the awareness of the environment around the water is a key feature of swimming in place' (Gould, 2019: 268). Gould's work has been instructive for me in thinking about the role of swimming in my own changing views of the world, especially her description of swimming as a practice of 'inter-animation'. Gould draws this term from Casey (2009), who writes that 'Bodies and places are connatural terms. They inter-animate each other' (327; in Gould, 2019: 269). Inter-animation is a way of thinking about relationality as alive and sparkling, as impacting and reliant on each other, as recognising that our individual consciousness of water and water ecologies is not the only outcome of that encounter. For Gould, it is the bodies being with water that defines swimming, more than the horizonal, self-propelled, out of depth-ness: 'My definition of swimming therefore is an expression of a living-sensing moving body as the creature inter-animates water' (Gould, 2019: 270).

Gould's more-than-human definition of swimming as inter-animation reflects so much of what is written in research about swimming in oceans. The inter-animated, ecological relationality of different swimming experiences is evident in Elspeth Probyn's (2011, 2016) description of 'swimming as a methodology', as she explores human–fish relationships. Probyn's swimming is of the vertical kind, immersed in water, head bobbing below to watch tuna as she swims in their enclosure. In this swimming, she is a part of the world of the tuna and must trust them to turn their powerful, several hundred-kilogram bodies as they speed like missiles through the water around her. Without Probyn's own body immersed with them in the water, the tuna would swim differently. Being immersed with them also helps Probyn feel her fragility in their domain. Karen Throsby (2013), and Easkey Britton and Ronan Foley (2021) reveal the central role of sensory experiences in swimming, and how bodies respond to immersion. For Throsby, the sensory joy of swimming 'is an affectively transformative experience', such as how it shifts one of her swimmer participants from feeling like a 'cranky sea lion' to a 'smiling dolphin' (2013: 15). Britton and Foley (2021: 74) found that for sea swimmers even preparing for immersion was a multisensory practice that included 'developing an awareness of place through direct contact/embodiment practices, such as breathing exercises or observing the sea conditions (tide, wind, size of waves) from the beach before swimming or surfing'. This is in line with Ronan Foley's (2017) previous work in which he describes swimming as an 'accretive' practice. His framing challenges the commonly expressed notion that swimming washes away our problems, to suggest that it also results in us accumulating skills, experiences, knowledges, memories and relationships. Each swim, no matter how many years apart, stays with us and impacts our relationships to swimming, to water and to ourselves.

Alongside these descriptions of outdoor swimming, Jayne Caudwell (2020) reminds us that layers of politics exist in swimming places, and despite its simplicity and affordability, swimming remains inaccessible for many people. In her work about transgender and non-binary people's experiences of swimming in the UK, participants described having avoided swimming for years as they did not feel safe or comfortable at public beaches or swimming pools. Private sessions at indoor pools offered inter-animating opportunities for 'relearning how to interact with water' (5), experiencing 'amazing freedom' (6), building supportive and trusting relationships and community networks, and 'renewing relationships with exercise and the self' (6). While the shared change-room facilities could remain a cause of anxiety, participants found 'being in the water was the safest and most enjoyable space' (7), and that it was a space of 'imaginative and transgender possibilities' (7). In one case, and similar to Throsby, Caudwell's participants described feeling like a dolphin to express the joy they experienced while swimming. Across all these conceptions, including those in a private session in an indoor pool, ecological aspects of swimming are significant. In water, out of our usual element, we cannot avoid how we're part of multispecies water ecologies. Even in pools where our survival is dependent on staying afloat, we are aware of how we do and do not belong in water. In all cases, the feel and volume of the water remind us we are in relation to other people, critters and things.

In her work about outdoor swimming, Kate Moles echoes Gould's definition of swimming as inter-animation. Moles writes that

> Swimming is an entanglement of cultural practices, situated accounts, and bodily encounters, which changes in form and meaning over time and place. It reflects, produces, and reproduces socialities, attachments, and connections between bodies and water. (2021: 21)

For Moles, swimming in rivers and the sea helped her 'consider the ways interactions and meaning-making occurs in and around bluespace in ways that disrupts and expands our understanding of social worlds and life' (Moles, 2021: 22). Moles's conception recognises the role of ecologies in how we experience swimming. She writes that 'relationships with places – green, blue, brown or any other color – are socially situated, culturally produced, and are neither inherent or inevitable', and that we learn to account for our experiences by 'using the available frameworks and narratives' (Moles, 2021: 23).

As in descriptions of accretion (Foley, 2017), inter-animation (Gould, 2019) and entanglement (Moles, 2021), swimming, especially in oceans, has shaped how I relate to the world around me.

Under the jacaranda, manuka and sequoia trees

Swimming in seas and oceans means making sense of depths and volumes, currents and waves, tides and winds, and the multispecies ecologies I'm immersed in. Each day I swim, I must adjust to the conditions as they are, to the critters who are there, and choose to take the risk or stay on the shore. On days of big swell, I swim out deep behind the impact zone of the breaking waves. On murky days I stay close to shore, in the comfort of shallower water.

Sometimes the expanse of the ocean is too big for me.

Sometimes, it's too much and I can't face the enormity of it. When I turn my head to breathe on the ocean side, I close my eyes against the deep blue and all that it signifies: my smallness, my frailty, my fleetingness, my insignificance, my vulnerability. I can't look into that blue void, into a world I can't truly know, full of life and death. Instead, I look down to be comforted by the tangible safety of sand and rocks and seaweed and corals on the ocean floor.

In the ocean I am always out of my depth, immersed in a world of not knowing.

Since March 2020, with pandemic lockdowns, there have been (are) many periods when I've not been able to get to the coast. But after the end of the first lockdown, my swimming world largely shrunk to the pool where I swim with my beloved squad. Some weeks, I was lucky to have that. The challenge of the unknown offered by the ocean seems more vast than ever. As I stroke back and forward along the length of the pool, I am locked into its confines. Pandemic lockdowns have brought our worlds in – shrunk them, retracted our boundaries, reaffirmed commitments to borders, limits, insularity, localism. I miss the Pacific Ocean, the Coral Sea, the Bass Strait, the Tasman, the Atlantic, the North Sea.

In the pool, there is no existential crisis to be had. I swim in straight lines of 50 metres × 20 or 40 or 60 laps. The regulated depth (1.65 metres maximum depth; 'No Diving'), the ordered tiles and lanes, the clear lines of the rectangle that contains us all offer comfort, safety and certainty. The water might cloud, but the right balance of chemicals can clear it. The water might cool, but the heater can warm it. The water level might drop, but a hose can fill it again. Leaves and sticking plasters and sunscreen might pollute the pool, but these are all fixed with careful maintenance. Chlorinated, sanitised, regulated, bounded; this is inner-city swimming in a pandemic.

Here, the pleasure is being in water. The effects of depth, volume and ecology are limited, so I focus on the sensory pleasures of being immersed, afloat and outside. I feel grateful for my access to the pool and the relief it brings to my life. I can move my body, enjoy being in water, catch up with friends, be seen. Even in my absence, I am accounted for.

In the pool, I have volume and depth. I matter.

But there are many days when even a swim in a pool has not been possible. There have been days and weeks and months when I was lucky enough to be able to lie in an inner-city park, under the shady expanse of a jacaranda or poinciana tree. The boughs of these trees extend over wide areas, so a few groups of people can sit, safely spaced, under their canopy. In the first lockdown, I would make regular trips to the park at the end of the street where I was staying to lie outside and read, enjoying the play of dappled light, the feel of the breeze on my bare skin, the clouds above, the birds in the branches, the insects crawling on my limbs. I felt the space above me, so high and potential. I felt the tree cocoon me, reminding me to be here now.

This chapter started during that first pandemic lockdown, as I lay under the jacaranda tree I've described above. It was a moment I captured in an Instagram post of the canopy above me, and the caption 'How to swim without water: Exploring possibilities under a jacaranda tree in an inner-city park'. The ideas had been brewing for a while – most memorably under tree ferns and manuka trees in Aotearoa/New Zealand and a towering sequoia tree in a friend's garden in Normandy in France. Looking up at these various trees, I wondered at my changing relationship to horizons and my increased yearning to be immersed in forests. Under these trees I noticed how I was experiencing the garden's and forests' surfaces, depths, currents and multispecies interactions in a way that was oceanic. Under the canopies of leaves and boughs, I thought of Phillip Steinberg and Kimberley Peters's (2015) and Karin Amimoto Ingersoll's (2016) work about oceanic ontologies, epistemologies and literacies, and the politics of who has access to these.

Those trees in Aotearoa/New Zealand and France were significant in how I came to recognise that oceans and swimming shaped my experiences of being on land, in part because of the forms of the spaces, but also because of what I was seeking from them: comfort, shelter, relief and quiet. The truth is that these trees offered me solace from the relentless exposure to the brightness of the sun and the expanse of the horizons that I'd been living with in each place. They helped me rein in the thoughts and emotions that filled all the available space I allowed them, and to move my view from the far horizon to my immediate surrounds and what lies beneath. Horizons and surfaces are important, and I still often turn my attention towards them. Looking at them helps me understand the scope of something, as well as the ways things connect. But to more consciously swim within the volume, to float above the depths, and to navigate the currents, waves and tides that characterise those expanses has been so helpful in how I position myself, and understand our ecological, relational complexities. Thinking with swimming – in oceans, tarns and pools – has strengthened how I approach my research work in real ways. Not only in how I make sense of the relationality of swimming in ocean ecologies, but also how I make sense of my research project as an ecology.

Reorientation: the limitations of swimming

Steinberg and Peters's 'wet ontologies' 'expands on recent attempts to destabilise the static, bordered, and linear framings that typify human geographical studies of place, territory, and time' (Steinberg and Peters, 2015: 247), through conceiving of a multi-state (liquid, solid, gas), sensual, mobile, wet worldview.

> It is in this context that we advocate thinking from the ocean as a means toward unearthing a material perspective that acknowledges the volumes within which territory is practised: a world of fluidities where place is forever in formation and where power is simultaneously projected on, through, in, and about space. (Steinberg and Peters, 2015: 261).

Applying an oceanic conception allows us to re-imagine capacities, interactions and flows within spaces out of the water. Instead of thinking about 'terrain' or 'landscapes', we can think about 'volumes', 'surfaces', 'depths', 'flows' and 'currents'. Such reorientations shift interactions and possibilities in different ways, including bodily and spatial interactions and possibilities.

In this discussion, I'm exploring ways that swimming is challenging my assumptions about contemporary 'human' relationships to and separateness from 'nature' (Plumwood, 1993). However, since I'm writing from Meanjin/Brisbane, which are the unceded lands and waters of the Jagera and Turubal people, I must remember how my knowledge is already partial, based on colonial injustice against traditional owners, and is only one of many ways of knowing here today (Lucashenko, 2008). Always close to my thinking about how swimming has shaped my ways of being and knowing are Karin Amimoto Ingersoll's (2016), Amberlin Kwaymullina's (2018) and Lauren Tynan's (2021) reminders that while narratives of building deep connection to water and place are common in activities like surfing and ocean swimming, these do not give settlers like me access to the ancestral, cultural or custodial relationships of First Nations and Indigenous people. That is, for me to have my worldview challenged by swimming does not confer me with new rights and authorities, nor does it challenge the colonial, patriarchal power relations that underpin my relationship to place or to swimming itself (Tynan, 2021).

These tensions run deep. Recognition of the limitations of my swimming knowledges must also include an acknowledgement that my relationship to oceans is based on growing up swimming in the ocean waters of the Arakwal people of Bundjalung country. Any relationship I have to the waters of my childhood home is as a settler-coloniser and is grounded in settler genealogies, timelines and histories. My knowledge of the coast and ocean there is partial, so even as I talk about how swimming shapes my thinking and relationships, I am still not attuned to and don't have rights to the communities of Arakwal and Bundjalung ancestors, spirits, histories and knowledges that are part of the water, land and sky (Bawaka Country, 2020; Lucashenko, 2008). How these impact my experiences remains unknown to me, but since swimming there means swimming among them, I want to recognise the partial and settler-colonial parameters of my knowledges and sensibilities.

I know there is much about my access to swimming that is built on colonial invasion and violence.

I know there is much I don't know about who and what is part of my swimming sensibilities, relationships and experiences.

I know there is much I have no right to know about the places I swim.

I know that swimming, which challenges my worldview so much, can only take me so far in a shift in thinking and knowing.

Attending to the politics of swimming in Australia means attending to how we are immersed, inter-animated, entangled in the politics of place. This is true for all places, but in settler-colonised countries it is especially pressing. The places we live can be our home, but settler-colonisers are always newcomers living on contested, stolen lands (Olive, 2019; Slater, 2018). In the United Kingdom, these politics play out differently, but there is a 'trespassing' movement for restored public rights of access to waterways in line with histories of public commons and rights to roam (Hayes, 2020). In the UK, acts of trespass to swim reject private custodianship of rivers, lakes and other water bodies as bundled up with land ownership. These politics reflect different manifestations of the same imperial politics of treating places as resources (Boyce, 2020). Such claims to access British waterways fall under different histories and injustices from those in Australia, but stem from, and perhaps reflect, the same foundations.

Attending to the politics of places is part of experiencing ecologies and recognises that people are always part of places too. Like
other First Nations people, Aboriginal and Torres Strait Islander
people describe themselves as being of Country, which accounts for
their own embodied relationships to places, including to ancestors,
spirits, histories and culture (Parmenter et al., 2017). To connect
with Country is a practice of caring for community and self – they're
the same. The importance of relationships to place in our relations
with place is instructive and inspiring, but it also comes with cultural
and ecological caveats (Spillman, 2017). Settler-colonisers, visitors
and newcomers must engage with the histories and politics of these
knowledges and practices, and to understand the limitations of how
they can be accessed and appropriated. As she navigates her own
continuing relationships to Country, trawlwulwuy woman, Lauren
Tynan explains that 'placing relationality and Country as the starting
point to research practice is vital'; however, 'relationality is not a new
metaphor to be reaped for academic gain, but a practice bound with
responsibilities with kin and Country' (Tynan, 2021: 2). For me to fail
to recognise the continued impacts of invasion, settler-colonisation
and white supremacy perpetuates environmental, colonial and cultural injustice (Kwaymullina, 2018).

The disappearing tarn

Kwaymullina and Tynan's points bring me back to the influence of
swimming on how I think about my relationships to ecologies, including all their human, multispecies, elemental and cultural aspects. It
reminds me how, even when I choose not to swim, I remain immersed
and entangled. A visit to what is known as 'the disappearing tarn' in
Hobart is an example of this. On that day, my friend and I got up early
in the dark, winter morning, pulling on jumpers, hats, thick socks
and gloves. A thermos of hot tea in hand, we drove the short distance
to the National Park carpark for the walk through the bush to the
mysterious body of water.

I'd heard about 'the disappearing tarn' over the years, through
reporting in national news. It is a body of water that collects after
sustained heavy rain in a particular spot on the side of kunanyi.
kunanyi – also known as Mount Wellington, the name bestowed by
British settlers establishing penal colonies in the very early nineteenth
century – is a peak of igneous rock and dolerite columns that rises

above the harbour city of Hobart, Tasmania. It's often-snow-capped presence is a defining feature of the city and, through my regular visits to friends who live in its foothills, it's a mountain I have come to have great affection for. The disappearing tarn is part of kunanyi's magic, but I'd never had the chance to visit it before. It's not a constant, nor even a regular, fixture, but it has become popular through news reports and Instagram posts shared to audiences keen for such treasures. Usually, I'd not be such a person. I'm excited to see beautiful places, but I travel mostly on my own and am usually lacking in motivation to seek out difficult locations. I find enough pleasure in knowing about their existence and don't necessarily feel the need to experience them for myself. But this time, with companions, I was happy to join the hike.

We were told by a woman who knew the way, that it would take over an hour to walk to the location. It wasn't an easy hike, on a wet, rocky, hard-to-follow track, but I wasn't concerned about this kind of bushwalking and was happy to be outside in the cold morning. I live in the sub-tropics where the summers are getting hotter and drier, so being in a wet, cold, grey climate feels precious. Much of the trail required navigating puddles and mud, as the tarn only appears after sustained heavy rain. But there was comfort in the tall eucalypts that surrounded us, their stringy trunks and low canopy protecting us from the wind, adding an easy intimacy to the walk.

Over time, I fell behind. I'm a strong walker, but the mud and, later, the stretches of loose rocks made me feel uncertain on my feet. My eyes take a while to focus in the morning, so my foggy, blurry vision made it hard to know where to put my feet. But I was just enjoying being under the trees so wasn't worried about my slow pace. I was comfortable for my faster friends to leave me with the trees and birds and cool breeze.

And I needed time to think.

I was in Tasmania as part of a month-long fieldwork trip. I was swimming with different ocean swimming groups as part of my research about how ocean swimming impacts our relationships to coastal and ocean ecologies, so I'd been thinking a lot about what it means to go swimming, and the ethics of swimming in different places. I swim in numerous different places, so I am considerate of the assumptions I make about my safety in a new location and about how I join in with different groups. I'm also aware that there are lots of things I don't know about the places I swim; the best entry and exit points, rocks beneath the water, hidden currents and dangers, animals, histories, community politics. At each place I'd swum on this trip, it was in the company of people who lived and swam there regularly. Like me, all of these people were settler-colonisers, and I was aware that in all the places I'd swum I'd not asked permission from traditional owners, nor learned much of their Indigenous histories. This was an issue I was thinking about during my walk.

I was ruminating on it because it is common for people to swim in the disappearing tarn, and it was assumed I would want to as well. But I didn't. It didn't feel right. I didn't know much about kunanyi, nor the cultural significance of the tarn. Perhaps there is none, but I'd not done the work to find out. I know kunanyi itself is significant for Aboriginal people in the region, that they avoid visiting the summit for various reasons, and that they are tolerant of visitors hiking the trails there. Sharnie Read told one news site that 'If we [Tasmanian Aboriginal people] go to the mountain, there should be good reason for that', and that 'I'd rather it wasn't dotted with tourists every day but we [Tasmanian Aboriginal people] do also promote that people should value and understand the cultural landscapes'; 'to do that they need to connect with it, but it's about connecting in a way that shows respect' (Hosier, 2020). In the same article, Theresa Sainty explained that 'kunanyi is here for people to enjoy but that doesn't mean hooning around, leaving rubbish and disrespecting the place because by doing that, you're disrespecting the people of the place and all that's gone before them'. Given all of this, I felt strange enough about walking on the mountain, so swimming in the tarn felt like the wrong thing to do. I decided I would wait until I arrived at the body of water to really decide, but I felt quite certain I would stay dry.

The forms of respect for place described by Sharnie Read and Theresa Sainty have helped me understand some of the other issues shaping my decision at the time. The tarn is an ephemeral occurrence. It comes and goes but never lasts long, and there is yet no consensus on why the waters gather there at all. As I walked, I thought about what might live and die there, and what might remain. I thought about the micro- and nano-plastics left behind by the many folk who visit the waters. Even if we carry out our rubbish, the swimwear, food wrappers and Gore-Tex jackets of the hundreds of people who visit the tarn each time it appears, leave traces. Of course, this is true for all water places, but the fleetingness of the tarn, it's place on kunanyi and it's Instagrammable popularity as a collectible destination in a time of high enthusiasm for cold water swimming, all assembled through my visit to emphasise the ethics of how we interact with, relate to and encounter this body of water.

Despite my questions, when we arrived at the tarn I didn't regret visiting. I'd never seen a place like it; a steep, tree-lined hollow of tumbled rocks that held crystal clear water the colour of blue-green glass. The surface was perfectly still and undisturbed by even a breeze. It was incredibly beautiful and I often return to look at the images I took of it. But I knew to swim there was not the right thing to do. Not for me. Samantha Walton (2021) made a similar decision not to immerse herself in the healing waters of Lourdes. In her explorations of the health and wellbeing properties of water and swimming, she travelled to join the long queue at the edge of the Pyrenees mountains. Not a religious person, Walton had 'come to Lourdes because I want to understand the promise of water as a medium for transformation' (23). Yet, Walton understands that 'Immersing yourself in the waters at Lourdes is not an act of science, but of faith' (24), and so, after hours of queuing with others on wooden benches, she left just as she reached the front. Despite the possibility and opportunity to immerse herself in the famous waters, the reasoning behind her doing so did not align with the stories of the water itself. As Walton writes, 'I know I will be invited through in moments, to take part in a ritual that means nothing to me. ... There's nothing wrong with me that this water can cure. ... There is no reason for me to be here at all' (47).

Like Walton, I knew to swim in the tarn would deliver me no meaningful transformation. In my case, given my questions about the stories of the mountain, it would have been the wrong thing to do. So I sat and admired the water and the curve of the space, wondered at whether this was a place that hosted an ecology that rose and fell with the water. Others dove into the frigid waters – a very cold, 6 degrees Celsius. Most people stayed in no longer than it took to get out again before scrambling up the loose rocks to dress quickly and wrap their hands around warm cups of thermos tea. Their joyful, flushed faces reflected the physical high that cold water swimming in such a beautiful location can bring, and I felt jealous of being outside the shared experience of their icy plunge. Their swim was meaningful to them, but my experience of the tarn did not feel lesser for not immersing myself in the waters there.

I'm still not sure of the ethics of my visit. I won't pretend I can justify hiking to the tarn through thinking and reflecting, because ultimately I wanted to go there and I did. But not swimming was the result of careful consideration of what was known and not known to me at that time, and about how the idea of immersion, inter-animation, entanglement with the mountainside waters felt wrong. For better or worse, my experience of not swimming was as relational to the ecology of the tarn as swimming there would have been.

Reaching the shore

Our relationships to water are never really still. They are always rippling, bubbling, stagnating and flowing, even if beneath the surface. Through swimming, and thinking about swimming, I have been finding new depths in my relationships to coasts and oceans. Lately, they are no longer so heavy with grief as they were; instead, new questions have emerged from swimming and once more the views across ocean horizons hold hope. Grief and pain remain, of course, and I still yearn for the comforting embrace of green, leafy canopies, but taking time to consider the ethics of swimming as an ecological sensibility has been helpful in understanding my own relationships to oceans. It has helped me re-imagine the complex ethics that shape any relationship to place, community and self.

Taking the lessons of swimming and of the water into my life on land is important, as it helps me explain ways of being and thinking that I have been struggling with, and to make sense of movements and spaces in more complex ways. I'm sure other sports and physical activities do this just as well for other folk, but the multisensory inter-animations of swimming have been particularly instructive for me. Making sense of how we move in relation to places, bodies, cultures, climates, histories, politics, economies and everything else cannot be navigated by taking one easy line. We bring too much to each encounter, each relationship, and so we need frameworks that will encompass that complex relationality.

I continue to immerse myself into vast waters that I can't be sure I'll emerge from, waters full of animals, chemicals, waves and ancestors, none of which I can control. I swim, I swim. I kick and pull and breathe and roll, slowly, surely moving through the volume of the world around me. I am small, I am vulnerable, but I must learn how to find my way when there is no lane to keep me safe.

References

Bawaka Country Including, Mitchell, A., Wright, S., Suchet-Pearson, S., Lloyd, K., Burarrwanga, L., Ganambarr, R., Ganambarr-Stubbs, M., Ganambarr, B., Maymuru, D. and Maymuru, R. (2020) Dukarr lakarama: listening to Guwak, talking back to space colonization. *Political Geography*, 81. doi:10.1016/j.polgeo.2020.102218.

Boyce, J. (2020) *Imperial Mud: The Fight for the Fens*. London: Icon Books.

Britton, E. (2018) 'Be like water': reflections on strategies developing cross-cultural programmes for women, surfing and social good. In L. Mansfield, J. Caudwell, B. Wheaton and B. Watson (eds) *The Palgrave Handbook of Feminism and Sport, Leisure and Physical Education*. London: Palgrave Macmillan, pp. 793–807.

Britton, E. and Foley, R. (2021) Sensing water: uncovering health and well-being in the sea and surf. *Journal of Sport and Social Issues*, 45(1), 60–87.

Casey, E. S. (2009) *Getting Back into Place*. Bloomington: Indiana University Press. 5:64, 1–12.

Denton, H., Dannreuther, C. and Aranda, K. (2021) Researching at sea: exploring the 'swim-along' interview method. *Health & Place*, 67, 102466.

Evers, C. (2006) How to surf. *Journal of Sport and Social Issues*, 30(3), 229–243.

Evers, C. (2021) Polluted leisure and blue spaces: more-than-human concerns in Fukushima. *Journal of Sport and Social Issues*, 45(2), 179–195.

Foley, R. (2017) Swimming as an accretive practice in healthy blue space. *Emotion, Space and Society*, 22, 43–51.

Gould, S. E. (2019) *Swimming in Australia: A Cultural Study*. Doctoral dissertation, Victoria University.

Gould, S., McLachlan, F. and McDonald, B. (2021) Swimming with the Bicheno 'Coffee Club': the textured world of wild swimming. *Journal of Sport and Social Issues*, 45(1), 39–59.

Hayes, N. (2020) *The Book of Trespass: Crossing the Lines that Divide Us*. London: Bloomsbury.

Hosier, P. (2020) What does Hobart's kunanyi/Mt Wellington mean to Tasmania's First Nations people? *SBS News*, 26 April. Available at: www. abc.net.au/news/2020-04-26/what-hobarts-mt-wellington-mean-to-tasmanias-indigenous-people/12141266 (accessed 30 August 2022).

Humberstone, B. (2011) Engagements with nature: ageing and windsurfing. In B. Watson and J. Harpin (eds) *Identities, Cultures and Voices in Leisure and Sport*. Eastbourne: Leisure Studies Association, Publication No. 116, pp.159–169.

Humberstone, B. (2018) Bodies and technologies: becoming a 'mermaid': myth, reality, embodiment, cyborgs, windsurfing and the sea. In M. Brown and K. Peters (eds) *Living with the Sea: Knowledge, Awareness and Action.* Abingdon: Routledge, pp. 183–195.

Ingersoll, K. A. (2016) *Waves of Knowing.* Durham: Duke University Press.

Kato, K. (2007) Waiting for the tide, tuning in the world – ama no isobue: soundscape of abalone diving women. In R. Bandt, M. Duffy and D. MacKinnon (eds) *Hearing Places: Sound, Place, Time, Culture.* Newcastle: Cambridge Scholars Press, pp. 214–233.

Kwaymullina, A. (2018) You are on Indigenous land: ecofeminism, Indigenous peoples and land justice. In L. Stevens, P. Tait and D. Varney (eds) *Feminist Ecologies.* Cham: Palgrave Macmillan, pp. 193–208.

lisahunter (2019) Sensory autoethnography: surfing approaches for understanding and communicating 'seaspacetimes'. In M. Brown and K. Peters (eds) *Living with the Sea: Knowledge, Awareness and Action.* Abingdon: Routledge, pp. 100–113.

lisahunter and Stoodley, L. (2021) Bluespace, senses, wellbeing, and surfing: prototype cyborg theory-methods. *Journal of Sport and Social Issues,* 45(1), 88–112.

Lucashenko, M. (2008) All my relations: being and belonging in Byron Shire. In Anne Haebich and Baden Offord (eds) *Landscapes of Exile: Once Perilous, Now Safe.* Bern: Peter Lang, pp. 61–67.

McMahon, J. and Penney, D. (2013) Body pedagogies, coaching and culture: three Australian swimmers' lived experiences. *Physical Education and Sport Pedagogy,* 18(3), 317–335.

Moggach, D. (ed.) (2019) *At the Pond: Swimming at the Hampstead Heath Ladies' Pond.* London: Daunt Books.

Moles, K. (2021) The social world of outdoor swimming: cultural practices, shared meanings, and bodily encounters. *Journal of Sport and Social Issues,* 45(1), 20–38.

Olive, R. (2019) The trouble with newcomers: women, localism and the politics of surfing. *Journal of Australian Studies,* 43(1), 39–54.

Olive, R. (2021) You can't hide from yourself in the water. Blog post, *Moving Oceans,* 13 December. Available at: https://movingoceans.com/multi-spe cies-communities/you-cant-hide-from-yourself-in-the-water/ (accessed 19 December 2021).

Olive, R. and Enright, E. (2021) Sustainability in the Australian health and physical education curriculum: an ecofeminist analysis. *Sport, Education and Society,* 26(4), 389–402.

Osmond, G. and Phillips, M. G. (2006) 'Look at that kid crawling': race, myth and the 'crawl' stroke. *Australian Historical Studies,* 37(127), 43–62.

Parmenter, J., Nelson, A., Crawford, E., Basit, T. and Dargan, S. (2017) My body's getting healthy and my mind is getting healthy with it: considering urban Aboriginal and Torres Strait Islander conceptions of health. *International Research Journal of Public Health,* 1(1), 1–11.

Peters, K. (2019) Invited panellist ACNB Berlin, Germany. (Dis)connections and the fluid spaces in-between', 7 November. Available at: www.ancb.de/sixcms/detail.php?id=19198198#.Yb_7131ByWB (accessed 30 August 2022).

Peters, K., Moore, A. and Brown, M. (2018) Conclusions: learning to live with the sea together: opening dialogue, creating conversation. In M. Brown and K. Peters (eds) *Living with the Sea: Knowledge, Awareness and Action*. Abingdon: Routledge, pp. 227–239.

Plumwood, V. (1993) *Feminism and the Mastery of Nature*. London: Routledge.

Probyn, E. (2011) Swimming with tuna: human–ocean entanglements. *Australian Humanities Review*, 51, 97–114.

Probyn, E. (2016) *Eating the Ocean*. Durham: Duke University Press.

Roper, L. (2018) *Wild Woman Swimming: A Journal of West Country Waters*. Edited by Tanya Shadrick. London: Selkie Press.

Slater, L. (2018) *Anxieties of Belonging in Settler Colonialism: Australia, Race and Place*. London: Routledge.

Spillman, D. (2017) Coming home to place: Aboriginal lore and place-responsive pedagogy for transformative learning in Australian outdoor education. *Journal of Outdoor and Environmental Education*, 20(1), 14–24.

Steinberg, P. and Peters, K. (2015) Wet ontologies, fluid spaces: giving depth to volume through oceanic thinking. *Environment and Planning D: Society and Space*, 33(2), 247–264.

Stronach, M. and Adair, D. (2020) Swimming for their lives: Palawa women of Lutruwita (Van Diemen's Land). *Sporting Traditions*, 37(2), 47–70.

Throsby, K. (2013) 'If I go in like a cranky sea lion, I come out like a smiling dolphin': marathon swimming and the unexpected pleasures of being a body in water. *Feminist Review*, 103(1), 5–22.

Throsby, K. (2016) *Immersion: Marathon Swimming, Embodiment and Identity*. Manchester: Manchester University Press.

Tynan, L. (2021) What is relationality? Indigenous knowledges, practices and responsibilities with kin. *cultural geographies*, 28(4), 597–610.

Walton, S. (2021) *Everybody Needs Beauty: In Search of the Nature Cure*. London: Bloomsbury Publishing.

19

I just want an earth of cool mysteries

Samantha Walton

to be rattling on a train towards nowhere

burst light flailing through fields

everything gold & green in diamonds

the land so ruched

you could press your hip to it

one look through glass

& I know I can fall in love instantly

unparcel my heart & drop it

in any old stream

chuck the old self out

like water

no ritual no ceremony

no body no other

I want a world of cool meetings

breath outside my mouth

the jouissance of

language soaked

& wet

a little slipping

a little breaking of boundaries

to be tipped from

the shell of myself

the edge so rough

& rain so ravaged

to meet the

insides of my

self

booming with the

song of some

impossible & distant

ocean

I have been thinking and living with the work of Scottish nature writer Nan Shepherd for a long time, and it is impossible for me to write on the theme of 'living with water' without her words trickling through my own. In her non-fiction, hybrid nature journal and memoir *The Living Mountain* (written in the 1940s, but first published in 1977), Shepherd reflects on the pleasure of lighting a fire and drawing water from the well when one isn't used to completing these once routine and mundane tasks. Touching water, touching fire, 'you are touching life', she writes, 'and something within you knows it' (Shepherd, 2011: 82). On the surface, it's a rather bland and nostalgic statement. 'Life' has a pleasing authenticity, evoking a homespun spiritualism and a sense that things were better in the more hands-on past. But Shepherd is saying something quite specific. She had a vitalist view of Life, and saw a generous, infectious *livingness* pulsing within the creatures, plants and landscapes she encountered. This view was reinforced by the enmeshed quality of Cairngorm ecology and, most importantly, by the presence of water. Whether it is trickling across the high plateau, welling up from the dark pools of the recesses, or quivering in the scarlet cups of *Cladonia coccifera*, water is tangible, visible and audible in the mountains. Water touches living things into existence, makes matter pulsate and become something else. Like the mountain, water is alive, and essential for both bare existence and pleasurable living. 'I only know that man can't live without it', Shepherd insists. 'He must see it and hear it, touch and taste it, and, no, not smell it, if he is to be in health' (Shepherd, 2011: 28).

Reading Shepherd now, it's tempting to see her as trans-corporeal before trans-corporeality, new materialist before new materialism. Her belief in matter's vitality finds confluence with these newer forms of ecological materialism, which have so shaped recent ecocritical perspectives on the body. According to Stacy Alaimo's description of the 'immersed subject of trans-corporeality', rather than existing in Cartesian pockets of self, closed off from the world, 'humans are not only interconnected with each other but with the material flows of substances and places' (Alaimo, 2010: 23–24). Water, air and nourishment pass through our bodies, 'substantially recomposing them in the process' (Spiegel, 2013: 86). Such thinking challenges subject/object relations and binaries of self/other, human/environment and inside/outside. It is a transgression of boundaries, a shift from living by or on water to living within, and living with.

Much scholarly work informed by trans-corporeality, quite rightly, focuses on the environmental politics of the body burdened by the flow of matter. As Alaimo puts it: 'Humans are vulnerable because they are not in fact "human" in some transcendent, contained sense, but are flesh, substance, matter' (Alaimo, 2010: 15). Vulnerability to material harm in the world is unfairly distributed, with poor communities of colour unjustly exposed to the influx of toxic matter, poisoned water, heavy metals, choking dust, and manifold other blatant and subtle environmental harms. Living with water also means living with the risks it transports into the flesh and distributes through its global ebbs and flows to bodies and ecosystems near and far.

With this violence and vulnerability adequately foregrounded, there is still good cause to celebrate the boundary-dissolving capacities of water, and to meet its acts of transgression (when it doesn't bring chemical harms) with love. There is something euphoric, rapturous, about the feeling of *oneness* in the world, which has often been described as either transcendence (meaning to float beyond the self and world) and immanence (to melt into it). In *The Second Sex*, Simone de Beauvoir describes the pleasure that comes from slipping through the boundaries between self and place, as an escape from social being – an achievement of a sense of 'liberty through a continuous reaching out to other liberties' (de Beauvoir, 1997: 386).

But these are psychological experiences, described in the terminology of the ecstatic spiritual and the numinous. Trans-corporeal thinking takes us a little further. Awareness of the material, liquid oneness of the body with its environment (the body/environment distinction falls away) may be experienced as a form of rapturous liberty. It unmakes the human/nature division which has been so culturally and ecologically ruinous. It frees the self, blocked in by its own supposed separation from and supremacy above the more-than-human.

In this poem, I wanted to write about all this, and the jouissance of living with water. Jouissance has a specific heritage within literary criticism, but here I am playing off of Elizabeth Povinelli's definition of jouissance as 'the painful pleasure of exceeding a law in which we were implicated, an enjoyment of a desire (*desir*), in the mode of rage or grief' (2011: 288). Punk anger takes us there, as does the agonising ecstasy of protest. In the poem, I wanted to explore the desire for trans-corporeal un-selfing, and the painful pleasure of exceeding the laws of individualism and human-exceptionalism. Of course, the earth is not an untouched pleasure ground, an unpoisoned bright green Nature, whose unspecifiable healing energies will replenish our own. Hence the grief, the rage and the desire to unmake laws.

At the same time, jouissance is pleasure, and ecological thought needs desire and bliss as much as it needs outrage. As Kathryn Bond Stockton puts it:

> Jouissance is the strangest glistening, a dark glamour of rapture and disruption. It shines and cuts and leaves its bearer not knowing what to make of herself – or her pleasure. She is left beside herself, feeling ecstatically severed from herself, seized by subtleties, strange to say, even though bliss is an overwhelming force. ('Spiritual joy,' says American Heritage; 'paradise,' 'seventh heaven,' 'cloud nine,' adds Roget's.) Bliss is a word for impossibilities, felt and grasped as such. Something (im)possible coursing through the body, bending the mind. Then, on a dime: rapid, luminous deteriorations. (Stockton, 2017: 101)

So, in this poem, it is water that is bending the mind, forming and unforming us, and distributing us throughout a living world that was there, and with us, all along.

References

Alaimo, S. (2010) The naked word: the trans-corporeal ethics of the protesting body. *Women and Performance*, 20(1), 15–36.

de Beauvoir, S. (1997) *The Second Sex*. London: Vintage.

Povinelli, E. (2011) The part that has no part: enjoyment, law and loss. *GLQ: A Journal of Lesbian and Gay Studies*, 17(2–3), 288–308.

Shepherd, N. (2011) *The Living Mountain*. Edinburgh: Canongate.

Spiegel, J. B. (2013) Subterranean flows: water contamination and the politics of visibility after the Bhopal gas disaster. In C. Chen, J. MacLeod and A. Neimanis (eds)*Thinking with Water*. Montreal: McGill-Queens University Press, pp. 84–103.

Stockton, K. B. (2017) PLEASURE: jouissance, the gash of bliss. In N. Giffney and E. Watson (eds) *Clinical Encounters in Sexuality: Psychoanalytic Practice and Queer Theory*. Brooklyn: Punctum Books, pp. 101–122.

20

Conjuring a swimming pond

Emily Bates

You cannot truly understand the Dutch landscape without considering water.

In fact, the country would probably not still exist were it not for the specialised engineering approaches to water redistribution and control set in place; hydraulic systems, dikes, polders, dams and dunes are what literally keep the country afloat. Over half the country, and its population, live officially under sea level, in a country also known as the Lowlands. It is a man-formed landscape, a sculpture of engineering and requirement. Water has been an essential element to the countries' historic wealth and power, and perhaps encouraged the seeking of naval and economic domination elsewhere.

During the pandemic, this adopted home of mine became more of an island due to travel restrictions, than the islands of my birth just an inaccessible splash away. On a residency with the Vincent van Gogh Huis museum in Noord Brabant, a southern province of the Netherlands, I explored the Dutch landscape and its relationship with water anew. The waterways that exist in the area could be considered the echo of a past era. The narrow yet very straight channel of the Turfvaart, for example, was created for the transportation of peat, pulled on long barges to the city, often by women and, later, horses. Peat brought great wealth to the estates through the removal of up to 7 metres of the land's surface, to provide fuel and speed the development and economies of the country. Although the waterways, polders and dikes are still essential to sustained living and farming practices, they have also distorted our ecosystems and are now having to be rethought with regard to new emerging realities of climate change and the increasing demands of population growth.

I began plotting out the historic and potential swimming ponds of my new temporary home on the de Moeren estate and its surrounding area, from the memory of recent discovery during my daily walks, and from research assisted by old maps. I was struck by recurring shapes and narratives. I found a mimicry across scale and function that spoke of a similar era in use and creation: a piece of broken ceramic found on an old lanc behind the estate's main house, and the floor plan of Atelier Richard Roland Holst (an artists' studio designed in the Amsterdamse School style by the first Dutch female architect, Margaret Staal-Kropholler, in 1918), shared the shape of a local pond.

It was the appearance of a photograph of Henriette Roland Holst (poet and founding member of the Dutch Communist Party), in a swimming pond located somewhere 'behind the rhododendron' in the woods of the Oude Buisse Heide nearby, that triggered an eagerness to plunge not only physically into the now dark stinky and stagnant waters, but also into these bodies of water as symbols and new springs releasing historic narrative and ritual. Wild swimming and forest bathing have become particularly popular wellbeing activities in Western Europe, during this era of pandemic. Symbolically and spiritually water has long been a reference of cleansing and renewal. Whether recreationally or as an act of mediation and personal ritual, the waters have been inspirational for artists and poets across time and location. German artist Joseph Beuys could not resist the act, himself performing *Aktion im Moor*, in de Peel, a swamp in the Dutch province of Limburg (east of Noord Brabant) in 1971. Primordial acts of reconnecting with ourselves, greater forces and nature seem to be essential once more.

I picked up a Japanese ink brush and black ink pot as my tools for the plotting of the ponds and shapes recognised. Tools I had not used in my working practice before, but that I had brought back from former projects in Asia. The black ink flows from the long hairs of the brush, following its own sensual pathway. It gushes and weeps. Darkens and glistens when layered. Wets the page and crinkles. A new rippling and plunging of the dark waters' surface, the submerging in the cold unknown depths of the swamps I encountered is echoed. A shudder of fear and vulnerability from both acts occurs within the first moments, slowly followed by the presence of acceptance, calm and pure knowing. A rush of emotion and release. I continued with the ink painting, attempting the familiar circle of meditation practices. Little did I know that hidden in woods nearby was another old swimming pond, formed from a perfect ring.

Index

EU authorised representative for GPSR:
Easy Access System Europe, Mustamäe tee 50,
10621 Tallinn, Estonia
gpsr.requests@easproject.com

www.ingramcontent.com/pod-product-compliance
Lightning Source LLC
Chambersburg PA
CBHW051954270326
41929CB00015B/2658